Lunch with the FT

FT
—
125
YEARS

Lunch with the FT
52 Classic Interviews

Edited by Lionel Barber

Foreword by John Ridding

Illustrations by James Ferguson

PORTFOLIO
PENGUIN

PORTFOLIO PENGUIN

Published by the Penguin Group
Penguin Books Ltd, 80 Strand, London WC2R 0RL, England
Penguin Group (USA) Inc., 375 Hudson Street, New York, New York 10014, USA
Penguin Group (Canada), 90 Eglinton Avenue East, Suite 700, Toronto, Ontario,
Canada M4P 2Y3 (a division of Pearson Penguin Canada Inc.)
Penguin Ireland, 25 St Stephen's Green, Dublin 2, Ireland (a division of Penguin Books Ltd)
Penguin Group (Australia), 707 Collins Street, Melbourne, Victoria 3008, Australia
(a division of Pearson Australia Group Pty Ltd)
Penguin Books India Pvt Ltd, 11 Community Centre, Panchsheel Park, New Delhi – 110 017, India
Penguin Group (NZ), 67 Apollo Drive, Rosedale, Auckland 0632, New Zealand
(a division of Pearson New Zealand Ltd)
Penguin Books (South Africa) (Pty) Ltd, Block D, Rosebank Office Park,
181 Jan Smuts Avenue, Parktown North, Gauteng 2193, South Africa

Penguin Books Ltd, Registered Offices: 80 Strand, London WC2R 0RL, England

www.penguin.com

First published 2013
001

Copyright © *Financial Times*, 2013

Articles by Rob Blackhurst, Kieran Cooke, Andrew Davidson, Beverley Doole,
Amity Shlaes and Nigel Spivey are reprinted by permission of the respective authors.
Illustrations by James Ferguson reproduced by arrangement with the illustrator.

David Hockney, *Self Portrait Using Three Mirrors*, watercolour on paper 24 x 18 1/8",
2003, Collection The David Hockney Foundation. Copyright © David Hockney, 2003
Photo Credit: Richard Schmidt

Set in 10.15|14.75pt Miller Text
Typeset by Jouve (UK), Milton Keynes
Colour Reproduction by Tag: response
Printed in Italy by Printer Trento

UK ISBN: 978-0-670-92284-0
US ISBN: 978-1-59184-649-9

www.greenpenguin.co.uk

Penguin Books is committed to a sustainable
future for our business, our readers and our planet.
This book is made from Forest Stewardship
Council™ certified paper.

ALWAYS LEARNING   **PEARSON**

Contents

Foreword

Lunch with the *FT* has long been a mainstay of the *Financial Times* weekend section, a consistently entertaining read, and a unique 'seat at the table' with the personalities and players who have shaped our times. This book is, therefore, a fitting way to mark the newspaper's 125th birthday – rekindling memorable moments and reacquainting ourselves with the protagonists from that history.

But these interviews also tell a broader *FT* story. They provide a reminder of some of the guiding beliefs and objectives that have served us well over the years, and will remain at the centre of our publication and our purpose. While many in media and publishing struggle to survive amid the forces of digital disruption, the *FT* remains in strong shape. This is partly because we have embraced digital delivery and innovative web formats. But it is mainly because of our sustained commitment to quality journalism and our confidence in its value and importance to our readers.

That commitment to quality is matched by our dedication to a global perspective. Our international expansion from the *FT*'s UK roots was well under way when our first lunch guest sat across the table in 1994. Since then, our branches have extended and flourished across the US, Asia and the fast-rising economies of the BRICs and beyond.

These portraits chart the evolution and revolutions of global society, which will always be at the heart of the *Financial Times*.

John Ridding
CEO, *Financial Times*

Introduction

From the very first mouthful, Lunch with the *FT* was destined to become a permanent fixture in the newspaper. The formula was deceptively simple: a conversation-cum-interview over an agreeable lunch. Since its debut in 1994 there have been more than 800 lunches, featuring presidents, playwrights, tycoons, film-stars, monks and more than the occasional oddball. Lunch with the *FT* has become an institution, as entertaining and enduring as the Lex column.

To celebrate this year's 125th anniversary of the *Financial Times*, we are publishing 52 of the best of the genre – one for every week of the year. Our list is an international who's who from the arts, business, politics and science. The selection pays due regard to gender and geography, but above all it seeks to meet the test once set out by Richard Lambert, a former editor of the *Financial Times*. The task of *FT* journalism, he reminded colleagues, is not only to inform but also to delight readers.

Lunch with the *FT* was conceived by Max Wilkinson, a crusty, enterprising editor of the *Weekend FT* with an acute sense of the absurd. He thought the new interview format would provide 'a ray of sunshine' in the paper. The rules were straightforward. The guest/interviewee would choose the restaurant, and the *FT* would foot the bill. In fact, the Wilkinson rules were broken on the very first outing.

The *FT*'s first guest on 23 April 1994 was Marco Pierre White, the celebrity chef-cum-restaurateur whom our interviewer (Michael Thompson-Noel) memorably dubbed 'the wild man of English cooking'. White, who had chosen one of his own restaurants in which to be amply wined and dined, rejected any notion that the *FT* would pick up the tab. The principle that the *FT* pays has otherwise mostly held firm, despite protestations from interviewees. What we view as a declaration of editorial independence has often been taken as a cultural insult or a poor reflection of the guest's own financial standing. 'Now I know why the *FT* is so expensive' was the barbed quip of billionaire Michael Bloomberg on failing to pick up a $96 bill in New York, where he is now mayor.

The original idea behind Lunch with the *FT* was to rediscover the art of conversation in a convivial setting. Good food was essential, preferably washed down with a decent bottle of wine to elicit insights and the occasional indiscretion. The combination led to some memorable encounters, notably a liquid lunch of biblical proportions at the Café Royal between Nigel Spivey, a Cambridge don and freelance *FT* writer, and Gavin Ewart, the 79-year-old poet. The next day, Spivey received a call from Mrs Ewart, saying that her husband had returned home happier than she had seen him in a long time. 'The second [thing] – and you are not to feel bad about this – is that he died this morning.'

Less fatal twists of fate feature in this book. In 1996 Jacques Attali, the *enfant terrible* of French intellectual life, announced halfway through lunch in Paris with Lucy Kellaway that he had to leave – to go to a second lunch. Apparently, gastronomic two-timing was de rigueur for Attali. Another mid-lunch upset saw Ronnie Wood, the ageing Rolling Stone, excusing himself from his oysters to take a call from the *Sun* newspaper inquiring about his teenage mistress. But the ultimate *bombe surprise* came from Yuko Tojo, the granddaughter of the Japanese prime minister hanged after the Second World War. She brought his remains to lunch in Tokyo with David Pilling, our Asia editor.

Many lunches in this book show the *FT* at its eclectic best. Naturally, there is star-power aplenty: Angelina Jolie, Michael Caine, Martin Amis and Sean 'P. Diddy' Combs, the hip-hopper-cum-business-magnate, who turned up in a Seventh Avenue soup shop in New York. There are statesmen and -women: Václav Havel, the Czech playwright-turned-president and father of the post-communist nation; F. W. de Klerk, who brought about the end of apartheid in South Africa; and Angela Merkel, in a revealing interview in 2003, before she became German chancellor and arguably the most powerful politician in Europe. There are fashionistas such as Tamara Mellon, the founder of Jimmy Choo, as well as a rare luncheon duet with Domenico Dolce and his partner Stefano Gabbana. And there are tales of the unexpected from General Rosso José Serrano, the Colombia police chief who cornered Pablo Escobar before the drug kingpin died in a hail of bullets.

Inevitably, lunch – like the *FT* – has evolved over the 18 years since its inception. In the age of the BlackBerry, the smartphone and still or sparkling water, the idea of a long boozy lunch is almost quaint. Reluctantly, the *FT* has occasionally accommodated the busy lives of the rich, powerful and self-important by agreeing to a breakfast, tea or the occasional sandwich. But even modest fare can produce scintillating copy. Just read Pilita Clark's opening exchange with Michael O'Leary, the potty-mouthed boss of the no-frills airline Ryanair.

Today's lunches reflect the *FT*'s global reach. We have an ABC (Africans, Brazilians, Chinese) of prominent persons which stretches all the way to Z (Zimbabwe's Morgan Tsvangirai, the battered opposition leader interviewed over sundowners by Alec Russell, formerly the *FT*'s man in Johannesburg).

There are also some excellent interviews which failed to make the cut: Emily Stokes filleting the ambitious author-soldier-politician Rory Stewart at Harvard's Kennedy School; Paulo Coelho talking about prostitutes and the Pope with fellow author A. N. Wilson; Sean Parker, the tech guru, telling John Gapper in Los Angeles that a million dollars 'is not cool'; or Roger Waters of Pink Floyd comparing himself to Shakespeare and Woody Guthrie – and ordering a £75 piece of gravadlax.

The job of an editor is, however, to choose. In this case, I would like to thank Lucy Kellaway, a founder luncher and a mistress of the art, as well as Matthew Engel, the *FT* columnist, for his splendid essay on the 18th anniversary of the Lunch published last year (www.ft.com/lunch). Leyla Boulton, who co-ordinated this book project with patience and skill, has been indispensable. I am also grateful to James Ferguson, the *FT*'s brilliant cartoonist, whose illustrations have graced Lunch with the *FT* off and on since 2004.

Lionel Barber
Editor, *Financial Times*

Arts

Martin Amis

Literary lion

The novelist and commentator has lost none of his appetite for a war of words. He talks about Islam, his father and the 'marooned ideologue' Terry Eagleton

By Lionel Barber

Martin Amis greets me with an uncertain handshake and a furrowed brow. He is smaller and greyer than I had imagined. Is this slight figure in a waistcoat the imperious author of a dozen novels whose trademark is sledgehammer prose? For several minutes Amis does not utter a word. He stares at the menu at Odette's, a restaurant in celebrity-packed Primrose Hill. The silence is awkward, perhaps calculated (I arrived seven minutes late). Finally, England's one-time *enfant terrible* speaks: 'The menu is very pig-oriented.' The voice is deep and gravelled; the accent a languid Oxford drawl. Amis orders his main course (roast quail), a glass of Chardonnay and, reluctantly, a green salad; then he excuses himself to smoke a roll-up outside. I place my order (a velouté of sweet corn, and organic salmon) and another glass of Chardonnay.

When Amis returns, I ask him about his running public feud with Terry Eagleton, the Marxist English literary professor. Eagleton has accused Amis of Islamophobia, castigating him for advocating strip-searches of young British Muslims and raising the threat of repatriation to Pakistan.

'I never wrote it and I never said it,' snaps Amis. He does, however, admit to favouring ethnic profiling at airports after an incident at Carrasco airport in Montevideo, Uruguay. Amis claims a security guard

searched his then six-year-old daughter and 'f***-f****d' her fluffy toy duck.

The novelist and his family have since returned home after two and a half years in Uruguay, the birthplace of his second wife, Isabel Fonseca. Plainly, the fluffy duck episode still pains him, much more than his spat with Eagleton, an academic colleague at the University of Manchester, where Amis has just begun teaching a popular course in creative writing.

'This is very minor stuff. He is a marooned ideologue who can't get out of bed in the morning without guidance from God and Karl Marx. This makes him very unstaunch in the struggle against Islamism because part of him is a believer.'

Amis employs a linguistic defence: 'I said quite clearly I am not an Islamophobe. What I am is anti-Islamist. "Islamistophobe" would be the right word, except that it's not the right word because a phobia tends to be an irrational fear and it's not irrational to fear people who want to kill you. So I'm anti-Islamist.'

I joke that the Amis–Eagleton feud is the equivalent of Manchester United versus Manchester City. Amis declines the opening. A tall, blonde Russian waitress arrives with the Chardonnay. I note that my last Lunch with the *FT* – with an Irish politician in Washington DC – turned into an epic drinking session. For the first time, Amis smiles.

It is time to switch to highbrow. I want to explore the relationship between Amis and his father, Kingsley, the distinguished comic novelist. What was it like trying to write great prose, knowing that every word was likely to be scrutinized?

'I never felt any kind of particular pressure. He wasn't an invigilator. It was nice having a kind of a lazy father, a very soft, sweet father. But lazy, jealous of his time . . .'

But while Kingsley liked his son's (award-winning) first novel, *The Rachel Papers*, he did not think much of his second, *Dead Babies*. 'That was a physical shock, like a blow,' he confesses, before switching the subject to his new creative writing course at Manchester.

What has drawn Amis to teaching? He picks at his quail and admits to 'a bit of paternal influence' (Kingsley taught English at Swansea University for 12 years). But the other two attractions are 'a vulgar curiosity about youth' and being forced to read great books.

In Amis's literary pantheon there is no place for younger writers, with the exception of his buddies Zadie Smith and Will Self. 'There's something humiliating about reading younger writers. You're more likely to be on to something if you're reading V. S. Pritchett, Saul Bellow . . . But any young squirt, you're not going to read except out of a kind of sociological curiosity.'

For Amis, the authors that really matter are Saul Bellow and Nabokov, followed by, among others, Tolstoy, Dostoevsky and Jane Austen. The novel he most admires is Nabokov's *Lolita*. 'I must know it as well as I know any book. But it's always different . . . You've got to read it every decade of your life because you are a different person.'

Amis's elder daughter is 10, but he still finds the novel enchanting, particularly the last 100 pages whose pace he previously thought tailed off. At about page 220, when Lolita leaves Humbert, there's a huge influx of energy, he says.

'Nabokov might have ended the novel around there, instead of having those three years trying to find her and finding her. That marvellous scene where Humbert goes to see her and her beauty's all gone, she's pregnant . . . I cried quite a lot towards the end. It's morally very complicated and very unreassuring.'

Morally complicated, unreassuring: that's Amis in a nutshell. His novels are savagely comic and unsentimental; his literary criticism uncompromising; his choice of vocabulary rich to the point of self-indulgent. (Over lunch, 'jocose', 'palpating' and 'adulterous assignation' trip off the Amis tongue, leavened by a stream of four-letter words.) The result is usually enlightening, invariably entertaining.

Feeling outgunned on English literature, I mention that I studied German at Oxford, his alma mater. Amis is intrigued and asks me if I have read Kafka in German. When I reply in the affirmative he embarks on his own aphoristic literary tour.

The shorter Kafka works best. The dream logic in *The Castle* is staggering but 'nothing odd works long'. The other literary rule: 'Tell a dream, lose a reader.' Joyce's *Ulysses* is a noble, beautiful book. And borrowing from Nabokov, *Finnegans Wake* is a snore in the next room.

According to Amis, the relationship between writer and reader is a love affair. Sometimes the writer falls out of love with the reader. It happened to Henry James, it happened to Joyce. But if it really is a love affair, then why is Amis so keen on impressing the reader (and me?) with his command of the English language?

'I am not a great user of obscure words,' he replies, with a straight face. But he admits to writing prose which is 'packed', 'slightly goading' and 'sort of in-your-face'. I want to ask Amis about male friendship, but he excuses himself for a second cigarette break, leaving his green salad untouched.

Male friendships are a vital part of Amis's world. His closest pal is perhaps Christopher Hitchens, the US-based author and polemicist. Their friendship goes back more than 30 years to when both worked at the *New Statesman* magazine.

Amis cites his father's friendship with Philip Larkin, the poet. Except between man and wife, there are fewer limits to candour and intimacy between male friends than between men and women, where sex has a habit of intruding on friendship. 'Sadly I reached the conclusion that Larkin didn't really reciprocate this love.'

I suggest Larkin was a bit of a cold fish. 'Yeah, and an envious bugger,' replies Amis, noting that Larkin was jealous of Kingsley's ability as a novelist, his metropolitan life and mainly his women. 'Larkin was a sexual sloth who hated spending money on women, though there were many poets who splashed their way through women, like today's footballers.'

Our conversation turns to 'The Hitch' and life in London in the late 1970s, the subject of a novel which Amis is working on. 'What we talked about was women and it was all very carnal, in incredible detail about encounters, but serious . . . And very clear about feelings that were not to be trifled with, and quite moral, given it was low-bohemia promiscuity, but certainly not heartless. Dirty but not heartless.'

I nod in mock comprehension. My peppermint tea arrives, alongside an espresso for Amis. It is time, again, to move away from boys' talk to politics. Next year Amis will publish a compilation of his writing on the 9/11 terrorist attacks, *The Second Plane*. 'If September 11 had to happen, I am very pleased it happened in my lifetime because it's just endlessly riveting and couldn't be weirder.'

The crisis of Islam, he argues, is a crisis of masculinity. He speaks of 'centuries of humiliation', first by the west, latterly by Israel. 'How do you get back God's favour? You come to a T-junction: one says "less religion";

the other says "more religion" and you turn to the right. Absolutely desperate.'

The west must speak out. 'When we declare we are morally superior to the Taliban, we'redeclaring ourselves morally superior to the 15th century.' Still, it is no mystery why moderate Muslims are reluctant to follow suit. 'They (the extremists) have the monopoly of violence, of intimidation.' Slowly, the Amis invective gives way to sober reflection. He confesses to feeling guilty about being absent from England during the July 7 bombings. One of his sons had a holiday job which, if extended, would have seen him at Edgware Road tube station at the time of the bomb.

Shortly afterwards, a journalist came to visit Amis in Long Island. He had been on a transatlantic flight where passengers were not allowed to carry a book. Amis exploded in anger at this 'hideous symbol of humourless literalism'. He spoke about having to make the Muslim community suffer.

Now he regrets those words – a rare retreat for the macho wordsmith. Maybe Amis, 58, is mellowing. Odette's, he reveals, was where he and Kingsley lunched together in his father's final years. He looks at his watch: 'How are we doing?'

As an opening chapter, pretty good, I say to myself.

Odette's

Regents Park Road,
London NW1

....

1 x velouté of sweetcorn with pickled mushrooms and salted corn
1 x pan-fried organic salmon with braised lentils and caramelized baby onions
1 x roast breast of quail, confit leg with celeriac salad, jelly consommé, summer truffles
1 x green salad
2 x glasses of Chardonnay Bouscade
1 x fruit juice
1 x mineral water
1 x espresso
1 x peppermint tea

....

Total   £66.94

Michael Caine

'I can never pour these bleedin' things'

The actor talks about class, cholesterol, Jack Nicholson and becoming a 'Google freak'

By Peter Aspden

Disappointingly, Sir Michael Caine does not, when we are introduced, look me firmly in the eye and declare, 'My name's Michael Caine.' Nor, during the course of our tea together, does he at any stage say, 'Not a lot of people know that', or – and this admittedly asked too much – 'You were only supposed to blow the bloody doors off.' Is there a greater deliverer of catchphrases in the history of cinema than Michael Caine?

He is, at 77, still an impressive figure, standing tall and possessing a rich baritone with which he fires jokes with deft and natural comic timing. The accent is much imitated and inimitable. 'They've got scones and clotted cream here,' he offers, and somehow makes it sound funny. I am not sure about the word 'clotted', I say. It doesn't have good connotations. 'That's just what I thought,' he replies. 'If it had just said "cream" I'd have had it.'

A shared concern for cholesterol levels established, we settle on smoked salmon and cream-cheese sandwiches and cups of tea, English breakfast for him and Earl Grey for me. We are in a suite at the slightly soulless Wyndham hotel in Chelsea Harbour and there is a barrage of helicopter noise outside, as if there is a nationwide search for a runaway spy going on. 'It is because we are next to the Thames,' says Caine knowledgeably (he has a flat just round the corner), the kind of thing Harry Palmer might say to put me off the scent.

ferguson

Now that dates both of us. Harry Palmer – star of *The Ipcress File*, Caine's breakthrough role – hit the screens 45 years ago. The longevity of Caine's career is not the least remarkable thing about him. In his new autobiography, *The Elephant to Hollywood*, there are poignant personal recollections of two movie stars who were brought down by the pressures of stardom: one is Heath Ledger, the other Rita Hayworth. That is some chronological range. But Caine is still going strong.

Next year he once more reprises his role as Alfred the butler in Christopher Nolan's third *Batman* movie. He won critical acclaim for last year's *Harry Brown*, a hard-nosed vigilante movie shot in his native Elephant and Castle – a tough inner-London district (hence the title of his book). These are high-profile roles, in challenging and/or lucrative films. That is a rare feat for any actor, let alone one in the latter part of his eighth decade. How do you keep getting such great parts? I ask him. 'I dunno,' he deadpans. 'I sit back and wait for my agent to ring.'

But it wasn't always like that. The autobiography starts at an awkward moment for Caine. It is the early 1990s, and he is shooting a belated sequel to the Harry Palmer films, *Midnight in St Petersburg*, in the Russian city. He goes to the toilet. It is, he recalls, 'the filthiest toilet I have ever seen in my life. No one had cleaned it out. And I suddenly thought, "What am I doing here?"' He makes the existential crisis sound as desolate as Beckett. It sounds like a forlorn experience, I say. 'It was just after the communists had gone. When we had lunch on location they gave us Geiger counters, to test the food for radiation. And of course the first thing we did was test the batteries!' He laughs loudly. 'You don't want a duff battery!'

'It was a low moment,' he confesses, turning serious again. 'But I was quite philosophical about it.' He saw the incident as a turning point. He was preparing to wind his career down, getting increasingly involved with his restaurant businesses and enjoying the easy life in his new apartment in Miami's South Beach. And then, wouldn't you know it, Jack Nicholson called. 'He was the catalyst,' says Caine. 'I had got to that stage in life when you wouldn't even send me a good script. I had done a couple of duff ones. And then Jack was doing a movie with Bob Rafelson in Miami, and asked me to come. He said, "Get off your ass and just do it." And that changed everything. Jack is the nicest and kindest person, it was such a joy working with him.'

The resulting film – the noir thriller *Blood and Wine* – didn't change the landscape of motion pictures, but Caine's appetite was refreshed, his career revivified. Along came *Little Voice*, *The Cider House Rules*, *The Quiet American*, Baftas, Golden Globes and an Oscar. He says one of the aims in writing the book is to inspire readers of a certain age. 'As they get older, people think, "It's over." But it isn't. It doesn't have to be.'

The food arrives. The sandwiches are triple-deckers. 'Blimey! They give you a lot, don't they? We will weigh 400lb by the end of this!' He offers to serve the tea but is flummoxed by a designer teapot. 'I can never pour these bleedin' things. Either nothing comes out or it all goes all over the table.' Between us, we crack it. Caine dutifully removes one of the slices of his sandwich and tucks in with relish.

Caine has a habit of saying nice things about everyone. He makes Hollywood parties sound like village green fêtes. He doesn't even have a bad word for Frank Sinatra, for goodness' sake. I am suspicious of this. When he first travelled there in the 1960s, was Hollywood not full of predators trying to shaft this presumptuous Limey?

'No, truly not. And you know why? Because I wasn't their idea of a Limey. I wasn't posh. I didn't have this superior English attitude. And I was all for them.' His love affair with things American started during the war. 'There were American soldiers parked in the local recreation ground and we used to make their beds in exchange for chewing gum and Coca-Cola. I didn't actually go there until *Alfie*.' His maiden voyage happily coincided with an Oscar nomination. 'But then I saw Paul Scofield in *A Man for All Seasons* and thought, "There's no point in turning up."' (Scofield duly won the award.)

Was he an innocent when he went to Hollywood? 'I was an innocent by Hollywood standards. What surprised me was the hospitality, how kind people were. Even the lawyers and agents were the nicest people.' I raise an eyebrow. 'Remember, I wasn't really competing with anyone. You weren't going to lose a part to me if you were Jack Nicholson.' And then, in 2000, there was the knighthood, which helped. 'They like a bit of King Arthur.'

Never mind that, this was a town that famously spat people out for its own entertainment, I say. 'It can do. But I wasn't successful until I was 30. And I was a very tough 30, not some giddy little girl.'

The toughening of Michael Caine is the most sobering part of the book. Born Maurice Micklewhite to a working-class family in south-east London 'with funny eyes, sticking-out ears and, just to round it all off, rickets', he was evacuated during the war to a couple who would lock him in the cupboard for the weekend while they went socializing. That's the kind of thing you read about in the Sunday papers, I say.

He shrugs it off. 'A lot of children had a very bad time.' But to be locked in a cupboard for a whole weekend? 'They weren't wicked people. They took in the children for the money, and then didn't want to look after them. They wanted to go away for the weekend and didn't want to cart these dirty tykes from London around with them. Of course, when my mother came, she nearly went to prison for assaulting the woman. She beat her up.'

He is unsentimental about the war. 'I benefited from it. For a start I ate nothing but organic food for six years. We had no sugar, no biscuits, no fizzy drinks.' He went on to serve in Korea. 'It was a nightmare at the time. But I saw the world, and mixed with people from all classes and societies.'

He speaks movingly of his parents, particularly his father, whom he describes as a 'hero', a market porter at Billingsgate, who read voraciously and had an aptitude for technology, building his own radio from scratch. 'He was a symptom of this country losing out on talent because of class,' he says. 'They never knew they had it, they never knew they lost it. But today computers will compensate for any bad education there is.' He pauses for a second, and free-associates. 'I'm a Google freak.'

What do you google? I ask.

'Everything. It's a wonderful thing. I had a gardener who didn't know much about gardening.' (Read this out loud in a Caine voice and it is somehow hilarious.) 'Every time I bought a plant I googled it to find out how to look after it, and gave it to him and said, "There you go."'

It can be a terrible distraction, I add. He evidently agrees. 'I was looking for a penthouse once. And so I put in "Penthouse". Oh my God.' I quickly wonder to myself how many people who hit the *Penthouse* website are actually after a penthouse. 'And it's a funny thing – you can't switch it off. I had to take it out of the wall. I had to take the battery out.' There is something endearing about this techno-porno nightmare. Perhaps Jack Nicholson should have been around, I almost say.

He says in the book that 1967's *Billion Dollar Brain*, the third Harry

Palmer film, featured an early version of the internet. 'I read that in the paper,' he says. He remembers an adviser on the set trying to explain it to him. 'I said, "What a load of bollocks. Just tell me which knob to turn."' I thought it was the most preposterous thing I had ever heard.'

Like many people, I say, I became fully converted to Caine's acting talents by his performance in *Educating Rita*, for which he gained weight, looked permanently drunk and gave a startling portrayal of vulnerability. 'I had never been offered parts like that. But it is the proudest piece of acting I have ever done. An English professor in a college – it was the furthest thing from me that you could get. It was the first time I completely disappeared.' Was it hard to let his ego go like that? 'I realized that I didn't have that kind of ego, worrying about looking great. I didn't care about that.' He reminds me that he was in repertory theatre for nine years before his big movie break. 'A different role every week. I love being an actor. And I love not being me.'

Caine spends his time today between his Chelsea flat and his 200-year-old converted barn in Box Hill, Surrey, spending part of the winter in Miami. His days in Hollywood are over (he lived there for eight years, as a vociferous critic of Britain's tax regime). There is a touching account of a mournful farewell to his press agent on Rodeo Drive. 'I went straight to Ermenegildo Zegna [he mangles the name magnificently] and bought a shirt.' Did the retail therapy have the required effect? 'I was all right. I got on a plane and went home.'

Home is where his heart is. He is 'besotted' with his three grandchildren, a strength of reaction that surprised him, and reveres family life. Both in the book and our conversation, he repeatedly pays tribute to his wife of 37 years Shakira, 'the nicest person in the world', with whom he has a daughter (he also has a daughter with his first wife, the actress

Wyndham Grand
Chelsea Harbour,
London SW10

....

2 x Traditional Afternoon
Tea (all incl.)
£30

2 x Scottish smoked
salmon with herbed cream
cheese
Royal English Breakfast tea
Earl Grey tea

....

Total £30

Patricia Haines). It is because of his family, he says, that his book is studiedly discreet about all those Hollywood parties. 'When you fall in love, that becomes part of your past. Like mumps and measles. I didn't want to go into all that. Not like Kirk Douglas – he named them all, Marlene Dietrich, bleedin' Marilyn Monroe, everybody!'

As for the films, he says, touching every piece of wood in the vicinity, they keep rolling in. As well as the next *Batman*, he is preparing for a part in a version of Jules Verne's *The Mysterious Island*, about which he is unexpectedly rapturous. 'I have grandchildren now. And I get to fly off on a giant bumblebee. I want them to see that.'

Sean 'P. Diddy' Combs

When Diddy met daddy

The rapper, model, actor and king of bling tells the *FT*'s Washington bureau chief (aka cat daddy) that come election day, the youth of America will have their say

By James Harding

When I go back and listen to the tape of my conversation with Sean 'P. Diddy' Combs, I can hear myself launching into loud, uncertain guffaws and then stopping the laugh short, because I am not altogether clear whether he is joking.

Take his response to the question of which man he wants to win the election: 'I don't answer. It would sway people. If I endorse a candidate right now, I mean the race would probably be over.' I laugh, then wonder if he is being serious. Does he genuinely think that?

The hip hop magnate is just saying that for fun, he says, and then pauses. 'No,' he reflects. 'I could. I think a couple of people could: I think Russell Simmons [the founder of Def Jam records] could, I think Jay-Z [a rapper] could, I think Eminem could. There are a lot of people who have a lot of power that could. I think Oprah [Winfrey] could.'

Or, for example, his answer when asked about running for office. 'No . . . This is me doing my good thing. I like to party a little bit too hard to be in public office,' he smiles. 'I don't think I would be the best person to be in politics, because I would feel so passionately about something, they would probably have to pull me off somebody's ass in the Senate.' I suggest he would do well in Seoul's wrestling ring of a parliament and he agrees: 'I would be a champion there, I would get a lot of things done in South Korea.'

Even his assessment of his effort to get black people and young people to the polls is half jest, half earnest: 'This is the thing right now, cat daddy . . . this is like a pair of bellbottoms. You know what I'm saying, your parents are just looking at you and they're not looking down and then one day they're like: "Oh shit, everybody has on bellbottoms,"' he says. 'You were late. In this world, it is going down. On November 2, it is going down and the revolution will be televised.'

And, I guess, that's the point: at the end of our lunch, I was left wondering whether he may, in fact, be in the thick of the most significant phenomenon of the 2004 election or just an entertaining sideshow.

I had dropped off the campaign trail for a day to talk to Combs about the Vote or Die campaign, his drive to get generally poll-shy young Americans to vote on Tuesday. And, to begin with, it seemed more glitter than power.

A beefy man in a black suit, black shirt and black tie escorted me up to reception at Combs's Broadway office, where I waited for a while in a meeting room adorned with racks of the ultimate 'bling bling' accessory: chrome hubcaps engraved with the Sean John signature logo. Sophie, his miniature Maltese, wearing a magenta bow in her hair and a diamanté dog collar, trotted in, sniffed my feet and left. When I was shown into Combs's modest, cluttered office, he was on the phone, complaining about being ripped off by a building contractor. He finished the call, got up and shook my hand: 'Hey, baby,' he said.

From there on in, it was all politics and some soup. Me talking to Combs about voter mobilization is a bit like sending Donald Trump to interview Dr Ruth about gardening: a white Englishman boasting a sizeable Van Morrison collection and biting at the ankles of middle age talking to an icon of black youth in America with a résumé of rap music hits and enviable lovers about one of the more obscure areas of political science.

Combs is known by many names for many things: Puff Daddy, party promoter, music producer and former boss of Bad Boy Entertainment; P. Diddy, rapper and friend of the late Notorious B. I. G.; Puffy, ex-boyfriend of Jennifer Lopez and successful defendant in a bizarre criminal saga involving shooting in a nightclub and charges of bribery and illegal gun possession; Sean John, model and marketing man for his own fashion label; Sean Combs, Broadway actor; Mr Combs, salesman of an ever-expanding circle of selves, and frontman of Vote or Die.

There are roughly 42 million Americans aged 18 to 34. Combs has reach well beyond African American young men, pointing out that nearly 80 per cent of hip hop is bought by white people. And what is true for both young white and black people is they have a lousy record on election day: 36 per cent of 18- to 24-year-olds voted in 2000, compared with 72 per cent of 65- to 72-year-olds. (Not that voting statistics are Combs's forte – 'I can't fuck with you on that,' he told me.)

The political apathy makes simple sense when Combs explains it in his part-fumbling prose, part-street poetry style: 'We come from the community of people that is like, "Politics is bullshit, politicians are full of shit . . ." Just growing up in Harlem and seeing nothing change,' he says. 'You have a lot of people in those communities, whether it is Harlem, the South Side of Chicago, Detroit, Watts, wherever; they don't feel connected. There is a disconnect.'

Combs spent his early childhood in Harlem. His father was killed when he was three. His mother, a former model, moved the family to the more well-to-do New York suburb of Mount Vernon, where Combs went to private school. He went to Howard University, dropping out to get into nightclubs and the music business. The rest is not quite history, but, certainly, fame. He admits he has had his 'ups and downs', a reference, among other things, to the deaths of nine people who were crushed in a stampede at an event he organized in 1991. But, he continues, 'God has blessed me with a talent to be able to communicate, to energize and synergize, like, my people, young people and minorities.'

Combs, who has ranted against George W. Bush before, says his current effort is non-partisan: 'If you just relinquish your power to one party, then you lose your power,' he says. 'I can't necessarily say that Democrats have made things better than they can be.'

At this point, the phone rings for perhaps the fourth, but not the last, time and our meeting turns into lunch. 'You want some soup?' I say, 'Yes please.' 'Bring an extra one for my man.'

And for the better part of an hour, we slurp soup bulked up with pasta in big cardboard cups from the local fast-soup store, Hale Hearty Soups. We agree it is good soup.

Back to the election. Combs voted for the first time in 2000. A couple of years ago, he ran the New York Marathon; it was called 'Diddy runs the City'. Really? 'Where've you been?' he asks back. I apologize: 'Washington.'

Anyway, Combs's point is that he raised money – a lot of it – for New York public schools and got fired up about the failure of government to address the youth constituency as it does the elderly, the unions and the veterans.

He is selling the ballot box much as he would a movie or an album. 'In the field of entertainment, right, people have said I'm a marketing genius. I didn't say it,' he says. I let out a laugh, halt and point out that he is happy to repeat it. 'No. No. No,' he says. 'You've got to understand my sense of humour. I don't take myself seriously like that. I'm strong on marketing, though, that's one of my strengths.'

Certainly, his case for luring young people to the polls has more life in it than the extraordinarily unimaginative schedule of stump speeches to partisan crowds that is the A–Z of electioneering in the last weeks before polling day. 'All of the political bullshit, statistics, numbers and all of the corny slogans,' he says. 'I give it to them real and raw. That the time is now. This is how serious it is. And you have the power.

'I'm on a different campaign trail. While Kerry and Bush are in fields with a bunch of white people waving flags, I'm in areas, I'm reaching out to people of more diversity – white, black, Latino, Asian. How am I doing that?'

He has no time for CNN or Fox News Channel; he promotes the vote through MTV, Black Entertainment Television and Clear Channel radio stations. 'I'm going to go into his nightclubs, I'm going to go into the areas politicians don't go. I'm going to go into the barbershops. I'm going to be on the mix tapes.' And he has recruited fellow stars, from Leonardo DiCaprio to Yoko Ono to Alicia Keys, to spread the same message.

The results, he says, are below the radar of the mainstream media, but will be felt on Tuesday night. 'It is not going to be regular. Voting is up in these communities . . . it is going to be staggering how much it is up.' I point out that others have tried to do the same before and failed. 'Nobody does it like me. There is a certain passion, it is a certain way to relate.'

As we near the end of our conversation, Combs leans back in his black executive chair and pulls back the curtain. From his window, he can look down Broadway and see a towering image of himself on a billboard sporting own-branded Sean John casualwear, his Mohican-tufted head bowed and his arm raised in the black-power salute. He will have an even better view in a few months, when they have finished constructing his office upstairs: 'I'm building the biggest office in the United States; 6,000 square feet,' he says, explaining that we have actually been talking in his temporary office.

There is something fitting about this, not simply because Combs has an ironic though vivid self-regard. Nor is it because this reticent 5ft 9in guy in sweatpants and a T-shirt seems like a man dwarfed by his own persona. Combs's image looms huge over Times Square, as if, facing uptown, past the chi-chi neighbourhoods that flank Central Park, he is summoning the ranks in Harlem to stand up and be counted. 'That's black power right there,' he says. 'Black power.' He grins, looking at the giant picture of himself. 'Right there.'

Gavin Ewart

The last toast for a poet

The bard's death, last week, was hardly the consequence of lunch with the *Financial Times*. But, with hindsight, the *FT* gave him a grand send-off

By Nigel Spivey

G avin Ewart is dead. The poet's death, last week, was hardly the consequence of lunch with the *Financial Times*. But, with hindsight, we gave him a grand send-off.

He had just recovered from a prostate operation when we met in high summer. But intimations of mortality were not apparent. Far from it.

Aiming to arrive on good time at the Café Royal, I found him already settled at the bar, fondling a large pink drink. 'Ah,' he said, without guilt. 'There you are.'

'I say,' I said, with anguish. 'That can only be a Negroni.' It was indeed a Negroni, the gin and Campari mixture with a velocity of intoxication that is both feared and loved by those who know it. This lunch would be, in the poet's own phrase, 'a thick one'.

Once upon a time the Grill Room of the Café Royal was a bohemian place. When Ewart came there in his youth, it was packed with chess-playing intellectuals.

The ripe Edwardian decor still gleams around the tables, but the earnest beards have disappeared. No wonder. A Negroni or three later, two bottles of Rully, and a wander into à la carte territory, and we had no trouble in running up a plump three-figure bill. At the time I was horrified. But glossed as a funerary banquet, it now seems fitting.

In fact, our chat began on the topic of the death of another poet, Stephen Spender. While W. H. Auden was Ewart's mentor, Spender was his first hands-on helper in the literary workplace.

'Hands on?' I queried, pruriently.

'Oh no, he never fancied me. He was a very decent man, too nice, probably, for his own good. You could tell from his face. He looked angelic from youth to the grave. Whereas Auden . . .' he paused.

'Had a face like an old potato,' I suggested.

'Exactly. Pure debauchery,' concluded Ewart. 'But always the superior craftsman. You know his lines, "For what as easy / For what thought small . . . Who goes with who / The bedclothes say", and so on. They're what my old English master used to call "poetry in pyjamas". Light, funny, sensuous.'

As it happens, Ewart's English master, T. C. Worsley, was for many years the *FT*'s drama and then television critic. The poetry in pyjamas that Worsley encouraged Ewart to write had its own success, even notoriety. And it was perhaps natural that he turned his skills to copywriting, with the Walter Thompson agency. He spent 20 years in the business. What, I asked him, were his triumphs there?

He mused. 'There was something for Andrews Liver Salts. We needed to convince women to take them. I think we succeeded. Then there was my new name for Bulmer's cider, "Strongbow". I just thought it was a good strong name, but it turned out that Strongbow was also a local hero of Herefordshire, where the cider is made. That tickled Bulmer's no end.'

He went into a reverie, perhaps induced by foie gras, which was an evident treat for him. 'You're too young for this one. But it was quite a hit.' And he began to croon: 'We must give them lovely Cheeselets, Twiglets must be on the scene. Do you get me, Mr Peek? You've said a mouthful, Mr Frean.'

Even when an aged bard is reciting his most banal work, it is enchanting. For a moment, the Café Royal returned to its inspirational heyday. Heads turned to catch the rhyme.

'Then,' he resumed, gloomily, 'they put me on to GKN screws. Technical copy. A screw is a screw is a screw. You can't write poetry about screws.'

This was a distinct admission of failure. For it was the singular hallmark of Ewart's work that you could indeed craft a poem from any subject whatsoever. I asked him if he were still turning them out.

'Oh yes. In fact I've just finished one. A paean of praise to the recently retired captain of the Scotland rugby team.'

'Wow,' I said. 'What rhymes with Hastings?'

'It's a wee ballad,' said Ewart, 'about how he and his team gave the Ivory Coast one of time's most tremendous pastings.'

I had to remind him that his collected works were out of print. 'But the good news,' I said, 'is that you've made the official grade. You're listed in Harold Bloom's *Western Canon* as one of the essential writers of the 20th century.'

A naturally modest man, he permitted himself an expression of enormous satisfaction. 'Yes,' he said. 'I noticed that. Up with Auden.'

It was, as I now see, the declaration of a life fulfilled: proving that good light verse has a place with good heavy verse in our lives.

Eventually we departed the Café Royal, in a moderately straight line; and when I saluted him on to a bus home, Gavin Ewart had the aura of a very happy traveller.

Zaha Hadid

Harnessing a global vision

The architect was a controversial choice to design the Cardiff Bay opera house

By Lucy Kellaway

I n the rag-rolled and marbled interior of Aubergine, a French restaurant in Fulham, the Iraqi architect Zaha Hadid looked all wrong. Too large for one thing and too flamboyant in a brilliant-lime-green pleated silk housecoat with a gash of crimson lipstick.

This woman is the queen of avant-garde architecture. For over a decade she has travelled the world winning competitions with her far-out, asymmetrical creations. Last year she beat nearly 300 architects in a contest for the Cardiff Bay opera house, submitting a design that has variously been described as a row of jewels, a freeze-framed explosion and a deconstructed pigsty.

But unlike her other work – most of which has never been built – the opera house may actually become a reality if the Millennium Fund decides during the next few weeks to pay £50m towards it.

'I like more funky restaurants,' she said in a husky voice, lighting the first of many cigarettes. I asked what she thought of the decor. 'It's not terrible, but I find it too fussy.' This was an understatement, judging by the look on her face.

Hadid knows something about restaurants, having recently designed one in Sapporo, Japan. 'The theme was ice and fire,' she said. 'Monochromic. The ground floor is ice, with one enormous sheet of glass suspended very low. Upstairs is the fire, with rubber sofas and fibre-glass – it is as though a tornado had started in the bar and hit the ceiling.'

'I see,' I said, although I didn't quite. A waiter minced up to our table. "'Ello leddies, I leet you 'ave a look at ze luncheon menoo,' he said.

Hadid exhaled slowly. 'I really don't understand a thing they say,' she said with the easy irreverence of one naughty schoolgirl to another. 'I don't find this French accent in English at all charming. It is like watching Peter Sellers. I mean! Send them to elocution classes!' She gave an eruption of a laugh.

She had chosen Aubergine because some friends had praised the food, yet so far so bad. Still, she brightened up on seeing a soup on the menu called 'cappuccino', and earned the unwanted approval of the waiter by choosing it. 'C'est la grande spécialité, madame,' he said.

Hadid rattled off the names of London restaurants that she did consider funky, though even these were not entirely to her liking as the service was poor. 'The problem in this country is that unless you go to the very top, you get terrible service. You really notice when you land in Switzerland. In America the service is more casual but they do accommodate you.'

This was the beginning of what turned out to be a global lunch. Even the most casual remark led to a comparison with foreign countries and cities, and in the course of one meal she mentioned Shanghai, Beijing, Japan, Hong Kong, Brazil, Vienna, Paris, Singapore, Tunis, Berlin, Switzerland, New York, Wales and, of course, Iraq.

It is most unlikely that she was trying to impress with this geographical name-dropping; instead the relentlessly international bent seems to have become part of her personality. Brought up in Baghdad, she went briefly to a minor girls' boarding school in England, lives in London but spends much time in New York, and is now working in both Vienna and Berlin. 'I fly twice a week and I am a doggy,' she complained. 'Finished.'

A waiter brought a dainty little *amuse-gueule* with a quail's egg on top, and placed it carefully in front of us. 'Bon appétit, mesdames,' he said.

I tried to get her to talk about Iraq and Saddam Hussein, but with little success. 'The Gulf war depressed me because there is no need for any wars,' she said. 'It was a very unfortunate situation. It is sad.' She seemed unwilling to elaborate. The fish cappuccino, which had just arrived, appeared to be meeting her approval. The soup, she said, reminded her of some dishes she had eaten in China. I felt relieved;

there is something powerful and original about her that made me want to please.

I rather crassly asked whether it was difficult being a relatively young woman – and an Arab to boot – in a business dominated by elderly white males. 'I am proud of being an Arab. Some people may have their prejudices but they can't help it,' she said easily. 'But there are two sides to everything. People surprise you by being so supportive.'

Even the notorious sexism of the construction industry she takes in her stride. 'They can't look at me in the face. They look at me here [pointing at her shoulder]. I say, "Why are you looking at my shoulder?"' She fixed me with her large brown eyes. If I were a developer I would have felt very small indeed.

However, it is not the chauvinism of developers that really vexes her, but their conservatism. 'They become so fixated with a particular idea that when you produce another they think either it's impossible or too expensive.'

Cautiously, I mentioned the Prince of Wales. She snorted. 'The royal family cannot be critical of things when they built that gate. The Queen Mother's Gate. Hideous.'

We ordered our puddings, and I pressed on, quizzing her about the high drama of the Cardiff opera house contest, which she won twice over, the first time meeting such hostility from the locals that she was asked to enter the competition all over again – much to the outrage of the architecture profession.

'I didn't take it personally. You have to be generous with people,' she said. 'Give them time and space to understand. The problem is that people in this country have seen so much garbage for so long they think life is a Tesco. When the highest aspiration is to make a supermarket, then you have a problem.'

She started to explain that what matters about a building is not what it is made of, or any of the details, but the space itself. 'Good space transcends taste and values. It's a weird, mystical thing. It's very difficult to achieve, but you know when you've got it.'

I asked her to describe the Cardiff space. 'It is a city of rooms. It has large rooms and small rooms. Different volumes. They stretch from linear to cubic to shadow. It is like a galaxy. You see objects suspended over your head. It flows like a river.'

I said it will be a great shame if these rivers, galaxies and cities never come into being, and if the Millennium Fund decides to finance a rival project for a tacky rugby stadium instead. 'We are doing our damnedest to do the best we can,' she said. 'We'll see what happens.'

Our lunch had started late and it was well after 3.30 when we finally gathered ourselves up and left. The other lingering diners stopped and stared as Hadid swept out.

They might have stared even harder had she been wearing one of the outfits that she used to attach to herself with pins. However, these garments took several hours to take on and off, and she has no time for that now. She hailed a cab to take her back to the office, and invited me to visit next time I was passing. So not going abroad today? Quickly, she explained: 'I was meant to be going to Brazil . . .'

David Hockney

A loaded paintbrush

The artist tells the *FT* why he has given
up on photography and turned to
watercolours instead

By Christopher Parkes

D avid Hockney lives in a world of his own imagining, where laws bend to the artist's will or whim. It comes accoutred with his rules of morality and manners, his principles of perspective, proportion and colour, and can be found in the space occupied by his home and gardens behind a scruffy boundary fence at the end of a dizzying drive to the very edge of the Hollywood hills. By 'chopping up space', a technique he applied to his opera stage sets, he has created a contiguous, benevolent environment where exterior and interior merge.

Down a gully, there's an iconic pool with ripples painted on the bottom to amplify the effect of the gentler stirrings on the water's surface. Up a facing slope, painted fishes dangle from a tree, swimming in their waterless aquarium.

Elevated walkways, decks, awnings and furniture adorned in Matisse's brilliant palette of blues, reds, yellows and greens – 'the colours of nature', he says – enhance rather than affront the more muted tones of the crowded, semi-tropical landscaping. A hall of mirrors, a gallery, a giant's paintbox stuffed with pencils and crayons; it is all Hockney.

His world even has its own private micro-climate – the smoke from his Camel filters that travels with him. Hockney is tickled by a *New York Times* picture of himself outside the gala opening of Frank Gehry's Walt Disney Concert Hall in Los Angeles. He is standing alone, his face barely visible through a wreath of smoke.

Over a lunch of sweet-glazed lamb chops and baked potatoes, prepared by his housekeeper, we are sharing a moan about how the petty restrictions on personal indulgence and busybody attitudes that nudged him out of his native England in 1978 have come to dog him in what-the-hell California.

'We had some buttons made that said "End Bossiness Soon",' he says. 'I wanted "End Bossiness Now", but I knew that was asking a bit too much.' He gives off a roar.

'But I'm only talking about out there,' he says, describing an overhead circle with his hand. Then, with a smaller rotation to encompass Hockney's universe: 'This is the real world and I paint it.'

He says he does not really care about what goes on outside. But that does not mean he is detached. Indeed, he ponders a good deal on what he calls 'the bigger things happening'. To Hockney, who relates only to things visual, these include the loss of 'veracity' in photography, exemplified on his studio wall by clippings of the staged Second World War planting of the US flag on Iwo Jima, and a more recent example from the *Los Angeles Times*, depicting an extraordinary illustrated apology for the publication of a digitally doctored photograph from the war in Iraq.

'Look at a photograph and you believe you are seeing something that once existed in time and space. That's not now necessarily the case. You don't need to believe a picture any more: it could be made up.

'I haven't figured out what that will do to us, but it will be something quite profound,' he says.

He recalls a 1989 visit to 'smoke-free' Silicon Valley to preview Adobe PhotoShop software that facilitates the manipulation of digital pictures. On the way back, he remembers noting what he had seen meant the end for chemical photography and the darkroom artist.

One effect, he says, now that digital technology has taken the art out of it, and put the mouse/brush in the hand of any snapper with a laptop and a few bucks' worth of software, could be that photography in all its forms may lose the position of cultural dominance it enjoyed in the 20th century.

He already knows how it has affected his world: those clippings mark the end of his involvement with the camera. The fate of his relationship with the medium was sealed, he says, during research for his last book,

Secret Knowledge – an investigation of the old masters' use of camera obscura and camera lucida in which the artist's hand and eye are in essence integrated into an optical device, providing the focus and the means for preserving an image. His experiments with the format ended with a series of camera lucida drawings that spanned 1999 to 2001.

Last year, in his longest stay in London since he moved to California, he discarded mirrors, prisms and lenses and drew 25 portraits from life in the most productive sustained bout of painting in his career.

Those scraps of newspaper mark a decisive point in the life of an artist who experimented with photography to substantial acclaim for 20 years. The collage *Pearblossom Highway, 1986* is one of his best-known pieces.

But it's not good enough for him now. 'I think the world is beautiful but we don't know totally what it looks like or how to make pictures of it,' Hockney says. 'Photographs aren't good enough. Frankly, they're not real enough.'

Pounding away at his thesis, he mocks a recent software advertisement that claimed it could make an artist of anyone.

'I had a good laugh at that. You can be an artist with a Bic pen!'

He is glad the copywriter recognized the importance of the human hand in art, even if it is holding a mouse.

'But as the Chinese would say, you need three things: the eye, the hand and the heart. Two won't do. Very wise, the Chinese.'

Which brings us back to another round of Camels and the first work he showed me in his studio an hour or so before: a small, smudgy reproduction of a 350-year-old Rembrandt drawing. Made in brown ink with a reed pen or possibly a sharpened stick, it shows a family group teaching a child to walk, sketched unaware, embraced by an aura of tenderness and attentiveness unmarred by the coarseness of the medium.

All Hockney said was: 'You can't do that with a photograph.'

Ignoring his sliver of angel cake, now lightly dusted with ash, he returns to his Rembrandt, devilled out of some dusty corner in the British Museum, and proclaims it a virtuoso piece. 'It doesn't shout "art" immediately. It shouts "humanity" first,' he says.

We have rambled through fame, fortune, a dismissive exchange on charges that he is a mere illustrator or 'the Cole Porter of figurative painting' and we are unintentionally back with the 'bigger things'.

Painting is in the dumps. Why? 'Because they stopped teaching it,' he says straight off.

At 16, Hockney went to art school in Bradford, Yorkshire, and spent four years learning drawing and being taught how to look and see before going to the Royal College of Art. 'The destruction started in the early 1960s. I witnessed it at the Royal College. I used to argue and they said, "Oh, it's David again – the old back-to-the-life-room story." I said, "No, no, forward to the life room."'

The requirement that secondary-school students must obtain A-levels to be admitted to art colleges continued the insurrection. But nothing is forever. Now, he says, there are young people – perhaps even prompted by the potential of the computer – who realize the value of being taught rather than hoping for the best from trial and error.

Hockney continues to learn. His new portraits are executed in watercolour, a difficult medium he had not used previously.

'I spent last year training my eyes not to see like a camera and, believe me, you've got to do a lot of work to achieve that,' he says.

In his studio, a dozen or more portraits hang in various stages of completion. There is a light littering of cigarette butts on the floor and an abandoned, unplugged jogging machine. 'I swim these days,' he says.

Chez David Hockney

2 x grilled glazed lamb chops
2 x baked potatoes with butter, green onions and bacon
2 x mixed salad
2 x angel cake
1 x Clausthaler near-beer
1 x San Pellegrino
1 x coffee
1 x tea

Back at the table, I ask him what is left. 'Oh, I'm painting now and it will grow. The more you understand what photography was, the more you begin to see that painting is necessary. I've got plenty to do but I've got to be left alone to do it quietly and I will. And I will show you what painting can do.'

He has already learnt that *Secret Knowledge*, recently published in Hungarian, its 12th language version, has given art historians and students new avenues to explore. More importantly, it has opened a way forward for the autodidact Hockney.

'I'm just beginning,' he says. '[The book] led me back to the hand and back to the hand with a loaded brush.' Just how loaded will be revealed at an exhibition of portraits and garden paintings planned for the Whitney Museum in New York in March 2004 and, to judge by the set of Hockney's jaw, in years to come.

'You can't go on saying art is this, that and the other and ignore the deep desire to see images of ourselves,' he says. 'If drawing is 30,000 years old, do you think that just because some theoretician comes along in 1960 and says there's no need for it, that we'll forget it? It's only a temporary disturbance. But then temporary things are disruptive,' he says.

'I'll avoid New York for the next five years. There's no bohemia there now, because bohemia is by definition tolerant of human frailty. It'll come back. All we need is a bit of tension and we'll all be smoking again.'

Angelina Jolie

'Acting is like being in therapy'

As she finishes her debut film as a director, the Hollywood star takes time out to explain why she doesn't love acting as much as she used to and why she dreams of crossing the Sahara by camel

By Matthew Garrahan

Watching Angelina Jolie stride through a restaurant is to be given a lesson in how to avoid attracting attention in public. She looks ahead impassively, her back is straight and she walks at speed so that she will have moved on before any diners, who think they might just have spotted the world's biggest female movie star, have time to do a double take.

Unlike the other diners in The Grill on the Universal Studios lot in Hollywood, I know she is coming, so although I am seated at the back of the restaurant I notice her as soon as she enters. She is dressed entirely in black – black shirt, black trousers, black shoes – her long brown hair falling over her shoulders, a Louis Vuitton bag clutched at her side. Suddenly she is standing next to me and I am scrambling awkwardly out of my seat to introduce myself. 'Hi,' she says, putting out her hand for me to shake, her face lighting up into a broad smile that almost knocks me off my feet. 'I'm Angie.'

We squeeze into a booth facing each other and a waiter asks if she'd like something to drink. I arrived 10 minutes earlier and am already halfway through an Arnold Palmer – iced tea mixed with lemonade – a

staple of California lunches. She orders a mint tea, flashing another smile.

She explains that she chose the location because she is using an office at the studio to put the finishing touches to her directorial debut, *In the Land of Blood and Honey*, a love story she also wrote, which is set in the Bosnian war. It's a low-budget affair with a little-known cast and today is her final day of post-production. 'This is the crazy day,' she says, looking at the menu. 'We're down to the wire. Today at four o'clock we make the call and it's all over. We're locked and there's no changing it.'

Lunch has taken a while to pin down. In addition to making films, Jolie, 36, has six children and a raft of humanitarian commitments with the United Nations as an ambassador with its High Commission for Refugees. Over the years her UN role has involved visits to camps in countries such as Sierra Leone, Pakistan and Ecuador.

She doesn't have an agent or publicist so our meeting was arranged after several weeks of email and telephone correspondence with a mysterious Frenchman called David. 'I've got good news and bad news,' he said one day. 'The good news is she definitely wants to do it. The bad news is you have to go to Malta.' Her partner, actor Brad Pitt, had been filming in Europe and she and the children were there with him.

We decided it would be better to wait until she had returned to Los Angeles, which is why we are now in a restaurant at Universal, home to Steven Spielberg's production offices, several soundstages and the sets of numerous television shows. Inside The Grill, framed prints of classic Universal releases such as *The Birds* and *The Creature from the Black Lagoon* hang on the walls. I had taken in the surroundings while waiting for Jolie to arrive but now she is here it is difficult to look at anything else. In person, her beauty is amplified; her eyes sparkle mischievously when she laughs, her celebrated lips frame a set of blinding white teeth. She rarely does interviews and is guarded at first – particularly when I broach subjects that she is reluctant to discuss. For instance, she doesn't want to tell me too much about her new film because she doesn't want to pre-empt the press campaign which is being lined up ahead of its release. But as she deflects these questions, there is a knowing smile and a shrug that is almost apologetic, as if to say, 'Sorry, it's all part of the game.'

The waiter has returned with her tea, and when it is poured Jolie adds some honey to her cup. We look at the menus again. 'There's a pasta in here somewhere,' she says when the waiter asks if we're ready to order. 'I'll have that with chicken.' I choose grilled salmon with heirloom tomatoes.

She tells me she has brought her daughters with her for this trip. She explains that she and Pitt tend to travel everywhere with their children and the family is never in the same place for long. 'We take turns working so one of us can be home with the kids.' They are apart when we meet, though. 'It's been hard – I've been [in Los Angeles] for a week and it's very unusual to separate for this long. I brought the girls so we're having a special girl trip. All the boys are hanging out with Brad . . . he's filming a zombie movie [*World War Z*].'

The Jolie Pitt family is a miniature League of Nations. Their eldest son Maddox, who is almost 10, was adopted in 2002 from his native Cambodia. Zahara, aged six, was born in Ethiopia, while Shiloh, the couple's first biological child, was born five years ago in Namibia. Pax, whom they adopted four years ago, was born in Vietnam and three years ago, Jolie gave birth in France to twins Knox and Vivienne. 'They are all learning about each other's cultures as well as being proud of their own,' she says. 'So it's not like just the boys get to do the Asian thing. They all have their flags over their beds and their individual pride. We owe Vietnam a visit, because Pax is due. Z wants to get back to Africa, and Shiloh too. So everyone takes their turns in their country.'

She has been to Cambodia this year, to shoot an advertising campaign for Louis Vuitton with Annie Leibovitz. An impoverished country might seem like an odd place for a luxury fashion house to shoot an ad campaign but the final decision was made by Jolie herself. 'To actually do it there, to highlight the beauty of the country, was something I was very happy to do because it is a place people should travel to,' she says. Indeed, she and Pitt have a house there – 'It's a little place on stilts.' Her fee from the campaign will go towards charitable projects in the country, she says, building on work she began with a foundation the family established in Maddox's name. 'It's focused on protecting mountains from deforestation, poaching and clearing landmines. We put it together for Mad so when he's older he'll hopefully take it over.'

Our food has arrived. Jolie's pasta is simple, with pieces of chicken in a tomato sauce. But my salmon is a part of an elaborate creation, built into a tower, with an ornate garnish of fennel, heirloom tomatoes and some other diced vegetables that I fail to identify. It looks ridiculous and when she sees my plate she bursts out laughing.

Given how much they travel I wonder where they consider home. 'Home is wherever we are.' Does she feel rootless? 'Yes, but happily. I'm very bad at staying in one place. I'm also bad at sitting still. I was a terrible student at school. But there's so much to explore in the world . . . so I love travel. If you can travel I think it's the best way to raise kids.'

This reference to her youth reminds me how much she has changed over the past 15 years since she came to prominence with her role in the high-school cyber thriller *Hackers*. Back then she seemed an archetypal Hollywood wild child. The daughter of actors Jon Voight and Marcheline Bertrand, she talked of self-harming in her teens and by her late twenties she had been married twice – first to *Hackers* co-star, English actor Jonny Lee Miller, and then to the American actor and singer Billy Bob Thornton. She had an interest in knives, acquired several tattoos – including one of Thornton's name on her arm (it has since been removed) and wore a locket containing his blood.

The controversies accompanied a rising career. In 2000 she won an Oscar for her startling performance as a patient in a mental hospital in *Girl, Interrupted* and soon became a fully fledged action star with the role of Lara Croft in *Tomb Raider* (2001) and in films such as *Mr and Mrs Smith* (2005). It was on that set that she first met Pitt and the pair have since become Hollywood's premier power couple, their fame magnified to the extent that they are, according to their friend, actor Matt Damon, 'like prisoners'. The media scrutiny shows no sign of letting up. Last year the couple sued the *News of the World* when it printed a false story alleging that they were breaking up; I ask if she shed any tears at the newspaper's recent closure. 'I did hear something about that . . . clearly I never read it. So it's hard to know how much of a loss it is.'

She has spent most of her adult life in the public eye. But the person I have read about before our lunch couldn't seem more different from the poised woman opposite me. Motherhood has changed her, she says, particularly with respect to her career. 'I've never not been grateful to be an actor . . . but I think when I was younger I needed [acting] more. I was trying to question things in life so you find these characters that help you find things and grow.'

She explains that her relationship with acting has changed over the years. 'It's like being in therapy, in a way,' she says, taking a forkful of penne and chicken. 'You're drawn to certain roles because they question something about life, or about love, or about freedom. You ask these questions as you grow up: am I strong enough, am I sane enough? Do I understand love, do I understand myself?' Now, she adds, 'I'm older and I know who I am . . . and I'm less interested in the character helping me answer something . . . than in being able to answer it for myself, as a woman, as an adult, with my family.' We talk about *Salt*, an action film released last year in which Jolie punches, shoots and kicks her way through the CIA, Secret Service and a cabal of rogue Russian spies. The title role was initially written for a man but the script was modified when it became clear she was interested. 'I'd just had the twins,' she recalls. 'I'd been in a nightgown for a very, very long time. And I was sitting in the hospital breastfeeding and reading this script in my nightgown, feeling so soft and mama . . . and I was flipping these pages and it was all fighting and shooting guns. I thought, "That's what I need. I need to get out of my nightgown and I need a gun." I'm sure many a woman who has been through childbirth has thought, "It would be nice to get a little physical, get a little wild . . . to remember what that other side is like."'

She says she is not thinking of quitting acting any time soon. 'But I don't love it as much [as I did]. I love being a mom.' She is, however, clearly excited about being behind the camera for the first time. 'I prefer it to acting,' she says. I ask if she drew on her experiences with the directors she has worked with. 'I think I've learnt something from all of them – even the ones I didn't like.' I try to get her to dish the dirt on the latter but she politely declines. She is full of praise for Michael Winterbottom, who directed her in *A Mighty Heart* (2007), the story of Daniel Pearl, the journalist who was abducted and killed in Pakistan. 'I also learnt a lot from Clint Eastwood [her director in 2008's *Changeling*] about how to appreciate the members of the crew, empowering them to do their job. I never worked with David Fincher [director of *Fight Club* and *The Social Network*] but I know him as a friend and have seen how meticulous he is, his attention to detail, how hard he works – even when you're too tired to go back into the room – to make sure that you've got it right.'

Fincher is in the frame to direct her in the forthcoming *Cleopatra*, but Jolie hints that we may see less of her on screen in future. 'As Brad and I get older we're going to do fewer films. I've been working for a long time, he's been working for a long time . . . we've had a nice run and don't want to be doing this our whole lives. There are a lot of other things to do.'

China is on her list of places still to explore, and she would love to see Burma, 'but not in the wrong circumstances', given that the country is under the control of an oppressive military junta. 'And Iran. I'd love to go to Iran.' Her dream, however, is to 'cross the Sahara. It takes 28 days . . . it would have to be on a camel. I wonder if I could do it in pieces and station the kids along the way,' she muses.

I tell her it sounds ideal for their nomadic family and we stand to say goodbye. There's no handshake this time, although she leans forward to kiss me on each cheek. Then she walks away through the now half-empty restaurant, out into the California sunshine, back to work.

Albert Uderzo

Asterix and the national treasure

The 78-year-old illustrator of the famously rebellious Gaul is somewhat at odds with recent violent protests in France

By John Thornhill

T he French sommelier, normally the most solemn of men, could resist no longer and approached Albert Uderzo to ask if he would like a little magic potion from the wine list. Asterix's 'father' smiled indulgently, as if hearing the quip for the first time, and opted for a splendid bottle of Pouilly-Fumé instead.

Uderzo, who along with René Goscinny invented the cartoon characters of Asterix, Obelix and the world-famous village of potion-drinking, boar-eating, Roman-bashing Gauls, is regarded as a national treasure in France. On meeting him, it is easy to understand why.

In spite of his 78 years of age, Uderzo sparkles with a gentle humour and a boyish charm, retaining an inquisitive interest in the foibles of the French and the wider wonders of the world.

In the chintzy pink dining room of the Hotel Raphael, close to the Arc de Triomphe, he is treated with fond reverence by the restaurant's punctilious staff. Dressed in a smart blue blazer, with a broad, handsome face and swept-back silver hair, Uderzo blends smoothly into the elegant surroundings.

The subject of the month has been the real-life violence that has raged across France's poorer *banlieues*, with 10,000 cars having been torched by disaffected youths. Uderzo has strong views on the issue, having grown up in an Italian immigrant family in Clichy-sous-Bois,

where the 'appalling' riots first erupted. 'I know this *banlieue* very well. In my day we had fun in the streets but we never thought about setting fire to cars,' he says indignantly. 'Sometimes I have the impression of living on another planet. The world has completely changed and I do not think it is for the better. It is for the worse.'

The illustrator seems pained by talk of social breakdown and the shirking of parental responsibility and visibly relaxes when the conversation turns to the contents of the menu – a matter of serious attention – and the origins and character of Asterix himself.

'You must go back 46 years,' he says with the cadences of a natural storyteller. 'Asterix was born in 1959. We met a publisher who wanted a cartoon book for children drawing on French culture and history. Asterix represents the first lesson of history that children learn at school.'

Goscinny, who wrote the words, and Uderzo, who drew the illustrations, let their imaginations roam freely in creating Asterix since little was known about the era in which the Gauls lived apart from the facts that they fought fiercely among themselves and were heavily influenced by Druidic rites. 'Little by little Asterix evolved into the person we know today. But,' he adds with a chuckle, 'if we had known how long Asterix would have gone on then we would have paid more attention to the details in the first album.'

That first album about the little Gallic warrior was published in 1961. Its opening sentences, repeated in every subsequent album, have become one of the most famous refrains in children's literature: 'The year is 50 BC. Gaul is entirely occupied by the Romans. Well, not entirely . . . One small village of indomitable Gauls still holds out against the invaders.'

The stirring tales of how a band of cunning Gauls outwits and outfights Julius Caesar and his legions have become an international publishing phenomenon. The albums, now beloved by three successive generations, have been translated into 110 languages and dialects – including Afrikaans, Welsh, Hebrew and Occitan – and have sold more than 320m copies.

Although Goscinny died of a heart attack in 1977, Uderzo has continued to release new albums single-handed – although he admits they lack the 'genius of humour' that spilled from the pen of his late collaborator.

In truth, the latest album, *Asterix and the Falling Sky*, the 33rd in the series, is not the greatest of Asterix's adventures, veering off into new territory by including alien characters inspired by Walt Disney cartoons and Japanese manga comics. It has, nevertheless, still proved a best-seller in the run-up to Christmas.

Contrary to press speculation, Uderzo denies this album was intended to conclude the series. 'No, no, no, it is not the last. Certain journalists believed this because the cover was the mirror image of the first Asterix album. That is indeed the case but it was not at all my intention to suggest it would be the last album. I can say that for one simple reason: my life is the work that I do. The day will never come when I will say that I have nothing more to do with this character. I certainly hope that I will have more ideas.'

Confessing that he does not frequent fancy restaurants (the Raphael hotel has been chosen by his publisher for its convenience), Uderzo opts for a simple meal of smoked salmon followed by filet of sole.

I am only slightly more adventurous in choosing salmon and the filet of bar. But there is sophistication in simplicity: the food is presented to perfection and is sweetly complemented by the Pouilly-Fumé.

To many readers, Asterix has come to personify the French, with their infuriating, and occasionally endearing, contradictions, their determination to defy the US (the modern-day Rome) and their defiance of a homogenized, globalized future. As one political commentator recently observed: 'Asterix is the citizen who is enamoured with liberty but thirsty for equality, the taxpayer who is pro-public service but anti-tax, the voter who would like to change everything but stamps his feet at the mention of reform. Asterix is neither from the right nor from the left but he is quite simply French.'

Uderzo says his Gauls were indeed created to reflect contemporary French characteristics but he suggests they also appear to enshrine eternal and universal values.

'In every country it is the same thing: the more we are under the sway of globalization, the more people feel the need to rediscover their roots,' he says.

It seems paradoxical that while Asterix, the character, is viewed as the champion of anti-globalization, Asterix, the international publishing phenomenon, is the undoubted beneficiary of a globalizing world.

'The Gauls are the French of today,' Uderzo says. 'But that raises the question: why do they work so well abroad? Perhaps it is because thanks to globalization we all resemble each other. We have the same tastes, the same desires, the same problems. I think that is important.

'Perhaps another reason is that Asterix has become a release valve for everyone. I think that is why he attracts young people, even unconsciously, because they do not like being under submission to anyone. They want a magic potion, not so that they can invade another country but so that they can defend themselves in their own home and quickly resolve all their problems.'

One of the most amusing features of the Asterix albums is the depiction of foreigners, be they Romans, Belgians, Britons, Germans or Spaniards, who are – mostly playfully – lampooned according to their national stereotypes, as seen through French eyes.

'Of course, we made the Germans very strict, very militaristic, with helmets that resembled a little those from the Second World War. The English were also made very British, especially when we translated their phrases into French. It was an idea of Goscinny, who spoke good English and who took these English phrases and translated them into the most astounding French.'

The nationalities that are so caricatured do not seem to have taken offence. Indeed, in the words of Obelix, these foreigners are mad: the sales of Asterix often appear strongest in the countries that are the most ridiculed. The Germans, for example, have bought almost 100m Asterix albums in total. Belgians and Britons are also big fans, although, curiously, Finland holds the record for the highest number of albums bought per head.

Asterix is also conquering new markets in India and South America. His publishers are even negotiating a Chinese edition.

The one market that Asterix has never truly conquered is the US, even though it was American animators, such as Walt Disney, who first inspired Uderzo to become an illustrator. He suggests that this may have something to do with the different formats of cartoons in the US, or a sense of cultural protectionism, or a different way of seeing the world.

'It is not only the Atlantic that separates us,' he says. 'The Gauls do not have any relevance to their culture. Someone who wears a helmet like Asterix's is thought of as a Viking. I think that perhaps it must have something to do with their total ignorance about our history. It is a pity, but *tant pis.*'

Neither of us wants dessert, so it is time for coffee. I seize the moment to pull out a copy of his latest album and ask him if he would autograph it for Jamie, my four-year-old son, who has become the latest recruit to Asterix's fan club. It is cheesy, I know, but one does these things for one's kids. Uderzo consents immediately and inscribes the book holding his pen between his middle two fingers in a remarkable grip. He then takes an album that his publishers have brought along and kindly autographs a copy for me too.

'There, I've written your name into it so I'll know if you sell it on eBay,' he smiles.

Perish the thought. I'd rather be biffed by Obelix than sell my latest treasure.

Ronnie Wood

'It's hard to get old and hard to say no'

With a domestic earthquake about to hit, the rock star talks about touring with the Rolling Stones, his new exhibition of paintings and a life spent battling the drink

By Rob Blackhurst

K eith Richards once said, 'If you are going to get wasted, then get wasted elegantly.' At 61, his fellow Stones guitarist, Ronnie Wood, embodies this louche creed. As he arrives in the reception of Dublin's elegant Shelbourne Hotel for lunch, cutting a path through huddles of overly nourished politicians and businessmen, he's dressed in the same size of superskinny jeans, 28 waist, that he's been wearing for the past 30 years, a pair of space boots that may once have belonged on an alligator's back and a tight black shirt undone to the chest: the fruits of a trip to Prada before his daughter Leah's wedding last month.

But, even from 50 paces, it's the luxuriant crow-black head of hair, flecked with only the tiniest hint of grey, that really marks him out as a Rolling Stone. As he greets me with a warm handshake and naughty, liquorice eyes, he says, 'I don't dye it either.' Alluding to his equally thin bandmates, he adds, 'We're all the same build, as well. It's a good thing I didn't join Fleetwood Mac.'

We take our place in a booth in the newly refurbished Saddle Room, which is all mirrors and velvet and upholstered in a garish shade that might be described as boudoir gold. Wood squints uncomfortably. 'Christ, it looks like Rod Stewart's trousers,' he says.

The Shelbourne is Wood's favourite Dublin haunt. 'I've a good old affiliation with this hotel,' he says. 'When we played the Point Depot five years ago we were based here. It was like the Stones coming home to my town.' Wood has lived in Dublin on and off since the early 1990s, when he bought a second home in the southern suburb of Sandymount, searching for a sanctuary for his art and music, and shelter from the British exchequer. He transformed the cow byre into recording studios and the stables into a personal pub called 'Yer Father's Yacht'. It seems a dangerous place for a fitfully recovering alcoholic like Wood; there are 20 more pubs within a square mile of his front door.

He looks at the menu reluctantly: 'I'm not really hungry at all,' he says. Eventually we opt for 12 oysters from County Clare followed by the seafood platter to share. Nothing stronger than caffeine is ordered, though Wood is going through another well-publicized bout of heavy drinking. 'A friend came over last night – I hadn't seen him for years. We had a few drinks. It ended up being seven in the morning.'

Though he has been woken up for the interview only an hour earlier, Wood is lucid and charming, especially when an espresso arrives to kickstart the conversation. I mention his latest art exhibition, *Ireland Studio*, a six-week show at his Scream gallery in Mayfair. The exhibition features paintings and pen-and-inks produced – mostly through the night – at his Irish pile over the past 10 years. Free of tour commitments – this year the Stones are on sabbatical after two and a half years on the road – he has been able to spend more time in Ireland with his two Great Danes.

Wood's interest in art dates back to the early 1960s, when he was a student at Ealing Art College, but he took it up commercially for 'grocery money' in the mid-1980s when he had blown a considerable portion of his Stones money on a cocktail of drugs and comically disastrous managers. He flicks through a pile of prints of the front garden of the Priory Clinic, where he has been a regular in-patient; moonscapes from the west of Ireland at night; and horses racing on the Irish turf. Sir Peter Blake and Lucian Freud are among fans of his art: 'He [Freud] told Mick [Jagger] that he loves my landscapes. That's a compliment, from the greatest living artist.' Tracey Emin is a friend: 'She's like my aunt. She rings me up every day to ask how I'm doing.' He pauses and confides mischievously: 'Tracey thinks she can draw.'

Most of his collectors are Stones fans in the US: 'The leading cancer-curing doctor in Florida – much to his wife's chagrin – spends most of his money on my paintings. She says, "Oh, please don't sell the house and buy another Ronnie painting!"' Though his portrait of the Stones in a Jacobean interior, *Beggars' Banquet*, sold in 2005 to a private collector for $1m, he is pricing his Irish landscapes at between £10,000 and £50,000. Deals, he makes clear, can be struck.

Wood has become a kind of official portraitist to the court of celebrity over the past decade – ever since Andrew Lloyd Webber commissioned him to paint the famous patrons of the restaurant The Ivy in the early noughties. Now a Ronnie Wood sitting has become as much a signifier of the upper reaches of stardom as a *Hello!* wedding deal. His waiting list includes the Stones-mad French president, Nicolas Sarkozy: 'I met him and Gordon Brown and he was desperately trying to put me on the phone with Carla Bruni. There are all these people like Scorsese, Clinton, Beckham . . .' but he trails off, as if bored of the fame whirligig: 'I'm trying to get away from the commissions so that I can do what I want,' he says. 'This new exhibition is more the stuff that I want to do – landscapes, dogs, horses.'

The plate of oysters arrives. Wood is a fan of their nutritional properties. 'They've got everything you need – all the vitamins and minerals. They keep the zinc up,' he says with a mock leer. Discussion moves to his other day job. I ask whether age has calmed Richards who, Wood recalled in his autobiography, used to hold an arsenal of guns and knives that would be drawn during band frictions. 'It's still on the verge, you know,' he deadpans. 'Murder is still quite an easy option. You have to be on your toes all the time.' Nevertheless, Wood is more appreciated now by his fellow Stones than he was when he left the Faces to join them in 1975. For years, as a latecomer who joined when the band had already made their fortune, he had to negotiate his fee on a rising scale for every tour and album. 'There was a 17-year apprenticeship,' he says. 'Charlie and Bill stood up for me. Nice of them to do that, because they could have carried on looking the other way. I'm part of the empire, finally.'

In spite of the Strolling Bones jibes, he thinks the Stones have never sounded better in their 45-year history than they did on the final dates of their tour at the O2 arena last August. He says there's 'talk in the air' of another tour next year.

It must feel odd, I say, to go from playing in front of a crowd of a million in Rio to sitting at home. He becomes melancholic. 'I'm more lost when I'm not on tour. I'm in a bit of a muddle at nine o'clock – "Where's the stage?" On tour there are people directing and supervising you. And then when you finish it's like, "Sit down and watch TV." Sometimes I get so bored I think I'll have a drink. I don't mean any harm but I just go off the rails.' He points out, however, that he did manage to catch himself last month when he checked in for treatment ahead of his daughter Leah's wedding so that he didn't miss the big day.

A torrent of alcohol runs through Wood's life. His account of his upbringing in a council house in Middlesex, the third son of 'water gypsies' who had left their barges for dry land, sounds like a preparatory school for a career in rock 'n' roll. His father, Archie, played in a 24-piece harmonica band that toured the racetracks of England. At home, there were weekend singalongs around the piano that got so boisterous that a crack appeared in the middle of the house. When the family lawn was dug up 1,700 Guinness bottles were discovered. This may sound impossibly romantic, but his relationship with drink turned darker when, while he was still a teenager, his girlfriend was killed travelling to one of his first gigs: 'When Stephanie got killed I sort of drowned my sorrows,' he tells me, 'and I suppose I've never looked back since.'

Does he worry about his own health? He's dismissive: 'Here I am at 61 and I've never felt better. I've never had a cleaner bill of health. I was just in the Mayr Clinic in Austria. They said, "We want to use you as an example of how we want people to end up." They said I had the body of a 40-year-old.'

As our seafood platter arrives, Wood dips straight into the crab claws. 'These are really cool. I don't know which sauce you put on them.' As he plumps for the shallots and vinegar, the conversation turns to Jimi Hendrix, with whom he shared a flat for six months in the late 1960s. 'He didn't think he was any good as a singer. I used to say, "Don't worry about that voice." He used to obliterate real life by being stoned all the time – and he couldn't handle it. He didn't realize how good he was.' His last memory of seeing Hendrix alive, the night before he died in 1970, is haunting. 'He was leaving Ronnie Scott's [jazz club]. He had his arm around a girl and he looked really sad. I went out after him and said, "Jimi, you didn't say goodnight."'

I try to lighten the mood by asking about the Wood clan – who all seem to have found jobs in the family business. He married Jo, a former model, 23 years ago after splitting with his first wife Krissie, another model. Jo is on the Stones payroll as his dresser and assistant on tour, in between running her organic beauty products business. His stepson Jamie is his manager, and his young- est son Tyrone is curating Wood's latest exhibition at Scream.

The 'Little Red Rooster' ringtone on Wood's phone sounds. He seems agitated. The call brings news, he says, of the *Sun* door-stepping his home in Kingston, south-west London. A few days after our lunch I realize that he had been given news that the paper was about to write a story about how during the week of our meeting, he was holed up with a young Russian waitress.

Whatever domestic earthquakes are going on in the background, he returns quickly to conviviality, suggesting we finish lunch with a drink elsewhere. Though he is great company, it's some- thing of a relief when his PR appears to steer him to his next engagement and saves me from making the decision. As we leave the hotel, the kitchen staff lift their ladles and knives in salute, out on the street car horns honk, and Wood poses for an endless round of photos with passers-by, loving every second of it. 'That's always been a big problem with me,' he says with a grin that fades to exasperation: 'I find it hard to get old and hard to say no.'

The Saddle Room

Shelbourne Hotel,
St Stephen's Green,
Dublin 2

....

12 x Clare Atlantic oysters	€33
1 x seafood platter	€44
3 x espresso	€13.50

....

Total	€90.50

Yu Hua

The famished road

His early heroes were drawn from the Cultural Revolution's tragic poster-boy outlaws. Now, post-Tiananmen Square, the novelist has the power to frame Mao, and bring peace to his belly

By John Ridding

T he fried pigs' livers with yellow wine were my idea – but the inspiration was really down to Yu Hua. In his masterpiece, *Chronicle of a Blood Merchant*, the downtrodden hero, Xu Sanguan, eats the dish in the belief it will restore his strength. So it seemed fitting to give it a try, even if we were rather more fortunate than Xu, sitting in one of Hong Kong's most venerable restaurants discussing the books that have taken Yu Hua from an *enfant terrible* of China's literary scene to one of its leading lights.

Blood, violence and hardship run through this body of work as they course through modern China, from the civil war to the Great Leap Forward, the Cultural Revolution and the other trials that bedevil the lives of Yu Hua's characters, typically ordinary people who both suffer and express their country's upheavals.

In truth, Yu Hua's bleak tragedies are leavened by uplifting themes of fortitude and family bonds. But they are still hard to square with the affable 44-year-old, who looks nearer his thirties, as he pauses for thought, dipping his chopsticks into the grey yolk of a '1,000-year-old egg'.

The traumas, like much of his writing, are drawn from experience. The son of a doctor and a nurse, he grew up in a hospital in the eastern

Chinese town of Haiyan, against the backdrop of the Cultural Revolution. 'When my father finished a surgery we would see his coat stained with blood,' he recalls. 'My mother would carry tins of organs out and pour them into a pond behind the hospital. In summer, the pond would be covered with so many flies it looked like a thick blanket.'

If home was where the blood was, the street outside was a stage for the brutality that features in many of his works. 'There was a lot of violence then – even in our small town. I saw with my own eyes people beaten to death on the street.'

Yu Hua started his own working life as a barefoot dentist. Given the macabre detail of his early works, it prompted Mo Yan, author of *Red Sorghum* (made into a film by Zhang Yimou), to comment: 'I've heard he was a dentist for five years. I can't imagine what kind of tortures patients endured under his cruel pliers.'

In the event, the patients were spared. Hating the job and jealous of the artists and writers he saw walking around town, Yu Hua determined to enter the local cultural council. With most novels and virtually all foreign books banned at the time, he drew inspiration from the 'Big Character Posters' that were plastered across the walls of Chinese towns denouncing 'capitalist roaders' and other traitors to Mao Zedong's causes. Many of these victims were known to Yu Hua before they were swept into public and, generally, tragic local dramas, and later into his bestselling books.

His lack of formal training led to a sparse writing style – prompting some critics to cite Ernest Hemingway as an influence. But Yu Hua has an alternative explanation. 'I went to primary school in the year when the Cultural Revolution started and graduated from high school the year it ended. That meant I never studied properly, and knew only 4,000 characters,' he says. 'That is why my style is sparse. Maybe Hemingway's vocabulary was quite small too.'

As the style of Yu Hua's books has evolved from experimental avant-garde towards more conventional narratives and commercial success, it is tempting to see a parallel with China's recent evolution. The suggestion is reinforced by the fact that this former tyro of the Tiananmen Square era, who was involved in the student-led protests of 1989, is now comfortable with China's recent development and his own move towards the cultural mainstream.

'There must be some connection between my writing style and the general situation of society at that time,' he acknowledges. 'When I started writing, my style was rather radical and the characters in my books were completely under my control. I wrote like a dictator. In the 1990s, when I wrote the longer novels, I found characters had their own voices. This was an amazing experience and fundamentally changed my attitude to writing. Maybe this is a coincidence, but it is in some way consistent with the evolution of Chinese society, from highly authoritarian to more democratic.'

It is, of course, a relative progression. Yu Hua is tolerated rather than endorsed by Chinese officialdom and sails close to the lingering winds of censorship. While he denies he is a political writer, he sees the 'truth of history' as his driving force and the messages of his books have strong political symbolism. An unfortunate character in the novel *To Live*, for instance, is bled to death during a transfusion to supply a party official, a literal expression of the extreme sacrifices demanded by the state. Arbitrary and ruthless decrees frequently dictate the fortunes of his characters.

'I don't think they see me as a model writer,' he jokes.

His books have never been banned – but neither does he expect official recognition or awards. 'I am comfortable with this position. A writer should not have a cosy relationship with the government.'

The tacit toleration of Yu Hua's books probably reflects his 'rear view' perspective and his focus on the monstrosities of Maoism. China's current regime acknowledges mistakes from that period, although it has so far rejected a 'reassessment' of the Tiananmen Square massacre.

Yu Hua believes those chapters have closed, drawing a curtain on all-consuming ideology. 'It is a good change. People may no longer believe in high missions and they are thinking of money all the time,' he says. 'These indeed may cause many problems in society. But no matter how problematic, it is better than using one ideology. Trying to make one billion people think the same, as in the Cultural Revolution, is the most dreadful thing.'

While the era of choreographed campaigns has passed, Yu Hua sees risks to stability in the localized protests that are now bursting through the fissures of China's widening social gaps. 'Almost all the political movements in China were started by Mao Zedong alone, and he alone could then regain control of everything; whereas today's small-scale upheavals are everywhere and they are not initiated by the government. When they come together to become a tide, nobody can control it.'

On a personal and professional level, this evolution removes the ideological targets that Yu Hua hit so unerringly in his previous works, challenging him to capture the more complex currents of contemporary China. 'Writing about the past is much easier than writing about the present. The present in China is constantly changing, and increasingly quickly,' he says. 'A European would need to live 400 years to experience such a sea change.'

Yu Hua has sought to chart this sea change in a new book due out in the summer. The two-part novel, still awaiting a title, records what he sees as the defining social shift in China – from the 'self-denial' of the past to the 'self-indulgence' and sensationalism of the present. 'Today's China is full of sensations. If you open the paper you will read about the most peculiar stories that could ever happen,' he says. He cites a story about a rich Chinese man taking his dog to a sauna and then placing the dog on a separate bed for a massage. Such a scene is a long way from the struggles of his earlier works. In those times, a dog would have been a bizarre luxury, or lunch.

The tone of the new novel will be dark. 'It is full of sarcasm and even more cynical than my previous novels, because I think that tone suits our age.' Despite this, or possibly because of it, he sees no problems getting it published. He has yet to show it to publishers, but has already received an offer for an initial print run of 300,000 copies – a reflection of the following he has built as a writer and as a narrator of China's unfolding history.

Amid the tumult of that history, it is a struggle to keep roots and memories intact. That is something that Yu Hua feels strongly about, personally. And as we move to the next dish – the head and legs of a lobster, with rice – it transpires that food is one way he seeks to preserve his own past.

'When I was a kid I was crazy about a local dish – rice cake with shredded pork. It is something you rarely had the chance to eat then. It no longer tastes that delicious to me today, but even so, I have to eat it at least once a month. Otherwise I would feel uncomfortable,' he says.

'I eat this to make up for the past, because I ate too little at the time. I was constantly hungry as a kid.'

His experience of hunger rumbles through many of the most moving scenes in his books. When, in *Chronicle of a Blood Merchant*, Xu San-guan is reunited with his first-born son, banished because of doubts over his legitimacy, their reconciliation is sealed over a bowl of noodles. In *To Live*, the mute and starving daughter is unable to protest in a desperate struggle over a single sweet potato.

Those days created demons as well as dramas. Shuffling his chopsticks, Yu Hua reveals that he writes for self-restoration as well as for his readers. 'I don't write to cure other people's souls. I write to cure my own soul. There are problems with my own soul, and I need to work on them.'

As the dim sum dessert arrives, and the warm and surprisingly potent Shaoxing Chiew wine takes effect, this soul is in good spirits. 'Sometimes I eat for the past. But today's meal is fantastic,' he exclaims. 'I feel I am eating for my present life.'

Yung Kee Restaurant
Central, Hong Kong

....

1 x fish maw with mushroom soup
1 x pigs' livers with yellow wine
1 x beef brisket in superior soup
1 x lobster ball in black bean sauce
1 x garoupa with bean curd
1 x lobster with rice in soup
1 x dim sum dessert
1 x Shaoxing Chiew wine

....

Total   HK$2,480 (£170)

Business

Prince Alwaleed

Royal subjects

Between diet tips and investment philosophy, the world's fifth-richest man explains why he is uniquely placed to bridge the divide between east and west

By Simon Kuper

When would Prince Alwaleed like to have lunch? At 6.30pm. Where? At his hotel, the George V. Does he always stay there when he's in Paris? Actually, he owns it.

The world's fifth-richest man, worth an estimated $21.5bn, tends to own things. There are his chunks of Citigroup and News Corp, not to mention EuroDisney, Canary Wharf, Hewlett-Packard, Time Warner, and so on. Though one of his grandfathers founded Saudi Arabia and the other was independent Lebanon's first prime minister, Prince Alwaleed bin Talal is considered practically a self-made man. He has even been called the Saudi Warren Buffett, chiefly for having turned an $800m purchase of Citicorp stock into a stake worth $10bn. Not content with being rich, the prince also believes he has a divinely ordained role to bring together 'east and west'.

I wait in the George V's lobby while the prince hangs with his buddies, Richard Parsons, chairman and chief executive of Time Warner, and Sandy Weill, chairman of Citigroup. Then he goes to pray.

When I am eventually led to his regular nook in the lobby, I discover that lunching with him is not exactly a tête-à-tête. It takes a while to identify him – moustachioed, bushy-haired and extremely thin – amid his entourage of aides. A cameraman slaps a microphone on my

lapel: our 'lunch' is to be filmed. To complete the multimedia experience, a television is playing a tape of BBC World on fast-forward.

Noticing my surprise at the crowd, the prince's private banker, Mike Jensen, jokes, 'Don't worry, you're not paying for this!'

'Only for three people,' corrects the prince. I had said the *FT* would buy him lunch, and the prince has decided to slap an aide on to our bill. 'I'll have my salad,' he tells the waiter. It's a rucola salad with tomatoes that is not on the menu.

The prince, 50, is observing the optional six-day fast after Ramadan, a doddle for him as he rarely eats in daytime anyway. Speaking in double-pace English, which he more or less mastered during a stint at Menlo College in California, he explains, 'I was very fat before. My peak weight was – do you want pounds or kilos? – 89 kilos. Then we went down to 60. No spaghetti, no bread, no butter, no meat. Complete moratorium. I eat only one meal a day.'

He has stuck to this regime for 15 years, although 'one meal a day' doesn't mean he never otherwise eats: he says he broke his fast 'just an hour ago' and his printed schedule for today lists dinner at 2am.

Prince Alwaleed doesn't just want you to think he is thin, however. He wants you to think he is a statesman. When his salad arrives, he ignores it as he explains his mission to unite people around the world. 'God blessed me with a lot of wealth. After 9/11 a major division took place between Saudi Arabia and United States, west and east, and Christianity and Islam. And I believe my role, because of what God blessed me, is to try to bridge the gap.'

The next day he will be signing deals with Harvard and Georgetown universities to finance some of their Islamic studies. It's all part of bridging the gap. 'That's why we focus on the east coast of America. Because that's where the decision-making process is, with all respect to west coast, north coast or south coast.'

The prince's most famous attempt at bridging failed. He donated $10m to New York City after the September 11 attacks. But he also called on the US government to 'adopt a more balanced stance towards the Palestinian cause'. Rudolph Giuliani, New York's then mayor, returned the cheque, and accused him of trying to justify the attacks. A Saudi newspaper later quoted the prince blaming 'Jewish pressures' for Giuliani's rejection.

Does His Highness regret his Palestinian statement? 'A friend of a nation has to say the truth any time. Although, if you ask me a question, 'If the Palestinian situation was resolved a day before 9/11, would 9/11 take place or not?' Most likely it would have taken place, yes. I have no problem. All my friends sitting here: Mr Parsons, Christian man; Sandy Weill, a Jewish man, from Israel – from, from, from US. Muslim, Christian, Jewish – I don't care about that.'

Indeed, by Saudi standards the prince is a liberal. Does he expect his uncle, King Abdullah, to move towards democracy? 'You use the word "democracy". I'll say, "people's participation in the political process". Because there are many forms of it. I believe, for example, in people's participation. I believe the fact that the municipal elections took place, there's an indication that at the end of the day King Abdullah has in mind the introduction of elections at the Shoura level, our version of parliament.'

I venture that there seems to be some dissent within Saudi Arabia. 'From what?' demands the prince. Well, from the monarchy. 'Where do you get that from?' The newspapers. 'Frankly speaking, I don't see that at all. Most people in Saudi Arabia are really for the government. And, frankly speaking, if you look at so-called dissent outside Saudi Arabia, it's only Saad al-Fagih [a dissident in London]. That's superb. Population of 16 million indigenous and six million expatriates, you have one guy going publicly.' It seems tactless to mention another prominent Saudi dissident, Osama bin Laden.

Yet as the prince knows, not everyone has a gleaming image of Saudi Arabia. Americans got particularly angry when 15 of the 19 hijackers on September 11 turned out to be Saudis. Did the prince take stakes in western media companies partly so that he could help clear up east–west misunderstandings?

He begins with the standard denial: 'My investment in the United States is not really to influence public policy.' But then he adds: 'When I meet Mr Murdoch of News Corp, that owns Fox News, and BSkyB, or when I meet Mr Parsons, who controls CNN, *Fortune* magazine, *People*, *Time*, America Online, I don't intrude into the management of these companies. However, I do convey to them the message about where I believe they went wrong. It's their discretion to decide what to do. My job is to open their eyes to things they may not have seen.'

Could His Highness give an example? 'One time CNN, they brought the Palestinians' so-called terrorist act against Israelis. I communicated to them, "Look, you have to give the other side of the equation. Look what the Israelis are doing to the Palestinians." And they did that. And they were censured and reprimanded by the Israelis. I do not claim it's my right to intrude. But I have to do my best to try to influence events.'

At News Corp, the prince is currently helping Murdoch rebuff an attack from the investor John Malone. No doubt it is for literary reasons alone that Murdoch's HarperCollins has just published the hagiography *Alwaleed: Businessman, Billionaire, Prince* by the former CNN anchor Riz Khan. The prince has a copy by his side. 'Foreworded by President Carter,' he remarks. Then he says, 'Yeah, it's being foreworded by President Carter. President Carter. By President Carter.'

'Wow,' I finally reply.

'President Carter,' he says.

Khan writes of the prince: 'He's fast-paced, incredibly organised, and a unique mix of Middle East and West . . . arguably, the hardest-working billionaire on the planet.' In the book, the great man's mother and Khan watch a video of the toddler prince chasing a goat until he catches it. She tells Khan, 'It showed me even then how determined my son would be.' What does the prince think of the book? 'I think it reflects . . . reality.' When President Chirac appears on the TV set, the prince murmurs, 'Ouf, Chirac!' and turns up the volume. We listen to Chirac intone about 'respect', 'justice' and 'equality'. The prince knows Chirac. 'I can meet any president, any king, any sultan, any president of a company. It's a very unique position.'

George V Hotel
Paris

1 x rucola and tomato salad
1 x ceviche de crabe
1 x chicken linguine
1 x Pepsi One
1 x grapefruit juice
1 x mineral water
2 x coffee

Total   €136

Does having lots of money make you happy? Only when you give it away, the prince reveals. 'When the tsunami happened, I was the biggest single contributor in the world. When the Pakistan catastrophe happened, I am the . . . single biggest contributor on the globe. I went to Pakistan personally. The prime minister told me, "Prince, your visit is more important than what you can pay us."'

We order coffee. When his arrives first, he insists on giving it to me, even though I have ordered a double and he a single. He resumes: 'Something else gives me a kick: when I get involved in something that's not successful, and all of a sudden it becomes good.' He says Citigroup, for example, was 'on its knees' when he first invested in it. 'And guess what: now it's the first global bank in the world and number one company. George V – piece of rubbish. When I bought it, you order spaghetti, they say, "We have no spaghetti, give you rice." Look what: you buy it, you shut it down, you fix it up. Guess what: number one hotel in the world, for five years.' In short, unusually for a famed investor, Alwaleed appears to invest for motives other than profit.

Still, he doesn't miss a trick. When I rise and thank him for his time, he replies, 'We have to pay the bill now.' Then he offers to pay after all. I refuse. Luckily the bill is within reason – another benefit of dieting. I depart for the bottom bunk of a second-class compartment of a night train, leaving Alwaleed to unite east and west until his scheduled bedtime of dawn.

Jeff Bezos

Dotcom omnivore, hahaha

The entrepreneur is as surprised as everyone else at his metamorphosis from New York banker to founder of Amazon, the online store

By Andrew Davidson

J eff Bezos, founder of Amazon.com, says he is an omnivore. 'I eat anything and everything,' he grins, and laughs loudly, with his trademark, full-throttle guffaw. Then he selects from the menu: salad of Belgian endive with apples and walnuts, and grilled sea bass. And later, a pudding. Oh yes, he doesn't want to miss the pudding.

We are sitting in the upstairs restaurant of Home House, the members' club on the north side of London's Portman Square that Bezos uses as a base for his flying visits. It is vast and grand with long windows and over-decorated walls, a paean to paint effects. Standing by the blue-veined, faux-marbled staircase you feel you are sinking into a giant Stilton cheese.

Bezos, 38, finds it cute, passageways to here and there, illogical ups-and-downs. He clearly has a romantic streak behind the brainy geek façade. Why else would the East Coast boy have chucked in a well-paid New York banker's job eight years ago to head west and set up Amazon in a garage in Seattle?

'Oh, I was never really a banker,' he says, flashing his deep-brown eyes. Well, he could be. Medium-height, trim, bald, sleek as a fish in his well-pressed chinos, shirt and blazer.

But he says he's as surprised as everyone else at what's happened to him. From 10 employees to 8,000 in little more than half a decade, generating billions of dollars of revenue, becoming one of the best-known entrepreneurs in America.

Wine? 'Nah, I don't wanna fall asleep, this is 5am for me!' He'd jetted in from America the day before and spent the evening at Gordon Ramsay's dining his European management. Today he's meeting the media to promote Amazon UK's fourth birthday. He should be tired already but if he is, I wouldn't want to meet him fresh. By turns incisive, giggly and earnestly loquacious, he is clearly button-bright, as you would expect from a man who read theoretical physics, electrical engineering and computer studies at Princeton. But he wears it all under a patina of infectious charm, which he uses to good effect.

I wonder what made him want to set up his own business? 'Oh, it was just a rational move,' he says, sipping his mineral water. He'd stumbled on a website in 1994 that showed internet use growing at 2,300 per cent, thought, 'Wow, I'll have some of that,' drew up a list of top ten products that would be good to sell online, plumped for books, decided on where the best place to hire software talent was, packed up the car and drove west.

Sounds so logical. What did his boss say? 'He said that seems like a pretty good idea, but an even better idea for someone that didn't already have a good job! Hahaha!' His huge laugh booms round the tall room. If you worked for Bezos, you wouldn't want open-plan.

In fact, his main base now is a converted hospital in Seattle, great views to the mountains, room for 800 staff. He has a small office on a middle floor, furnished with a door desk like everyone else. A door desk?

'Yeah, an old door on 4x4s,' – trestles to us – 'we all have 'em.'

Why?

'Big and sturdy and cheap.'

Isn't that a bit pretentious for the CEO, too?

'No, because symbols are important and good symbols are not pretentious.'

Nicely answered.

'Thanks, hahaha.'

Later he tells me one of the things he hated about a stint at Bankers Trust – sounds like a banker to me – was the way furniture became a symbol of status, typifying how inward-looking the organization was. 'That was where I learnt what a credenza was. A little desk with drawers thin enough to hold one sheet of paper. If you qualified for one, you must be important. I mean . . .'

So here he is now, the man with the logical dotcom idea that's grown and survived the crash and is just beginning to make money (first profit in last quarter of 2001), who's got a wife and two little boys and a beautiful home on the lake a mile down from Bill Gates, and appears on Oprah Winfrey as her favourite entrepreneur and gives to her charity and works on a door desk and seems so unspoilt by it all. Why him?

'I dunno,' he says, methodically chasing the last walnut round his plate, 'but I think the essence of entrepreneurship is a strange combination of being flexible and stubborn. Successful entrepreneurs are both, simultaneously – the trick is knowing when to be flexible and when stubborn.'

So when is he stubborn? Over his father, for one thing. His parents divorced when he was one, and he never saw his dad again. His mother remarried and he calls his stepfather, a Cuban-born oil engineer, 33 years at Exxon, his 'real dad'.

No interest in contacting his – as he calls him – 'biological' father? No, and it's cost him not a dollar in therapy fees, he laughs. That's stubborn.

Bezos is also meticulous – he turns over his sea bass to squeeze lemon juice first on one side, then the other – and undaunted by what the rest of us just wouldn't attempt.

He attributes that to his maternal grandparents, who ran a ranch in Texas. He spent summers there as a kid. 'They were very self-reliant, miles from the nearest city. Granddad did his own vet work, fixed old bulldozers.'

And now he's comfortable with the iconic status he's achieved, the endless media attention?

'Yeah, it's OK with me,' he says, chewing. 'I mean, nobody likes answering the same questions 10,000 times, it's just dull. But hey, this is more fun than most interviews because you're asking me some new questions.'

What do you normally get asked? 'Like, when are you going to be profitable? My mom has a framed *Newsweek* article from 1996 saying that it will take at least five years for us to be profitable. I don't know whether people don't remember, don't listen or just aren't interested.'

His mother and stepfather, his brother, who runs a small advertising agency, and his sister, who has recently moved to Seattle, all own stock in Amazon. Bezos himself has close to 30 per cent. That made him very rich when it hit its peak at $113 a share, and he is still a dollar billionaire now with the share price below $20. He shrugs.

'Pannacotta with raspberries, I'll take some of that and a latte with skimmed milk,' he grins at the waiter. What next? He talks about the changes in technology uptake that could benefit Amazon but no firm predictions: the businesses that run on one forecast, he says, always screw up.

'You're better being able to deal with lots of scenarios. Boy,' he adds, spooning up the pannacotta, 'this is good!'

And his working hours? 'I do 60 a week, any less I get bored, any more, tired. I mean, what do people do who do less? How do they fill the time?'

Family, hobbies, television. He frowns, as if he doesn't quite understand.

Doesn't he watch *Frasier*, set in Seattle?

'No, never seen it.'

And books, the bedrock of his business? He gets them passed on by his wife MacKenzie, who has been writing a novel for nearly a decade. Is he in it? 'No, I don't think so.'

What's it like? 'Psychological novel, more Updike than Roth, more *Remains of the Day* than Updike.' Ah.

'I like that painting,' he says, gesturing at the large contemporary canvas opposite, depicting a woman holding a lily beside a man sleeping in bed. Does he buy art?

'No, not really.'

Holidays?

'I want to take more.' He and his wife are aiming for four children – meticulous again – but could squeeze in some trips if the grandparents step in to help.

Anyway, time to go, questions to face downstairs on profit and Wall Street and dotcom survival. Looking back, does he think he has been smart or just lucky?

'Yeah, you go from running a business in your garage to building a multinational, there's a tremendous amount of luck involved, and good timing.'

Smart luck? 'Well,' he says, his little-boy grin widening further, 'I am quite happy with just dumb luck, yunno? Hahaha!'

Anatoly Chubais

The history maker

The Russian politician-turned-businessman ran the Kremlin for Boris Yeltsin, brought privatization to Russia and enraged a nation

By Robert Cottrell

The love affair between Muscovites and Japanese food is a mystery to me, but a welcome one. Izumi has some of the best, which is one reason I am pleased Anatoly Chubais has chosen it as the venue for our lunch.

My second reason for being pleased is that it gives me a chance to revisit old haunts. Izumi occupies a big 19th-century house on Spiridonovka, a quietly prosperous street where I rented a long, thin, gloomy flat when I first moved to Moscow in 1995.

Soon afterwards I discovered the previous occupant had plunged to his death from what was now my fifth-floor balcony, while caught in the midst of a diamond-smuggling scandal. I moved out a few weeks later.

Frankly, if Chubais had proposed a hotdog at the railway station, I would have agreed as readily. Here is a person who privatized Russia, ran the Kremlin for Boris Yeltsin and is commonly ranked among the dozen most influential men in the country.

We are due to meet at 2pm, early for lunch in Moscow on a Saturday. But my guest has another appointment at 4pm, he explains – with the prime minister, Mikhail Kasyanov. And if that sounds like name-dropping, it can be bettered. We were going to have lunch the previous Saturday, but Chubais cancelled at the last minute. President Vladimir Putin had summoned him.

We have taken a private room at the suggestion of Chubais's office, and it proves to be a happy fudge of style and comfort. There are scrolls and tatamis and a low Japanese table but beneath the table is a pit. We can sit on the edge of it and dangle our legs happily beneath, instead of scrunching them up and pretending to be comfortable.

The first thing that strikes me is that he is on time – a pleasing gesture in a city where time gets treated more cavalierly the higher up the social scale you go. The second thing I notice is that he has lost a bit of weight since I last saw him a year ago, a process in which Japanese food has doubtless played its part.

The third thing I notice, when the picture menu does its rounds, is his courtesy to the waitress, a Russian girl wrapped up in a Japanese gown. His talent for enraging the public at large is matched by his talent for charming them as individuals.

I stab my finger at a photograph showing a generous-looking plank of mixed sushi and I deduce that Chubais has done something similar. The assortments that arrive after 10 minutes look much the same.

He orders green tea and I follow his example. I could have wished for something stronger but the prospect of Kasyanov hangs over our meal.

We begin to talk. Ten years have passed since his privatization programme, a fire-sale of state factories, forced capitalism of a harsh and wild kind on Russia. It made a few people very rich and left a lot of people very poor. Most Russians hated him for it.

I ask him what he thinks now of the results. 'What we finally have,' he replies, 'is what we were thinking about then . . . But it took much more effort, it brought much more pain, it cost far more than we had hoped.'

But the main point, he continues, is that it was done at all. Because of it, Russia will have private property for generations to come. 'And I did it,' he says. 'With all the mistakes. Despite all the criticism. I did it.'

He has no regrets, either, about getting Boris Yeltsin re-elected president in 1996. He took over the campaign when Yeltsin had a popularity rating in the low single figures and was so ill with heart problems he could barely speak a coherent sentence. A clique of tycoons bankrolled the election, then rewarded themselves with state assets worth billions of dollars for which they paid very little. Russians blamed Chubais for that also.

'If I found myself in the same situation,' he says, 'I would make absolutely the same decision.' It was 'a fundamental historical choice'. The asset-stripping that followed was 'the price we paid for not allowing the Communists back into the country'.

By this time we are well into our sushi, which is good but not spectacular. The usual question about sushi in Moscow is not 'Is it fresh?' but 'Has it been thawed properly?' I reckon this is fresh.

Talking of 'fundamental historical choices', I ask Chubais about the most dramatic of them all: the decision taken by Yeltsin to use tanks against the Russian parliament in 1993 when it challenged and blocked his authority.

The event still divides Russians. At this point I see the merit of our private room. His reply would start a fight in half the bars of Moscow.

'If the country had not paid this small blood in 1993,' he says, 'it would have paid huge blood in the next two or five or ten years. The decision for Yeltsin, personally, was fantastically difficult. And that is why finally he lost his political momentum. He had to live with the results of it. Only one person, Yeltsin, could know the real price of his decision when you say to the defence ministry, "Shoot! With tanks!"'

He admires Putin, whom he thinks is making courageous long-term decisions in economic and foreign policy. But he also surprises me with his reply when I say that some in the west think Russia is turning into a police state.

'The fear is not only in the west, it is here, too,' he says. 'We can't just push it aside and say it is stupid. No, it is serious. There are political forces not far from Putin who would support exactly that style of development for Russia. But there are political forces strongly opposing it, including the Union of Right Forces [a centre-right party of which Chubais is a leader]. We should not just discuss if it will happen or not. We should fight against it.'

The time is coming for Chubais to leave. These days he runs UES, Russia's national power company, and I imagine Kasyanov wants to talk to him about the price of electricity. He decides against dessert and seems faintly irritated when a plate of creamy sticky things arrives, compliments of the house. I see him off, pay the bill and wander out on to Spiridonovka.

It looks little changed but then it always was a posh street. More of Moscow, and of Russia, is catching up with it. The privatized economy is beginning to work. In a sense, Russia is coming round to Chubais's way of thinking.

And he is still only 46. For all his protestations to be happy in business, I would eat my chopsticks if he did not have his eye on the Russian presidential election of 2008, when Putin's second term is over. And at Izumi, the chopsticks are made of stainless steel.

Henri de Castries

It's a duty call

Did President Sarkozy offer him the finance ministry? Just because he isn't saying doesn't mean the Axa CEO is risk-averse: he is a freefall parachutist, after all

By Adam Jones

F rance can often resemble a loose federation of two very different nations. One is inhabited by state employees hostile to the free market and globalization. The second houses dynamic, multinational companies of world renown. Each is exasperated by the other's antics.

If the giant businesses that make up France's CAC 40 stock-market index were ever to give up on this fragile union and secede, Henri de Castries would be a strong candidate to be their first head of state. The boyish 53-year-old is one of France's most respected managers, having already notched up nearly eight years as chief executive of Axa, the acquisitive Paris-based group that is among the world's biggest insurers. His stature is such that last year there had been talk that he had been offered – and had turned down – the job of French finance minister.

We meet on one of those days when secession seems like a good idea. France's transport network is paralysed by the first day of a strike against public-sector pension reforms proposed by President Nicolas Sarkozy. Luckily, de Castries has chosen Laurent, a restaurant within walking distance of both Axa's HQ and the *FT*'s offices.

Situated near the Elysée Palace, on the site of a former hunting lodge of Louis XIV, Laurent offers a form of lunchtime theatre in which the Parisian elite is both audience and cast. We are seated at one of the prime window tables, which feature curved banquettes that allow all

diners to face inwards and scan the room. I spot Serge Weinberg, chairman of Accor, the hotelier. A leading economist strolls over to chat. He is a friend of de Castries, but not all bonhomie is spontaneous at Laurent. 'When two people are supposedly on bad terms and want to show the world they are speaking to each other, they come here – half an hour later it is in the press,' de Castries tells me.

Laurent's menu leans towards refined French classics, including frog legs and calf head. I opt for trompettes de la mort mushrooms served with egg on a Parmesan biscuit, followed by pigeon with a ravioli of its giblets; de Castries chooses the mushrooms, then scallops with more mushrooms and borage. Our chaperone – Axa's head of corporate communication – has the all-vegetable starter and the fish in seaweed butter. There is a murmured exchange between the sommelier and de Castries but it is not clear that a bottle has actually been ordered. Anxious not to have one of those teetotal Lunch with the *FT*s that prompt mocking letters from readers, I receive reassurance that wine is on its way.

Past encounters with de Castries have established English as the language in which we communicate (he speaks it extremely well). I begin the interview by asking about his remarkable family tree, which groans under the weight of achievement. One notable de Castries served as naval minister under Louis XVI, for instance, sending Lapérouse – France's answer to Captain Cook – on an epic but ill-fated expedition to the Pacific. 'There is a painting, and I don't know if it is in Versailles or the naval museum, showing the king, Lapérouse and himself, looking over the map in preparation.'

There are also illustrious names on his mother's side. His maternal grandfather, Pierre de Chevigné, was a hero of the Free French who also acted as de Gaulle's wartime ambassador to the US. When Henri was a boy, de Chevigné recounted to him how he was with Roosevelt when he learnt of the invasion of Sicily by Allied troops. With that kind of upbringing, ambition was natural. 'The tradition was to do things,' he says.

With the backing of his family, de Castries broke with custom by not choosing a military career, although he did perform his national service in a parachute regiment, where he developed a passion for freefall. He has jumped more than 100 times. Now that his children are relatively grown up he says he may take it up again.

After military service, de Castries went to the Ecole Nationale d'Administration (Ena), the civil-service school that was created to help rebuild post-war France and whose alumni are notoriously powerful and clannish. His was a particularly stellar intake. Classmates included Ségolène Royal, the Socialist candidate in the last presidential election, and Dominique de Villepin, the former prime minister.

Yet Ena is not an experience he would recommend today. Just as he was advised not to attend Saint-Cyr military college, de Castries says he is telling his children not to become *énarques*, steering them instead towards business school and other experiences that offer better preparation for what he sees as the big challenge of the age: getting France to accept globalization.

As we mop our runny egg yolks, de Castries tells me that one of the reasons for the prominence of his Ena class was that they graduated in 1980, shortly before François Mitterrand was elected president, evicting the centre-right's Valéry Giscard d'Estaing from the Elysée. This gave early career momentum to those members of his class 'who had decided that they would be Socialists, some by conviction, others by . . .'

He giggles and fails to complete the sentence. I'm intrigued. So which of your contemporaries were Socialists of convenience, I demand, suspecting that he means Royal. He won't say, however.

The young de Castries was a fan of Giscard d'Estaing. He still is, citing his 'outstanding' mind. The octogenarian former president had recently called de Castries to ask for a briefing on the crisis in the debt markets. The Axa man was dazzled by the way he devoured the background material.

'I think Mitterrand was a guy with a vision but totally amoral,' continues de Castries. He is even more scathing about Jacques Chirac, the president who came next. 'Chirac was a combination of the two worst things: amorality plus absence of vision.'

As for Sarkozy, de Castries praises him for unblocking European policy-making and for his university reforms but says a question mark still hangs over the government's willingness to rein in public spending. So what about this old finance-ministry rumour, I ask: did the president offer you the job? 'Ask him,' he says, laughing. There is a long pause, but instead of moving on I let the question sit on the table among the crumbs from our sourdough toast. He is too courteous to leave it there.

'It is a complicated question. I mean, I like what I do at Axa. I have spent 18 years of my life there. We have a goal. I don't want to leave . . .

I think I am serving my country by doing what I do at Axa as well as I would in a political position.'

Enough politics: de Castries notices the arrival of Hervé Aaron, a noted art and antique furniture dealer. He happens to be in discussions with de Castries – a collector of 17th-, 18th- and early-19th-century French art – over a particular painting. (The sighting is not a good portent for the negotiations, de Castries later jokes, since it means that Aaron 'is not starving'.)

Some antiques chitchat follows, punctuated by mouthfuls of pigeon and sips of smooth Bordeaux (although the *FT* is paying, I have no idea how much the wine costs – it tastes expensive, but not alarmingly so). I return to a topic we had touched on earlier in the meal, namely that of risk, and people's perception of it. It is hard not to conclude that the French currently have an unhealthily low tolerance for risk, manifested in demands for excessively secure jobs and retirements. Does de Castries – whose job involves rational assessments of the probability of bad things happening – agree that this excessive caution is more pronounced in France than other countries?

He does. 'I think it is particularly accentuated in France but it is a problem that is common to all the old societies that feel threatened by globalization,' he says, blaming a shortage of authority figures willing to calm people down. 'I think the world was much more threatening to previous generations than it is to the current one.'

But are insurance companies blameless? I'm thinking of how some people fear retirement more than death now we are living longer. Isn't that partly because insurers advertise the downside of greater longevity – possible sickness and dependency – to win more fees from pensions and other investment products? I ask.

'Well tried – but I don't buy that,' he counters, seeming to enjoy a bit of needling. In order to mitigate the risks of old age, the facts must be laid out well in advance, he says, stressing that dependency is going to be a massive social issue.

I change tack. A few days beforehand, I had scanned through the terms of pet insurance Axa sells in the UK. It offered up to £2m of cover against damage caused by a domestic animal. Surely that constitutes scaremongering: how often do pets wreak such costly havoc? 'If a young child is severely injured by a dog biting him, how much is this going to cost?' he replies.

It is time to order dessert. Normally, de Castries sticks at two courses but he sometimes makes an exception for Laurent's vanilla ice cream, and will do so today. I choose the (excellent) pear roasted with ginger. The chaperone has ice cream.

Earlier in the lunch, the former paratrooper had outlined his rather gung-ho willingness to seek out and then master risks in his career and hobbies ('I don't like bonds, I prefer equity,' as he puts it). I ask whether there aren't a few areas in which he – like everyone else – harbours irrational fears. Apparently not. 'Life is a gift, so you should say thank you every morning and why would you be fearful? You know that one day it is going to end. If you have strong beliefs' – de Castries is a practising Catholic – 'it is not a problem.'

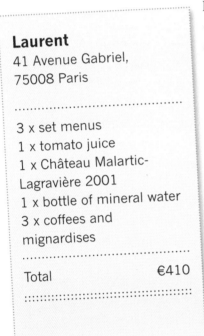

Laurent

41 Avenue Gabriel,
75008 Paris

....

3 x set menus
1 x tomato juice
1 x Château Malartic-
Lagravière 2001
1 x bottle of mineral water
3 x coffees and
mignardises

....

Total   €410

This recognition of mortality has seeped into his leadership of Axa. Succession planning is already under way; it would, after all, be unforgivable for the boss of an insurer to fall under a bus without having sketched out a plan B. He won't say how many dauphins are jostling for the right to follow him. But with demographic trends being what they are – and if the example of Giscard d'Estaing is anything to go by – there is a decent chance that de Castries will remain influential in France for decades.

By the time we leave Laurent, it has been a leisurely two hours. We emerge into bright sunshine. Before we part, he observes that it would have been a wonderful day for hunting. Confronted by such an urge, a de Castries from an earlier age would no doubt have ridden off straight away with hounds in tow. But this is 21st-century France and some of us at least have to get back to work.

Oleg Deripaska

Alloys and allies

The Russian metals magnate has entertained Peter Mandelson and George Osborne, yet has been humiliated in public by Vladimir Putin. The *FT* meets the teetotal billionaire in a London restaurant

By Gideon Rachman

I t is a sunny summer afternoon in London, and the courtyard of St John restaurant is bright and airy. Inside the dining room, however, things are much darker. There is little natural light, the walls are white, the lamps are black and the waiters pad silently around in the gloom.

St John has a reputation as a restaurant for people with a serious interest in food – which makes me wonder why Oleg Deripaska has arranged to meet there. Deripaska, a 42-year-old tycoon who made his fortune by dominating Russia's aluminium industry, is known for many things: his enormous wealth, his prowess as an industrialist, his political connections and the rumours about his past that have seen him denied visas to visit the US.

But he has never been noted for an interest in food. I had been briefed that he is a man of few words, who eats and sleeps very little and seems to survive on a diet of green tea.

As I wait for this phenomenon to make an appearance, I study the menu. St John is favoured by the most enthusiastic of carnivores and the choice is Dickensian and sounds slightly stomach-turning: devilled kidneys, beef mince on dripping toast, smoked eels. In a dark corner, a Japanese tourist is eagerly scooping out the marrow from an ox-bone.

I look up to see Deripaska striding into the room. There are no body-guards in evidence, although I assume that they must be stationed outside. It is a hot day and the photos I have seen of Deripaska suggest that he favours the 'smart casual' look, so I am not wearing a tie. But Deripaska is dressed formally: blue suit, blue shirt, blue tie, blue eyes – all slightly different shades. He is around 6ft tall, well built, lean and with closely cropped brown hair.

Most entrepreneurs like to talk about the old days and how they got started. It is usually a safe, relaxing way to begin an interview. With Deripaska, however, the origins of his business empire are the most sensitive topic of all. At the beginning of the 1990s, just as the Soviet Union was collapsing and the old state-run industrial behemoths were being sold off, he was a student. By the mid-1990s, aged 25, he had acquired a stake in a smelting factory. By the end of a turbulent and bloody decade in Russian business and politics, he had emerged as a tycoon controlling a huge swathe of the Russian aluminium industry.

In 2008, *Forbes* magazine listed Deripaska as the ninth-richest man in the world, worth about $28bn. He was hit badly by the global financial crisis and by the collapse in the demand for commodities. But even now, after a near-bankruptcy and a restructuring of his debts, *Forbes* estimates his fortune at about $10bn.

As we settle back in our chairs, I ask him what qualities he had needed to prevail in the industrial struggles of the 1990s. He points out that he was a star student at school in southern Russia – 'I was very good in maths and physics. In the Soviet time, we had a lot of Olympic-style competitions for different disciplines: I was always winning in my region.' Deripaska went on to study nuclear physics at Moscow State University. He says that in the height of the Soviet era, he would probably have ended up doing military research. But the old system was breaking down as he was graduating. Like a lot of his contemporaries, he went into business.

Deripaska says that from an early age he was fascinated by factories: 'My mum brought me to my first job when I was 12. I started electrical work at her plant. She was an engineer, a technical expert, at one of the plants in the south, and in the summer she brought me in and I learnt how industrial things work: casting, electricity, maintenance, everything.'

Deripaska is not feigning his interest in industrial processes. Few doubt that he has hugely improved management at all the Soviet-era plants he has owned and invested in. And yet more than energy and intelligence were needed to emerge at the top of the pile in the chaos that was post-Soviet Russia. The aluminium industry was particularly noted for violence and many people involved in the business ended up dead. I ask Deripaska if he had known what he was getting into, when he first got involved. 'Not in the beginning,' he laughs, 'it was my nice surprise. Don't forget I'm from a military family. I was in special training in the army. I am tall, sporty and – how do you say – you can always protect yourself . . . I have very strong security. Even now.' He says he triumphed over the criminal elements as he rose to the top.

Many of Deripaska's critics will take issue with that version of his rise. Michael Cherney, one of his most important business associates in the 1990s, is currently suing Deripaska in court in London, claiming that he was defrauded out of a significant chunk of his metals empire. Deripaska denies owing Cherney anything and denies that he was an associate. An associate of both men was Anton Malevsky, who has been described in court as the leader of an organized crime gang. Deripaska has said that he was forced to work with Malevsky and Cherney, who extorted money from him. Cherney denies this allegation. Deripaska also insists his aim was to clear out crime in the industry.

But in 2001 Malevsky died in a parachute accident in South Africa. Malevsky's death sounds like something from a crime thriller or a Bond movie. I ask Deripaska, as pleasantly as I can, whether he believes that Malevsky's death was a genuine accident. He blushes, glances down at his table napkin and laughs softly – 'I have no idea,' he replies.

I blunder onwards – 'Because it sounds like something out of a movie. This guy dies in a mysterious parachute accident.' I ask whether Malevsky was a criminal. Deripaska's manner is pleasant but cagey: 'It's very difficult for me to go into detail,' he says, 'because of the case. I think my lawyer will try to have a hearing in court. It will be open; and I'm prepared to be open.'

Our conversation is interrupted by the arrival of a waiter. Deripaska ignores the starters and chooses one of the less gory items on the menu – lemon sole. I opt for a pork chop with fennel. Defying the usual clichés about Russians, Deripaska is a teetotaller, so we order some sparkling water. After a little while, the food arrives. I wait for my guest to tuck in but he makes no move towards his fish. After about 10 minutes, hunger gets the better of me and I cut into my Gloucester Old Spot chop. A few minutes later, Deripaska seems to notice that I am eating and says, slightly absently, 'Bon appétit.' Without evident relish, he slices off a small piece of white flesh.

It is clear that Deripaska is a highly disciplined survivor. He got through the aluminium wars of the 1990s. When other Russian oligarchs fell out of favour, he survived again. Mikhail Khodorkovsky is in prison and Boris Berezovsky is in exile in London, but Deripaska is still in business. The financial crisis of 2008 posed another mortal threat. I ask Deripaska how close he was to going out of business – 'Very close,' he replies. 'I remember certain bankers in February 2009, trying to explain to me that there was no chance.' He points out proudly that, in fact, no debts have had to be written off.

The strain of the financial and economic crisis in Russia seemed to sour his relations with Vladimir Putin, who by then was prime minister. In a famous confrontation in the small Russian town of Pikalyovo in June 2009, Deripaska was subjected to a televised humiliation, as Putin ordered him to sign a document, safeguarding the future of a local factory, and then added caustically, 'And give me my pen back.'

Some regarded the confrontation as a sign that Deripaska's days were numbered. Others saw it as a carefully staged mock-confrontation between close allies. Deripaska insists that neither version of events is right. Putin, he says, was simply misinformed about the facts. 'But he called you a cockroach on television,' I protest. 'That is exactly the point,' Deripaska replies, 'it was not against me. It was against other people who were trying to run away from the business.'

Certainly, any misunderstanding appears to have been cleared up. A few months later, the Russian government agreed to prolong vital loans that kept Deripaska's business empire intact, when many analysts were convinced that it was on the brink of breaking up. As Deripaska sees it, the government simply realized that he was far better able to rescue a precarious situation than any state-appointed bureaucrat – 'They have no idea what to do to restructure the company . . . Because, if you're bankrupt, afterwards you lay off automatically more than 2m people . . . You can't just kill a big white elephant and say, "OK, I have done the right job."'

Some analysts put Deripaska's remarkable survival down to his impeccable political connections. He is married to the daughter of the chief-of-staff of a Russian former president, Boris Yeltsin. (They have two children.) He is also reputed to be close to both Putin and the new president, Dmitry Medvedev. In Britain, he befriended Lord Mandelson, the godfather of New Labour, and hosted George Osborne, now Chancellor of the Exchequer, on board his yacht. But Deripaska denies being particularly well connected. He says he was bewildered by the fuss that the British press made over his connections with Mandelson and Osborne, and professes never to see either Putin or Medvedev socially.

I ask him about the big question in Russian politics – whether Medvedev is really independent of Putin. He chuckles and skirts the question but adds that the two men represent different generations and have different outlooks. Will Putin and Medvedev run against each other for president in 2012? Deripaska says that nobody really knows – 'I think at some point they will discuss this,' he says, laughing heartily.

With his business empire safe, Deripaska's worst worries seem to be over. But there are still problems on the horizon. There is the London court case. And there are his continuing problems with entry to the US. Last year, he was allowed to visit the country twice. But these seem to have been specially arranged visits. I ask him whether his visa problems are over – 'I don't know. I don't care,' he replies. I remark that it must be annoying 'because it's very damaging to your reputation'. 'History will judge,' he replies quietly. Hasn't it been damaging to his business interests, I ask, not to be able to travel freely to America? 'Yes, but it gives you more opportunity . . . When they started making a problem, I just went to Japan and I got much more.' His companies are also taking an increasing interest in China.

Despite his problems in the US, Deripaska has powerful friends and allies in the west too. Bob Dole, a former US presidential candidate, has lobbied on his behalf. Nat Rothschild, a scion of the famous banking family, is a close confidant. James Wolfensohn, a former head of the World Bank, has also been a business partner. Deripaska's western defenders portray him as a great industrialist and a patriot. Questions about his past tend to be brushed aside – or dealt with by references to the murky origins of the fortunes of some of the great American industrialists and philanthropists of the 19th century. (Deripaska is also a big donor to charity.)

Deripaska himself, although he has a ready laugh, is earnest and ascetic. I notice that he has eaten just one half of his fish. The waiter reappears. I am feeling a bit peckish and hope that my guest will order a pudding. But Deripaska just asks for a black tea without sugar and I settle for a coffee.

As the lunch draws to a close, I ask him if he is ever tempted to go into semi-retirement and just enjoy life, like his friend the London-based Russian oligarch Roman Abramovich, who has bought a football club, acquired a new girlfriend and dabbles in modern art. Why not cash out? I ask. Deripaska looks faintly indignant – 'And do what?' he asks. As well as his current industrial interests, he wants to invest in nuclear power and in space exploration.

We walk out into the sunshine together. A large black car is waiting for him, just outside the restaurant, and a large man in a black suit is holding the door open. Deripaska steps in without a backward glance and the car moves silently off. I still feel vaguely hungry, so I walk down to Pret A Manger and buy myself a fruit salad.

St John
26 St John Street,
London EC1

....

lemon sole	£18.40
Old Spot chop	£20.80
1 × double espresso	£2.50
1 × Assam tea	£2.50
1 × bottle of sparkling water	£3

....

Total (incl. service) £47.20

In September 2012 Mr Deripaska and Mr Cherney reached an out-of-court settlement in their case over a $1bn stake in UC Rusal, the world's biggest aluminium producer.

Stephen Green

God's banker

The executive chairman of HSBC, who is also an Anglican priest, breaks bread and discusses the ethics of globalization, moral ambiguity and being rewarded for failure

By Lionel Barber

S tephen Green arrives three minutes early for lunch but apologizes for being late. Tall, soft-spoken and wearing a dark suit, the 60-year-old executive chairman of HSBC is courteous, almost to a fault. We are at a small table in Le Pont de la Tour, a Thameside restaurant favoured by City bankers during the Blair–Brown boom. (Green originally favoured another City restaurant, the Bleeding Heart, but feared the name was an invitation to poke fun at him.) There are lunch guests on the terrace outside but inside the place is empty, testimony to the Blair–Brown bust.

The timing of our gastronomic encounter in the shadow of the Tower of London could not have been better. Hours earlier, Sir Fred Goodwin, disgraced former boss of the now state-controlled Royal Bank of Scotland, had bowed to popular demand and surrendered a third of his £16.6m pension pot. As a conversation opener, the capitulation of Sir Fred is irresistible.

'I am not going to talk about individuals,' says Green, firmly. I push back, gently. The smile turns into a squirm. 'No, no, no. That's not fair . . . No . . . Not even off the record.'

Green's reluctance to pronounce judgment is curious on two counts. First, he is an Anglican priest who has thought long and hard about right and wrong. Second, he has written two books about ethics and

business in the age of globalization, and it's the publication of the second, *Good Value*, that, I remind him, is the reason we are having lunch in the first place.

Happily, a waiter arrives before our verbal skirmish goes any further. We study the menus. Green orders soused mackerel as a starter, followed by roast cod. I go for gazpacho and then roast chicken. In search of common ground, I suggest a shared side order of spinach. Then I return to the ticklish question of bankers being rewarded for failure.

The previous evening, Mervyn King, governor of the Bank of England, had delivered a stern speech at the Mansion House, admonishing bankers for failing to absorb the lessons from the global financial crisis. The Bank of England, he suggested, was like a church where the congregation turned up for weddings and funerals but paid no attention to sermons. 'Yes, I was there,' says Green, as he glides into a two-minute discourse on the governor's plans for tackling systemic risk to the banking sector. It's fascinating but not exactly relevant. What does Green say about bankers receiving handsome pay-offs when they have driven their institutions into the ground?

Green, sipping a Virgin Mary, counters with studied even-handedness. One must distinguish between bonuses and pension rights. Then again, there have been 'market distortions' regarding pay, not just in the financial sector. The era of 'my word is my bond' is over but people should not be starry-eyed about the age of the gentleman banker when insider trading was rife. Most important, 'rules are never sufficient to enforce morality', a theme we will return to during our 90-minute lunch.

I press him on the principle of restitution. Green refers me to the biblical tale of Zacchaeus, a corrupt tax superintendent who gives his ill-gotten gains to the poor. Once again this amounts to an artful dodge: Sir Fred may have been incompetent but nobody is suggesting he was corrupt. More fencing follows. Green simply will not be drawn into personal criticism. It is time to switch subject.

Green was ordained in 1988 and is a non-stipendiary minister attached to a church in London. He has stuffed *Good Value* with biblical references but also many literary ones, especially from Goethe's *Faust*. He studied German at Oxford University – as did I, a few years after him. Green later switched to Politics, Philosophy and Economics, on the grounds that PPE was of more practical use than medieval High

German. Nostalgia overcomes me and I challenge him to recite the opening verse in part one of *Faust*.

'*Habe nun, ach! Philosophie, Juristerei und Medizin . . . Durchaus studiert*' (I've studied now philosophy, jurisprudence, medicine through and through), says Green, deploying a more than passable accent. I join in, but he trumps me by invoking Faust's thumping declaration: '*Im Anfang war die Tat!*' (In the beginning was the deed.) The bookish banker is in full flow, eyes alight, long arms ranging across the table. Passion for German culture is a rarity in contemporary Britain.

I am mindful we still have to discuss the grand theme in his book – the ethics of globalization, personal responsibility and social progress – but first I ask about his circuitous route to the top of HSBC, formerly Hongkong and Shanghai Banking Corporation, and now one of the world's biggest financial institutions.

After university Green worked in a centre for recovering alcoholics ('a vicar came to Oxford and inspired me') before starting his career as a civil servant at what was then the Overseas Development Administration.

'The furthest I got was Paris,' he recalls. Frustrated, he won a Harkness fellowship to the US, completing a master's degree at the Massachusetts Institute of Technology. In 1977 he joined McKinsey, the management consultancy, and stayed until 1982, when, at 34, he was headhunted to join HSBC in Hong Kong. He has been with the bank ever since.

Our waiter arrives with gazpacho and mackerel, along with the bread basket. Munching a roll, I ask Green what were the highlights of his time in Hong Kong. It was, he says, setting up new business systems, then frets that he sounds like an 'anorak'.

Green, with his wife Janian and two daughters, returned to Britain in 1992 when HSBC bought Midland Bank. He published his first book in 1996, which sought to reconcile serving God with serving Mammon. This is a genuine dilemma for Green, made more acute by the global financial crisis.

Good Value wrestles with the demands of individual responsibility and the market but it is set in a broader economic and historical context. Green's ambition is to make the case for globalization as an inevitable, progressive force and as a human phenomenon.

'Let's look at the positives: human cross-cultural fertilization and enrichment; the delivery of economic development around the world; higher productivity . . . and in recent times globalization has lifted hundreds of millions of people out of poverty, particularly in China and India. These [benefits] are material, spiritual and cultural.'

And the negatives? 'There is something about the market system which is inherently unstable,' says Green, referring to financial bubbles from tulip mania in the 17th century to the 21st-century crash originating in the subprime lending market. 'This is a tiger we are seeking to ride by its tail.' Other negatives, says Green, include social marginalization and climate change. Green is in full flow so I pass on reminding him of HSBC's disastrous foray into the subprime arena with the 2002 purchase of Household Bank in the US.

By now, he has polished off the cod, and my chicken is surprisingly succulent. It is time to press Green on his sunny view of social progress, especially in Britain, which he argues is less racist, less class-ridden and less sexist than a generation ago. 'Well, I don't know whether you can measure it . . . and it's not like these things have disappeared. But about 80 per cent of this country considers itself middle class. I doubt that was true then.'

Green's preoccupation with ethical responsibility and social progress has deep roots, no deeper than his admiration for a relatively obscure Jesuit priest, palaeontologist and philosopher, Pierre Teilhard de Chardin, whose masterwork *The Phenomenon of Man* was first published posthumously in 1955.

De Chardin might be characterized as a sort of Thomas Friedman for the religiously inclined. Whereas the *New York Times* columnist is the bestselling author of globalization primer *The World is Flat*, the Frenchman saw the world as a sphere, both literally and metaphorically. In his book, Green quotes de Chardin's view that the evolutionary ascent of human beings occurs in two stages. First, humanity expands around the globe, both in quantity and spiritual development. Second, in the 20th century, as the planet is increasingly populated, a collective memory is formed. Thus globalization is about something far deeper than economics, commerce and politics. Green tells me, 'It is about the evolution of the human spirit.'

Green speaks in a calm, unruffled cadence but also with inner conviction. Disarmingly honest about personal matters, he confesses, for example, that he wrote his book with the assistance of the former *FT* journalist Richard Addis (once a novice Anglican monk). The two exchanged numerous drafts, often at weekends.

Even more striking is how he deals with his book's second grand theme: the 'pervasive moral ambiguity' that he detects inside human beings and the outside world. At the end of the book, for example, there is a passage of poignant self-examination in which Green describes visiting Weimar, the home of Goethe at the time he wrote *Faust*, and which is close to Buchenwald, the notorious Nazi concentration camp.

'We tell ourselves we cannot imagine working with human skin as if it were leather. But perhaps I can see myself getting caught up in such an ordinary procedure as this,' he writes. 'I can see myself losing sight of ulterior objectives, motives, values – becoming so engrossed in a debate about whether regulation a or b applies in situation x, that I no longer notice what x actually stands for.'

Green's admission is superficially shocking but, as he argues in his book, can an individual ever know for certain whether he or she would have the moral courage to stand up to tyranny and totalitarianism?

Bringing the conversation back to the present, I say that the parallels with contemporary capitalism are obvious. Too many bankers followed the letter but not the spirit of the law. I wonder, therefore, whether it is fair to draw a distinction – as many Europeans do – between Anglo-Saxon capitalism, which elevates individual self-interest, and Calvinist capitalism, which emphasizes the collective good?

'I am a European,' says Green, with passion. 'And so are you.' He sees the British as European, and as a committed pro-European he believes there should not be a distinction. I stand reprimanded. But I still want to explore whether Green believes in the innate superiority of different capitalist models, particularly the Anglo-Saxon emphasis on share-holder value. He says, 'Shareholder value cannot and should not be elevated to the exclusion of all else. It is a by-product of providing goods and services. When the by-product becomes the end, then we distort the whole market. The market is necessary but not sufficient. So "No" to market fundamentalism.'

It is a nuanced view of shareholder value but he makes his point emphatically – and as he does so, with a sweep of those arms, Green knocks over a glass, sending a flood of water over my notebook. He is mortified: 'I suppose that's going to be published,' he says, half pleadingly. 'You bet,' I respond, mopping up a sea of watery blue ink with a crisp white napkin.

Our waiter arrives with napkin reinforcements. We skip dessert and opt for herbal tea. I ask Green what he is reading at the moment. It's *Der Turm* (The Tower), Uwe Tellkamp's prize-winning 2008 novel set in the twilight years of former communist East Germany. He is ecstatic about this epic, nearly 1,000-page, book.

And this brings him back once again to the 'heights and depths' of German history and culture – and reveals a surprising ambition. Green's dream is to write a history that captures the linear development of German culture and history: from Henry IV's walk from Speyer to Canossa, where the German Holy Roman Emperor sought to reverse his excommunication; through to Martin Luther, the Thirty Years War, the unification of Germany, Nazism, and finally a reunited Germany regaining its moorings in a united Europe.

There is enough material here for another lunch, let alone another book.

We must leave, although the herbal tea has still not arrived. As we walk out, I am left with a thought: as God's banker, Green may have a bleeding heart but he really does possess iron in the soul.

Le Pont de la Tour
36d Shad Thames,
London SE1

....

gazpacho Andaluz	£8.50
soused dayboat mackerel	£8.50
roast cod with crushed potato	£16
roasted supreme of chicken	£16
spinach	£3.75
bottle of still water	£3.95
Virgin Mary	£4
Le Pont Smoothie (Iced Tea)	£7

....

Total (incl. service)	£76.16

Lord Hanson

Cigar ban has Hanson fuming

The *FT* met the industrialist before he announced the break-up of his conglomerate this week

By Nigel Spivey

H anson hails from Viking stock. So does Spivey. Eye to eye at the altitude of 6ft 2in, we measured each other up. Hanson's ancestry lies in Huddersfield; Spivey's, around Leeds. Perhaps our forebears once shared a longboat, and pillaged south Yorkshire together. Then their ways parted.

The Spiveys disowned a regrettable past – the surname is said to mean 'sheep-stealer' in Old Norse – and took to evangelism. The Hansons, meanwhile, relinquished pillage for haulage. Theirs was the road to riches. Transporting goods around the country is the olden basis of the present global Hanson empire. 'I don't care if people know about my salary,' breezed Hanson the Bold. 'I implemented Greenbury rules before they were even invented. You can tell the readers of your left-wing paper precisely what it is.'

(For the benefit of the *Financial Times*'s two or three Marxist faithfuls, let us get that over with: £1,362,000 a year.)

We met at The Berkeley, round the corner from Hanson's headquarters in Grosvenor Place. Although it is elegant and roomy, the prices are modest, the fare decent and uncomplicated. It amused Hanson, plainly a regular at our corner table, that the bill would be met by this left-wing paper. 'My host will have this,' he would say, with a ducal wave, 'bring a

bottle of house claret for my host.' His trim charm never faltered. Well, hardly ever. We shall come to that.

Hanson belongs to a select caucus of Anglo-American advisers to Conrad Black, the media emperor. Included in the membership are Margaret Thatcher and other such oracles of the right as William F. Buckley. Hanson himself is a journalist manqué. And not so manqué, either. Just before we met, he had been peppering the press with the thoughts of Chairman Hanson on Europe, roads and education. I had seen his blast of Euroscepticism (in Black's weekly, the *Spectator*), but not the roads and education. These were two hobby-horses which he happily exercised over our lunch.

'Road tax should be for roads,' he declared. '£23bn a year we pay to use 'em, and precious little of that gets spent where it should – repairing the highways, building new ones. The government's simply ignoring the constituency of drivers, and listening too much to these good earth people.'

Good earth people?

'The hippies you see blocking us in the Mendips. Not Friends of the Earth at all, just rent-a-mob.'

One would hardly expect a Viking-turned-haulier to think otherwise: especially when a chunk of his conglomerate interests lies in the production of road-building aggregates. Warming to my role as buccaneer from the left-wing press, I opined that in an overcrowded island like ours, it was time to abandon roads and cars.

He snorted: 'Yes. And abandon all our growth prospects, too.'

'But you value your place in the country,' I protested.

'So?' replied Hanson. 'Peter Palumbo's got a motorway going straight past his estate. He's not stopping it. He's planting trees to screen it off.'

I wondered (to myself) what the non-Palumbos do if, for some petty reason, they lack the capacity to put a forest between themselves and one of Hanson's highways. Hanson himself migrates for five months of the year to Palm Springs in California, where he likes to nip around on a bicycle. Before I could point out that the rent-a-mob folk prefer two wheels to four, we were on to the next hobby-horse.

'Schools,' Hanson cantered, 'are turning out morons. They come to us for employment, but they're utterly unemployable. Arithmetic, spelling – no better than 10-year-olds. There's nothing we can offer them. I blame this child-centred education. What about you?'

I muttered something about computers turning children into vegetables. And something else about overcrowded classrooms. These were not factors in Hanson's analysis.

'Teachers need a shake-up. Kids aren't at school to enjoy themselves. It's time teachers did some teaching. Don't tell me it's underfunding. We spend more of our national income on education than the Germans or the Japanese.'

I asked when he thought the rot had descended on British education. 'About 30 years ago,' he said. 'Yes, well,' I said, 'the government's got a lot to answer for.' 'Nonsense,' said Hanson. 'It's the teachers. Obdurate lot, won't take change.'

The morons issuing from British schools will not find work in Hanson's company. His son, however, is doing well. Was he being groomed for succession?

'Robert came in completely of his own accord,' said Hanson. 'Surprised me. I never put him up to it at all.'

He admits that the City is not well disposed towards his conglomerate, or indeed any conglomerate. His holdings range from cranes to cod liver oil. I asked him if his many interests outside Britain had developed because of Thatcher's torpedo on British industry. 'Margaret didn't shut things down,' he snapped. 'Only you academics say that, in your ignorance. She enabled.'

Then a more immediate bone of contention was set before us. Hanson ordered me a chocolate dessert, and asked if the *FT* would run to a cigar. Surely, I said. A *garçon* was summoned.

'I am sorry,' said the *garçon*. 'We have many complaints about your lordship's cigars. Cigars no longer permitted in dining room.'

The moment is frozen in my mind. Lord Hanson's features were corrugated with fury. The waiter, meanwhile, looked as careless as anyone might – anyone who did not know that another chunk of the Hanson conglomerate is rolled up in Imperial Tobacco. I drew an expectant breath.

'Since when,' hissed Hanson, 'has this ruling been in force?'

'Manager he decide last week, sir.'

'Manager will be hearing from me,' said Hanson, ominously, and convincingly. Then, recalling his composure, he said to me: 'You see? These minorities, like the road-wreckers, dictating to us. We have to make a stand. This place may just have lost a very esteemed customer.'

I feared we two erstwhile Vikings were thus far united on little enough, so I was glad to be able to sympathize with him on the cigar issue. We parted, in fact, on what I took to be friendly terms. 'You must come and have lunch with me,' said Hanson. 'Of course,' I said, as one does. But I hardly anticipated that while I was still settling the bill, a call would come from Hanson's secretary, asking if I could come to lunch three days hence.

Lunch with Hanson Revisited, at his flat on the Brompton Road, deserves a brief description. It was a manly occasion, and the cuisine reflected Hanson's robust Yorkshire virtues. A densely packed soufflé, a hearty stew of British beef and mince pies served with cuts of farmhouse cheese. Other guests included Richard Addis, the boyish new editor of the *Daily Express*, and Kenneth Baker, former home secretary, who is a non-executive director of the Hanson Company.

Cigars proliferated with impunity. Talk turned from roads (inadequacy of spending on), to education (abysmal quality of). Baker declared that teachers should spend more time in the classroom. 'Start at seven-thirty, teach till five. None of this clocking-off in mid-afternoon. Time to end those 16-week holidays, too.'

There were puffs and clinks and grunts of agreement. Hanson basked in the convivial business of gentlemen setting the world to rights over a good meal and a smoke. And the curious illogicalities that surface on such occasions duly arose. Having comprehensively impugned the teaching profession, the gentlemen then deplored the failure of John Major to attend the funeral of the London headmaster murdered in his own playground. 'It was a focus of national concern,' we agreed. 'He should have been there.'

I walked meditatively to the Tube station with another guest, Nicholas True. True is a former member of the Policy Unit at the prime minister's office, whom Hanson is sponsoring to chronicle the post-war demise of British education. 'The City doesn't like his business,' said True. 'But he's a good sort. Don't you find?'

'Yes,' I said. 'But then, we were brothers in another life.'

And, I should have added, there are many ways to reach Valhalla.

Mo Ibrahim

The bounty of Africa

The Sudanese billionaire helped invent the
mobile phone in the 1980s. Now he wants to
use his fortune to promote good governance
among Africa's leaders

By William Wallis

Mo Ibrahim, one of Africa's wealthiest entrepreneurs,
doesn't have that much in common with Johnny Depp,
Madonna or Kate Moss. So I am somewhat surprised
to find myself waiting for the Sudanese telecoms mogul
turned philanthropist at Cipriani in Mayfair, an Italian restaurant that
features regularly in the gossip columns.

There are no A-list celebrities for the waiters to pamper today. The
clientele looks cosmopolitan but professional, business rather than glitz.
The tables are filling up fast, so I request what passes for a sheltered
corner to give my tape recorder a chance above the din of wine-fuelled
deal-making.

Ibrahim calls to say he is running late. When he does arrive, he looks
suave in a cravat, smelling mildly of pipe tobacco. We have met before.
But his energetic, straightforward manner is as disarming as the first
time. He asks after my family and, having apologized for the delay,
explains his choice of restaurant. It is proximity rather than celebrity
that brings us here: Cipriani is around the corner from his Portman
Square offices. 'The food is also great,' he says. Neither of us is particularly hungry. Ibrahim professes to be on a diet and says lunch slows him
down. But the menu does inspire an appetite.

Until recently, the mention of Mo Ibrahim outside the circles of
telecoms buffs or African business aficionados tended to elicit the

response: 'Mo who?' Google him since he sold Celtel, his African mobile-phone company, for $3.4bn and he starts popping up in the company of Bill Gates and Warren Buffett.

This is perhaps more for the audacity – some say hubris – of his new, philanthropic mission than for the size of his fortune. Where Gates has decided to do battle with micro-organisms wreaking preventable havoc across Africa, Ibrahim is taking on a more visible, if equally pernicious, enemy of African development. After we have ordered our starters – on his advice I go for pasta, he opts for carpaccio and Parmesan – Ibrahim turns to this latest project: persuading African leaders to rule more wisely, more fairly and for shorter periods.

A decade building mobile-phone networks across the continent has convinced him that business and trade, not charity and aid, will ultimately bring prosperity to Africa. But neither tactic can succeed without a radical shift in the way the continent is governed.

'The country is so lush, so green,' he says, recalling a flight over Kenya before the violently disputed outcome of December's elections. 'How come the people here could ever be hungry? Look at these spaces, huge, endless spaces, animals, water. I came to the conclusion that unless you are ruled properly, you cannot move forward. Everything else is second. Everything.'

African leaders, Ibrahim continues, look to retirement as they would to the edge of a cliff, beyond which lies a dizzying fall towards retribution and relative poverty.

'We don't have financial institutions for ex-presidents to go and run, or boards of great companies. There is life after office in other parts of the world. I just read that Tony Blair was paid half a million pounds to make a speech in China. People like Blair always have a place in society, they have secure financial futures,' he says.

Ibrahim believes he has created an attractive alternative to clinging on to power. Every year he is offering $5m of his own money to an African leader who is judged to have ruled fairly and resigned, with grace, to an elected successor.

He knows the continent too well to think that this project, which is accompanied by detailed rankings on governance standards in 48 sub-Saharan African countries, will have an immediate impact. Nor does he expect there to be a worthy winner every year. But the first benefactor of his prize, Joachim Chissano, who led Mozambique out of civil war and through a decade of economic recovery before stepping down, gives him cause for optimism.

'I think there's a new breed of African leaders who are trying to do the right thing in and out of office,' Ibrahim says. 'I was so impressed when we couldn't find Chissano to tell him he had won the prize. It turned out it was his birthday and he was spending it in the bush somewhere between Congo, northern Uganda and Sudan [mediating between the Ugandan government and Lord's Resistance Army rebels].'

There follows a flurry of insightful anecdotes about some of the African leaders he knows best, interspersed with digressions into recent events – South Africa's bitter leadership struggle, the precarious aftermath of Nigeria's flawed elections and the war in Sudan's Darfur province.

Ibrahim's own background was modest. His father, a clerk, took his young son and family away from Sudan to Alexandria in Egypt, where Ibrahim spent his formative years. In those days he saw himself as a Marxist. 'I ended up being a businessman unwittingly. I wanted to be an academic; I wanted to be like Einstein,' he says as the waiter puts down a plate of Dover sole with artichokes in front of me, and Ibrahim tucks into monkfish dressed in capers and cornichons.

Phones were a fascination for him early on, and it was this fascination that took him in the early 1970s on an engineering scholarship to the UK, where he eventually gained a PhD, and a career that started at British Telecom. A combination of serendipity, an engineer's eye for the transformative power of technology and a belief in Africa have kept him at the cutting edge of the telecoms business ever since.

In the 1980s he led the team of engineers at BT Cellnet that took the car phone out of the car, pioneering Britain's first mobile-phone network. But he tired of working for such a large corporation, and with $50,000 set up his own consultancy, Mobile Systems International (MSI). This went on to design digital cellphone networks in Europe, Asia and Latin America.

At first Ibrahim says he couldn't read a balance sheet or write a business plan. 'So I just managed the company by cash. For six years it kept growing. The first year we made a profit of £200,000. The second year we made a profit of £500,000. Then £1.2m, then £2.5m, then £5m . . .'

By 2000, Ibrahim's consultancy had 800 employees. He sold it to Marconi for $900m, and reinvested the funds into Celtel. At the time the dotcom bubble was about to burst, and the margins of IT companies were thinning. But sub-Saharan Africa, where most people had never used a phone, let alone owned one, had been overlooked by the big players, who deemed it too poor, corrupt and risky.

'All my life I have been in this industry. Then here is a situation where you have huge unsatisfied demand for a service that doesn't exist. You don't have competition with fixed lines as you do in Europe. It was a no-brainer that the cellular route would be a great success in Africa.'

On cue, mobile phones have been proliferating in Africa in recent years faster than anywhere else in the world. Ibrahim believes that they contributed about 1 per cent to the nearly 6 per cent GDP African countries on average enjoyed in 2007. In the process, millions of lives have been connected and changed.

Celtel has been among the more innovative companies, penetrating rural as well as urban areas, using phones for banking and, more recently, eliminating costly roaming tariffs. But it was held back, Ibrahim says, by the reluctance of banks to lend it money: 'The largest loan we ever had was $190m, but when MTC [of Kuwait] bought us out, they went to the same banks and won billions. This shows you what African companies are up against.'

By the time of the sale in 2005, Celtel was nonetheless operating in more than 14 African countries with 20 million-plus subscribers. At the bottom end, mobile-phone companies are competing for the same dollar that buys a square meal or a bottle of beer, Ibrahim says. But their success has helped galvanize other service industries to venture beyond the resource-driven bubble economies in which many multinationals have operated on the continent.

On that note, we both decline a tray of pastries, and opt for black coffee. Ibrahim appears one of those rare billionaires who has not let good fortune separate him from his more humble roots. Nor has his Sudanese wife, an oncologist, who 'after we sold out said, "I don't want diamonds or a private jet. What I really want is a state of the art hospital in Khartoum for the treatment of breast cancer."'

Women, he believes, are the real hope for the continent. 'They are more honest with money and they don't go around murdering people.'

There is a very long way still to go, he adds. But Asian demand for African commodities has brought about a turnaround in the terms on which the continent trades. Globally there is a new grasp of Africa's potential.

'It's not that we are any longer hanging our hopes on some nationalist leader or supposedly benign dictator,' he says. 'The fact that people have access now to TV, to newspapers, to phones, and some have access to the internet, means you can no longer keep the truth from them so easily. That is another fundamental change.'

Today Ibrahim splits his time between the foundation he has created and a private equity fund. With this he hopes to replicate Celtel's success in other sectors, investing in companies with the potential to link Africa's fragmented markets. Some critics contend that in such a difficult business environment, Ibrahim must have bent the rules. So, I ask him, as we leave, is he not too good to be true? For the first time a hint of irritation passes across his face. But he chuckles and brushes aside the question. He has always believed in social justice, he says, and being a businessman, it turns out, is not incompatible with that. And this, as much as anything, is the lesson he wants to impart.

Cipriani

23–25 Davies Street,
London W1

....

1 x carpaccio and
Parmesan
1 x fresh pasta
1 x Dover sole and
artichoke
1 x monkfish in caper and
cornichon sauce
1 x Peroni beer
1 x bottle of sparkling
water
2 x black coffees

....

Total   £118

Michael O'Leary

'It was either that or McDonald's'

The controversy-courting, cost-cutting chief executive of Ryanair does not want to eat in a fine Dublin restaurant. He prefers a pre-packed bagel and a 'menacing' chicken salad in his office at the city's airport

By Pilita Clark

Here,' says Michael O'Leary, shoving something the size of a small grapefruit wrapped in red and white cardboard over the table in his office at Dublin airport. 'Lunch.'

There is an awkward silence.

You do not expect a banquet from a budget airline boss who has threatened to make his passengers pay to use the toilet.

And you do not want to upset a man who calls regulators 'rapists', rivals 'arseholes', and advises customers wanting a refund to 'f*** off'.

But what exactly has he given me here? Eventually, I make out the words on the wrapper and blurt, 'Oh! A bagel!'

'It's got pesto,' says O'Leary. 'It was either that or McDonald's. I figured you for a bagel girl.'

For himself, he has procured a grim-looking chicken salad, entombed in thick plastic, also from somewhere in the airport down the road. An aide arrives with two takeaway coffees. So begins lunch with one of the world's best-known, least-loved and more improbable airline chief executives.

I had tried to persuade O'Leary's press officer that lunch in the office

FERGUSON

would be dull. Surely there was a restaurant he liked in Dublin? No. Lunch with the chief executive of Ryanair would be a Ryanair lunch: at the desk, just your basics, all expenses spared.

In the world of aviation, Ryanair is a phenomenon, a no-frills behemoth that has grown from a tiny operation which, in 1985, used to fly 5,000 passengers a year between Ireland and London in a single plane so small that, according to the company, its cabin crew had to be no taller than 5ft 2in. Since he took over in 1994 O'Leary has relentlessly expanded, with 200 aircraft flying more than 60m passengers a year to 150 European destinations, from the Canary Islands to Constanta in eastern Romania.

Recession has sent bigger, older airlines around the world hurtling into the red. Yet Ryanair has fared much better, coupling average fares of just €32 with a ruthless drive to cut costs and push up revenues by charging for everything from checking in online to buying a cup of coffee on board.

In the middle of this year Ryanair had the highest market value of any airline in the world, after Singapore Airlines. On the day we meet, it is getting ready to announce another quarterly profit and expects to make at least €200m this year.

None of this is evident from Ryanair's Dublin airport headquarters. Plastic sacks of wastepaper are piled at the entrance. Boxes are stacked up in corridors inside. The paintwork is scruffy, the carpet tired.

The open-plan office feels barely as wide as one of Ryanair's Boeing jets, and nearly as cramped. There is a single aisle dividing tightly packed teams of surprisingly young-looking workers into departments such as marketing, sales and planning.

It looks less like one of the airline industry's financial success stories and more like a scene from the television comedy *The Office*. Except the workers in *The Office* have bigger desks. And down at the end, peering out from behind the glass walls of his own modest office, is O'Leary.

Wearing jeans, open-necked checked shirt and sneakers, he looks a bit tired and pale up close. This could be because he and his wife Anita Farrell, a former banker, have three children under the age of eight. Or because he seems in a permanent state of exasperation with an endless number of irritants, including his own staff.

As I try to prise off the worryingly sturdy wrapper on the bagel, he says there are two 'great things' about lunchtime in an out-of-the-way office like Ryanair's. 'One, there's nowhere to go and eat,' and two, the only time staff are allowed to use the internet for personal reasons is between five past one and five to two. 'So they all tend to stay at their desks at lunch hour!'

The staff get another pasting as he moves on to talk about management consultants ('should all be euthanized') and MBAs ('bullshit'). 'MBA students come out with, "The customer's always right,"' he says, adopting a whiny voice. 'Horseshit! The customer's usually wrong! And, "My staff is my most important asset." Bullshit! Staff is usually your biggest cost!'

It is hard to say how serious he is about this. Ryanair did once say it had issued a memo banning employees from charging their mobile phones at work to save on electricity bills. But this always sounded like another PR prank by O'Leary, whose flair for using the media is boundless.

Airline entrepreneurs have often revealed a talent for doing their own PR. Richard Branson flew in a hot air balloon for Virgin Atlantic. Stelios Haji-Ioannou wore orange jumpsuits for EasyJet. But O'Leary takes the practice to new heights.

It is not just his willingness to dress up as the Pope to publicize a new route to Rome. Or his (so far unrealized) threat to charge passengers to use the lavatory. It is the sheer savagery of his blasts that make him stand out on the featureless plains of modern corporate life.

For 20 bracing minutes, he runs through a list of his more egregious enemies. There are the 'cretins' and 'twerps' in the Civil Aviation Authority, the British body that regulates the 'bloody evil empire' of BAA, the airport operator whose London monopoly was recently broken up, after prodding from O'Leary, who had griped incessantly about its charges.

There is the 'big bloody supertanker' of Boeing, the US aircraft maker that O'Leary has been badgering for months to sell him 200 new jets at recessionary prices. And there is, visible right outside his office window, one of his most hated foes: Aer Lingus, the struggling Irish flag carrier for which O'Leary has made two thwarted bids in the past three years. 'There it is,' he hoots, jumping up out of his chair to point out a large squat building facing away from his own. 'The gulag!' He would clearly like to make a third offer for Aer Lingus, but knows this would mean trouble with its 'bunch of bearded, sandal-wearing union bosses', not to mention Ireland's 'utterly useless' politicians.

And then there is that other source of endless aggravation, Ryanair's passengers. Especially the ones wrecking his efforts to shave luggage-handling costs by checking in their cases (for an extra £30) because they are 'too mentally bloody lazy to travel with carry-on bags'.

Surely he doesn't seriously expect anyone to go on a three-week holiday with just a carry-on?

'Oh, for God's sake, of course you can for three weeks,' he says.

'I can't.'

'You can.'

'I don't want to.'

He stares at me, then admits his wife feels the same way.

'My wife goes away on holidays for a couple of weeks, and she wears bikinis and a few flip-flops, but she needs her 40 pairs of shoes,' he says theatrically. 'What do you need 40 pairs of shoes for?'

So, who exactly is the ideal Ryanair passenger?

'Our ideal passenger is someone with a pulse and a credit card, who will follow the simple instructions to lower our costs to the maximum.'

By this point, hunger is driving me to make a fresh attempt on the bagel wrapper. Off it comes, and there sits a sad-looking bagel containing a pile of pesto, tomato and cucumber. I start picking at it. O'Leary's salad sits menacingly on his desk, untouched.

This is a typical lunch for him, he says, when he isn't at the gym.

What does he like to do in the gym?

'Look up and down a slim girl's rear,' he says. 'Sadly there's not that many of them. They're a bunch of old sweaty farts.'

Though greying a little, O'Leary is, at 48, not that old. Before he became a loud-mouthed chief executive, he was a tax accountant, before that a businessman's son, expensively educated at some of Ireland's best schools. According to one newspaper's estimate he is worth more than £300m, partly thanks to a 4 per cent stake in Ryanair. But for years now, he has been saying he will retire 'in two or three years'. So what is it today?

'Three years,' he says, suddenly trying to look serious. By then it will be time to 'Tesco-ize Ryanair', by which he means time to ditch him for someone more suitable for a larger, more sedate operation.

'In certain respects I am our best salesman,' he says, explaining the 'pantomime villain character' he plays for the airline is done purely for the free publicity (the net spend on advertising last year was €5m, he says, not much for an airline Ryanair's size). 'But I'm also negative in that a lot of my antics detract from the fact that Ryanair has the youngest fleet of aircraft, the best punctuality record, delivers a terrific customer service.

'I think you need me for the rapid growth and for the in-cost reduction initiatives, but once they're all done you then need to hand over to somebody who's a bit more respectful of politicians and bureaucrats, talks about caring about the environment and old people and f***ing jungles and fish in the sea and all that shite.'

Goodness knows what O'Leary will do if he ever retires. He claims to have no interest in holidays. 'I go to the Algarve with the family for two weeks, because I have to. And I can build the sandcastles with the children. You know, the sandcastle's fine for the first five minutes, and after that it's, "Oh Jesus, will someone come and rescue me!" I'm praying for a crisis.'

What about close friends? 'My wife, occasionally. My children on a good day.'

He hates the theatre. Only sees films when dragged by his wife, 'just for marriage maintenance reasons'. His main interests, apart from Ryanair, consist of farming, football and racehorses, of which he has a few including one called War of Attrition, which won the Cheltenham Gold Cup in 2006. I had always assumed this was an O'Leary-esque joke at a rival's expense – Aer Lingus, perhaps – but he says the animal had the name when he bought it.

There is a strange lack of sophistication about O'Leary. His success has made him one of the industry's most prominent airline chiefs, his name constantly on the lips of his peers, his business model aped around the world. Willie Walsh, a fellow Irishman and the chief executive of British Airways, once told me, only half joking, that O'Leary's success had even driven other airline executives to copy his dress sense: 'You get these CEOs who, because O'Leary doesn't wear a tie or a suit, feel that to have any sort of respect, you can't wear a tie.'

Yet his world-view has curious gaps. At one point, I ask him what he thinks of other well-known figures in his industry. Stelios? 'A rich kid who got off his arse.' Richard Branson? 'A genius in the way he has made a fortune out of the Virgin brand, but he doesn't add up to much.' But, when asked about Tony Tyler, chief executive at Cathay Pacific, one of Asia's biggest airlines, he looks blank. 'Never heard of him,' he says. 'Anyone in the airline industry outside of Europe, I wouldn't know who the hell they are.'

There is also something rather quaint about him. He doesn't have a BlackBerry, there is no computer on his desk. He even claims not to have an email address. 'Email is rubbish. If there's something important, I'll send a fax, or we'll speak.'

Each day a team compiles two reports on paper for him, one for sales, one for punctuality, which give an instant overview of how the business is performing. He gets up and grabs a sheet showing the day's bookings, the month's sales, next month's sales, available seats, how it all compares with the same month last year, and so on. 'Business should be simple,' he beams.

Lack of email does not stop him being an enthusiastic correspondent. When UK advertising standards authorities chided him for claiming Ryanair's flights were faster than the Eurostar train, he sent them a copy of *Everyday Maths for Dummies*. Journalists who write about him sometimes get an unsolicited, though frequently charming, missive. A colleague on the *FT* who wrote a column comparing Ryanair to Aeroflot received a two-page letter along with the latest 'Girls of Ryanair' calendar, featuring bikini-clad photos of Miss Check-In and Miss Fuel Pump, a regular production that O'Leary insists uses only company cabin crew.

Ryanair HQ
Dublin airport

2 x takeaway coffee	€3.60
1 x chicken salad	€5.50
1 x pesto, tomato, cucumber bagel	€5.50
Total	€14.60

The admiration is reciprocated, at least in the financial media. On a cabinet in a corner of his office is a dusty collection of awards sent by the likes of *Barron's*, the financial magazine that has named him one of the 'world's most respected CEOs' ever since it started handing out the award in 2005. 'Barf!' says O'Leary, looking embarrassed, when asked about the prizes.

His constant obsession with cost-cutting, however, not to mention his foul mouth, has also spawned less adulatory attention, such as the website www.ihateryanair.co.uk, dedicated to what it calls 'the world's most hated airline'.

Before today, I say, every person I spoke to and said I was having lunch with Michael O'Leary reacted with horror or pity. Doesn't he find it wearying to be such a hate figure? 'It would be wearying if you weren't growing by 9m passengers a year,' he says. 'We know, fundamentally, that we have huge public support.'

Outside, the light is fading. My flight home is getting near. My bagel is still there, still half eaten. O'Leary's salad still sits on his desk.

A few days later, I get a letter from O'Leary, thanking me for taking the time to come to Dublin to see him and hoping I enjoyed my 'five-star gourmet lunch'. By the way, he adds: 'I forgot to charge you for the coffee, so you owe me one.'

George Soros

The billion-dollar memory lapse

The financier has moved on to higher things since Black Wednesday 1992, when he broke the Bank of England and made a fortune – or was it a Thursday?

By Daniel Dombey

I t is the hottest day of the year, apocalyptic chords are crashing around an empty church and George Soros is describing his messiah complex. The man who made $1bn in a day by betting against the Bank of England always thought he was set apart. As a child, Soros had what he calls 'messianic fantasies'.

'I felt I was putting in time until I found my place in the world,' he says, his rasping voice a reminder of his central European origins. 'I was ill at ease in the position in which I was.'

Today, however, he finds himself in a locale designed to nourish outsize egos – Mosimann's, a dining club in a former Presbyterian church. It is staff training day and the place is deserted. But we are going to be served all the same, having booked a private room for £150.

As we drink at the bar overlooking what was once the aisle, a Wagnerian crescendo swells behind us. It is the kind of music you might want to invade Poland to. No wonder the establishment's corporate clients find it so invigorating.

Soros, however, is in a different league – so engagingly Olympian that he affects absent-mindedness about his greatest coup – Black Wednesday, 16 September 1992. That day, when Soros successfully bet the

British pound would be devalued, broke John Major's government, led to the election of the Labour party and entered political folklore as an unforgettable date. But not, it seems, to the man who made the most money out of it.

'Was it Wednesday?' he asks. 'It was Thursday, I think.'

'Wednesday,' I confirm. 'Definitely Wednesday.'

'Was it?' he asks again, seeming to distance himself from his former self.

Today, the 75-year-old no longer moves markets. He admits his Quantum Fund, so feared throughout the 1990s, is not a major player. But if anything his ambitions are now even greater. Soros has set up a network of charitable foundations that span the globe, prides himself on having helped the 2003 'rose revolution' that toppled Georgia's President Eduard Shevardnadze, and has poured money into opposing the administration of George W. Bush.

He has also written nine books, most of them over the past decade, dedicated to his pet theory of 'reflexivity'. Having just read the latest – *The Age of Fallibility* – I want to stave off the moment when we start exchanging abstract concepts.

Instead, as Soros nurses his Campari and soda, I ask about 1944, the year when the Nazis invaded his native Hungary and killed hundreds of thousands of Soros's fellow Jews. Soros himself had to deliver deportation notices. And yet it is the year he terms the best in his life.

'It was undoubtedly the formative year,' he says of that time, when his father obtained fake identity papers that saved the family's lives and those of many others. 'I was very close to my father and he imparted his entire wisdom in a practical demonstration of what you have to do to survive. A lot of my subsequent adventures in the financial world and my philanthropic philanderings were very much influenced by him, by this.

'I learnt then that there are times when the normal rules don't apply,' he says. 'Also the fact that it might be more dangerous to be passive – it can be less risky to take risk.' He leans back, discomfited by the heat.

Soros is by turns imperious, grandiloquent and humble. He revels in some of the more gushing ways he has been described, such as 'the man who broke the Bank of England' and the 'stateless statesman'. Yet he also listens, nods and offers up unflattering adjectives for himself and his arguments when I ask whether he is not simply a billionaire playing at being a big thinker. 'Arrogant', he suggests at one point; 'obscene', he volunteers at another.

I remark on the difference between him and his father, whom he calls the biggest influence on his life. Both were shaped by their experiences in world wars – his father in a Siberian prison camp during the Russian revolution. But afterwards Soros senior never sought money or power.

'In some ways he was broken by the experience,' Soros says of his father, a lawyer who pioneered the world's first and only Esperanto literary magazine but wound up running an espresso stand in Coney Island in New York. 'He avoided the limelight.'

There is a rustle behind us and Anton Mosimann, the chef and proprietor of the establishment, appears, smiling, bow-tied, moustachioed. He, like Soros, has a philosophy – his website says that chicken should taste like chicken and fish should taste like fish – and he has written even more books than the billionaire.

'You're not open today?' asks Soros.

'We have some food for you,' Mosimann assures us and before long we are led to the back of the church, down past a set of firedoors, to the Davidoff Room – a sponsored dining area intended to resemble the inside of a humidor.

This is not the first time Soros has seen the back of a restaurant. After he came to the UK in 1947 (his father dissuaded him from going to the Soviet Union), he had a variety of odd jobs while studying at the London School of Economics. At one time he worked at Quaglino's, then a stylish London eaterie, and subsisted on profiteroles. He also spent time as a trinket salesman and a swimming pool attendant.

But it was his studies at the LSE that proved more influential – particularly his fleeting contacts with Karl Popper, the philosopher who preached the merits of an 'open society' over the totalitarianisms of Nazism and communism.

What swayed Soros was Popper's insight that, since mankind could make mistakes, societies should be receptive to new ideas rather than based on rigid doctrines. He himself went further, arguing that people are bound to be wrong. This is where his talk of 'reflexivity' comes in. The idea is basically that people's misconceptions interact with reality – whether through driving down a currency or promoting an idea such as President Bush's war on terror. Soros swears the theory helped make his fortune.

'I really have no problem with being rich,' he smiles. (It's a big weight off my mind, I think uncharitably.) He says he allows himself minor indulgences, such as keeping a permanent staff in his London flat although he spends most of his time in the US.

He made his way to New York to work as a hedge fund manager in 1956 and his father joined him the same year. Two decades later, after he had made his first $30m, he had a midlife crisis. 'I was knocking myself out. I really thought long and hard about what I needed more money for,' he says as he digs into an endive salad. 'As part of that process I decided to set up the Open Society Fund.'

Soros calls the network of organizations he finances 'a cross between a foundation and a movement'. It has subsidized ministers' salaries in Georgia after the rose revolution, saved scientists in the former Soviet Union from starvation and seeks to promote government transparency, human rights and a free press. It has even supported the Hungarian zither players' association.

But it is for making money that he is best known. Stories abound about Soros the financier – about how he lost millions in Russia and Japan, about how he always wanted to raise the stakes. His $1bn profit on Black Wednesday, for example, came because he had bet $10bn. Investing also brought him pain – because of his fear of losing what he had risked. Despite all of Soros's talk of reflexivity, he admits he often sensed trouble with his investments because of an ache in his back.

He no longer has the same appetite for risk – partly because he wants to see his foundations endure after his death. That means the days are over when he gambled his entire wealth in a single day.

'It's a relief not to be dependent on the market,' he says, adding that he sees his legacy as his books and his philanthropy. 'The money is a means to an end; the end is a philosophy translated into action.'

Nor has he given up trying to win support for his 'conceptual framework', even though he long ago confessed that he could not make head or tail of his own writings.

Who are his books written for? I ask, prodding a fork into my beef tartare and watching egg yolk slide out of it. Soros tranquilly munches his salmon, stopping to remove a hint of mayonnaise from his thumb. 'Students,' he replies. 'People who are still forming their view of the world.'

Students? But the last 50 pages of *The Age of Fallibility* are a reworking of a 43-year-old text that even Popper, his old mentor, wasn't much interested in.

'Well, I have a sense that I haven't got my ideas across,' he says. He says the book is an attempt to study US society, which he faults for re-electing Bush and hence, in his view, making the world a more dangerous place.

'I basically wrote it to clarify my own thinking,' he adds. 'The ultimate audience, so to speak, is me.'

He also wants to change public opinion, and in the last US election undertook an anti-Bush speaking tour – something, I suggest, that may amount to a rich man's folly.

'Since I'm a rich man, whatever folly I commit is a rich man's folly,' he half laughs, half splutters.

And isn't it strange that a billionaire should write a screed against US consumerism and the way business seeks to stimulate desires?

'I have been successful within the capitalist system,' he replies. 'Who better qualified to criticize globalization than somebody who flourishes within it?'

The meal has overrun its time. We grab an espresso and then he leads the way back up to the main building, sliding past what appears to be an empty dessert trolley. At the main door, Mosimann and his staff line

---

Mosimann's Private Dining Club and Private Rooms
London SW1

1 x Campari and soda
1 x tomato juice
1 x ceviche
1 x endive salad
1 x salmon
1 x beef tartare
2 x glasses of white Burgundy
1 x bottle of mineral water
2 x espressos

up to say goodbye and Soros ambles to his unpretentious chauffeured Citroën.

Days later the bill still has not arrived. I have little idea how much our meal has cost the *FT*. But, by any calculation, it came to far less than Soros made during a tenth of a second on Black Wednesday. Or Black Thursday. Or whenever it was.

Shaw-Lan Wang

'It's true, I am a woman'

In a rare interview, the Chinese newspaper magnate reveals how she revived a French fashion house – and why she can't forgive the Japanese

By David Pilling

Madame Wang enters the room at some velocity. The first thing I notice are her super-large eyebrows, arched like croquet hoops above her heavily made-up eyelids. Then I take in her fashionable haircut, short with a jagged fringe. Her hair is dyed dark auburn, edged with little tufts of smoky grey. Next I register her mandarin-collared *qipao* in leopard-skin print, slit to the thigh. I know it is a *qipao* because she later tells me emphatically in her raspy, helium-filled voice: 'I always wear my Chinese dress. I am not Japanese. This is a Chinese *qipao*. It is not a kimono.' Over it is a black, cowl-neck vest. The outfit is finished off – if that's the word – with a chunky lord-mayor's-style neck chain.

Normally when journalists write about what women are wearing, they get letters complaining that they would never discuss men in the same way. That may be true. But the 70-year-old Madame Wang is the owner of Lanvin, the oldest surviving French fashion house, which she bought in 2001 and helped revive. To talk about what she is wearing seems appropriate, even essential. For the record, I am dressed in a grey suit, slightly rumpled after two cramped flights, one overnight, and a floral-patterned shirt by Marks and Spencer.

We are in Taipei, where Shaw-Lan Wang was brought up after moving to Taiwan from mainland China at the age of seven. Specifically, we are in a 34th-floor dining room in the luxurious surroundings of the

Taipei World Trade Center Club. I had arrived early and been ushered into the private room by a posse of women in grey skirt-suits. In the room, small but perfectly appointed, is a round table with a white table-cloth already set for two.

After she catches her breath, Madame Wang, as she refers to herself, reaches into her mouth to remove a piece of gum. She secretes the little green ball in her handbag, Lanvin presumably. Wang rarely gives interviews. She seems unsure as to how this one came about. 'How did you get in touch? Through my PR in Paris?' she asks. I am not entirely sure either, since the encounter was also arranged for me. Yet somehow here we are, thrown together in this little windowless room of a Taipei skyscraper.

Madame Wang was born in 1941, the Year of the Snake. Although her family was from the coastal province of Zhejiang, she started out life in Chongqing, the wartime capital after the fall of Nanjing to the Japanese. Her father, a colonel in the army of Chiang Kai-shek, the Guomindang leader, came to Taiwan in 1947. Two years later Chiang himself led a full-scale retreat to the island after being routed by Mao Zedong's Communist forces.

In 1951, her father founded the *United Daily News*, a staunch supporter of the Guomindang authoritarian government. Wang, who studied journalism in Taipei, worked as a reporter on the paper. She married an air force pilot and went to live in Switzerland with her husband, where she spent 12 to 15 years. She doesn't remember exactly. One day, she received a phone call from her father asking her to return to Taiwan and run the paper. 'I could not refuse.'

'What do you like to eat? You like kitchen or beef?' she asks. I take the former to mean chicken. Madame Wang's English, spoken choppily and with the hint of a French accent, is less than perfect, though it is leagues ahead of my terrible Chinese. She speaks with little concession to English grammar, omitting pronouns, tenses and even verbs and nouns. Gaps are filled with the most splendid mimes. Over the course of lunch, she acts out blind, short-sighted, dizzy, happy, drunk, dead, injured, crazy, terrified and a few other things besides. Much is achieved through facial expression. On several occasions, in place of saying 'good', she jabs her upturned thumb in my direction. Once, in somewhat less generous mood, she brings her hands together and twists as if strangling a chicken.

She orders several dishes. The waitress returns with succulent cold cuts of chicken, pork and duck. As Madame Wang takes a bite of the accompanying kimchi, I ask how her newspaper is surviving competition with the internet. 'It's not enjoyable to get information from the internet,' she says. 'A good book can touch your heart. But I have never had anything touch my heart on the internet.' But has the internet touched her sales? How is the paper faring in the face of online competition? 'The quality of the press is going down all around the world,' she persists. 'People have lost respect for the press.'

Two plates of grilled beef arrive. 'Chinese style,' she announces. I abandon my internet inquiries – she isn't sure whether her newspaper charges for its online version – and move to her more recent passion, Lanvin. How did she come to buy the struggling fashion house and how, in particular, did she come to hire Alber Elbaz, the designer whose appointment has transformed its fortunes? The purchase of Lanvin is easy. 'I have a friend in Hong Kong and he has dressed in Lanvin for more than 30 years. I thought, "He would be very proud if I was the owner."'

As for Elbaz, the Moroccan-born designer had been pushed out of Yves Saint Laurent after it was bought by Gucci. Embarking on a spiritual world odyssey, Elbaz contemplated giving up design altogether to become a doctor. Instead, he called Wang out of the blue, imploring her to bring him to Lanvin. 'Please wake up the Sleeping Beauty,' he said. 'I was in Cannes with a friend on a big boat,' Wang recalls. 'Alber called, "Can I meet you?" I say, "Of course. I will come to Paris."' She had never heard of Elbaz, but has been quoted as saying she 'smelt something meaty and fragrant' about him. To me she says, 'He showed me his press book. The first fashion show, he called "Homage to Yves Saint Laurent". "Good," I thought. "He knows respect." I was introduced to a lot of people. But with them I didn't have that feeling.'

Whether or not it was the meaty smell, Wang's instinct has served Lanvin splendidly. Under Elbaz, its reputation and sales have flourished. He makes clothes with a classic cut, to be worn year after year, not just for one season. 'Alber's dresses make women feel beautiful and easy. The first show he did was for winter. The fabric is quite thick. But all the dresses could swing. It's because of the cut. Normally, thick fabric is very stiff. But he makes you dance with your dress.'

A steamed fish appears, evidently too early. Wang sends it away. Elbaz's dresses are not overly revealing, she says, miming flesh spilling out of a low-cut dress. 'They don't show everything.' I had read that Elbaz didn't like his clothes to be thought of as sexy, certainly not in the full-on way associated with Gucci's Tom Ford, the man who deposed him at Yves Saint Laurent. 'I don't think so,' she says. 'Sexy is good. It's a compliment. But you have to have class. Not . . .' She leaves the sentence unfinished but treats me to another mime of a bosom bulging out of a dress.

The fish reappears. This time it has been cut in two, the part with the head for her, the tail for me. 'Everybody loves Alber's dresses,' she is saying. 'Before I [used to] say Alber's dress is for anyone from 18 to 81.' But she recently met an 85-year-old Chinese artist wearing a Lanvin dress. 'So pretty.' Wang's granddaughter, who is just 11 and evidently being groomed for greatness, also wears Lanvin. 'The dresses are very elegant and simple, so the range of our customers is very big.'

I ask if she enjoys the fashion shows, the parties and the glamour. 'Alber and my director go the parties. Not me,' she says, spitting out some fish bones into her hand. 'I don't like those kind of people or those kind of parties. I am not a jet-set person.' She has lots of famous friends but she meets them in private, she says, reeling off names of actors, actresses and kung fu stars. She's off on a tangent, telling a story about when Jackie Chan annoyed the Taiwanese by suggesting that Chinese people needed to be controlled and that democracy in Taiwan was chaotic. 'Jackie, he's very honest and straight. I called him and said, "You are great. You have a very big market. If people here are stupid, don't come."'

We talk about the recent thaw in relations between Taiwan and mainland China. Although she is an anti-communist and counts among her friends several Tiananmen Square dissidents, she says the government in Beijing has changed. 'Now, I agree with what they are doing. They are disciplined. Before you have the law, don't give too much freedom,' she says, wagging her finger. 'You have to teach people to respect the law, even if the law is bad.'

The waitress brings in some lusciously green and crisp snow peas with scallops. There's barely room on the table. She continues on the China–Taiwan theme, saying it has been more than 60 years since the two separated. But unification is not so easy, she says, referring to the strong sense of Taiwanese independence. 'We Chinese all have patience. Next generation, let's see what that brings. I think in China one day, if they have freedom of the press and liberty of election, we can negotiate to become one big China.

'We have no reason to hate each other. The Japanese killed many, many Chinese and Asian people. Why don't the people hate the Japanese?' she asks, referring to the relatively warm relations between the Taiwanese and their former Japanese colonists. 'War kills, but not the way the Japanese kill. They use . . .' Here she mimes the stabbing action of a bayonet. 'They kill women and babies with their cruel methods. People say forgive, but I say, "I cannot."'

To this day, she says, she refuses to meet Japanese people, notwithstanding the fact that she is currently negotiating to buy back the Japanese licence to Lanvin, previously sold to trading house Itochu. 'It doesn't matter what title they have. If people say, "Madame Wang, this is such and such," I never give my hand. I never say hello to Japanese.' She turns her head disdainfully. 'Bye bye. I don't care what they think.'

The waitress offers to wrap up the left-overs. 'For my driver,' says Wang. Two egg tarts and two portions of taro pudding are served. The egg tart, with divinely crumbly pastry, is the best I've tasted. I had read somewhere that she compares the dual role of newspaper magnate and fashion-house baroness to having a husband and a lover.

Taipei World Trade Center Club
34F, No 333, Sec 1,
Keelung Rd, Taipei City,
Taiwan

. . . .

cold cuts of chicken, pork and duck with kimchi
Chinese-style grilled beef
steamed fish
scallops with snow peas
egg tart
taro pudding
pear and papaya
jasmine tea

. . . .

Total not disclosed

Which is which? 'Who told you I said that?' she flashes back. 'Since my husband died I don't have any lover. So how can I compare my husband to a lover?' The important thing is to throw yourself into both. 'If you run a business, you have to love this business with all your heart. Before, when I ran a newspaper, I sleep for maybe two, three hours a day. I am

so excited.' Now she has cut back and handed over day-to-day management to her nephew. With Lanvin, too, her strategy has been to step
back and give Elbaz the freedom to create.

The waitress brings pear and papaya. I nervously broach the subject
of who should pay for this feast. Wang's assistant had warned previously
that, under no circumstances, would Madame Wang allow the *FT* to pay.
I try anyway. 'I am meant to invite you,' I say timidly. 'The *FT* really does
insist on paying.' The riposte is swift and brutal. 'Here in China, no.
Never, never, never,' she shrieks. 'This is my domain. Even if you are
Chinese, you cannot pay.'

I figure it is useless. Besides, she is already wrapping up, telling me
that on no account am I to refer to her as a Taiwanese businesswoman.
'I don't consider myself Tai-wan-ese,' she says, drawing out the word.
'I am Chinese. And I don't consider myself a businesswoman either,' she
adds without explanation. Then she softens. 'It's true, I am a woman.
That I cannot say anything about.'

Steve Wozniak

The wizardry of Woz

The engineering genius admits he'd like another bite of Apple

By Richard Waters

The Hickory Pit, set on a particularly faceless strip in the faceless Californian city of San Jose, does not look a promising place for a heart-to-heart. Inside the concrete shell is a cavernous, diner-style hall that is aching to return to the 1950s: rows of booths decked in candy-pink and blue plastic, veneer table tops, fluorescent lights.

Steve Wozniak looks right at home – which, it turns out, isn't surprising, given the amount of time he has spent here recently. It is easy to walk right past one of Silicon Valley's legendary computer engineers. A waiter gestures to the back of the hall, but I see only two men bent over handheld gadgets connected by a cable. A polystyrene box with the remains of the ribs they have just eaten is on the table.

The waiter insists that Woz, as he is widely known, is back there, and a second pass reveals that one of the game-players is indeed the man I have come to have lunch with. Only he has already eaten.

In an explosion of explanation, Wozniak says he and his companion are playing *Tetris*; did I know he was once the world champion? Had I played *Breakout*? He designed that one for Atari in the days before video games were written in software, when they were baked into the machine's hardware. Almost at once he has launched into a description of how those early circuits worked, reliving the four days and nights it took him to work out how to put all the dots in the right places on the screen.

'You hook up all the wires on the chips so that the chips alternate one,

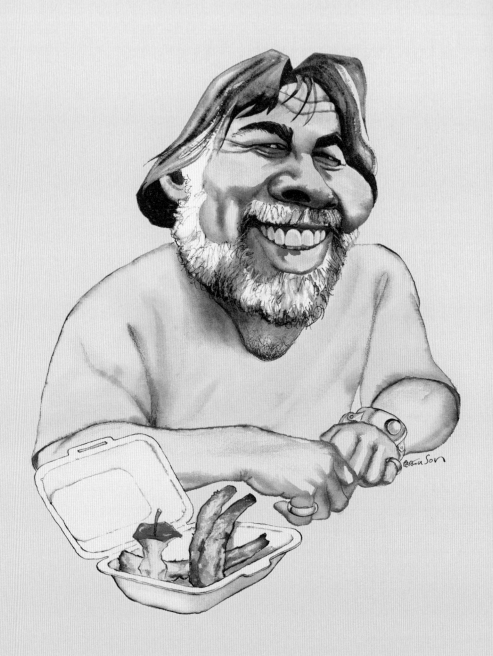

zero, one, zero, click, click, click, click,' he says, tapping it out, getting the memory from the early 1970s down pat.

This obsessive engineer, his beard now greying and chest-hair sprouting from the top of his yellow T-shirt, is the other half of the Apple myth. These days Steve Jobs may be better known, but Steve Wozniak's place in Silicon Valley folklore is just as strong.

He was – indeed, still is – the primal computer nerd, a bearded whizz who rode a boyhood love of electronics to spectacular early successes of the computer industry. The Apple II, a machine he designed single-handedly in 1976, is reckoned by many to be one of the most impressive engineering feats of recent decades, a machine that laid the blueprint for the desktop and laptop machines that have become central to modern life. It turned him and Jobs into stars and multimillionaires, and launched the personal computer revolution almost overnight.

We are sitting here now because Wozniak has written his memoirs. To be more precise, he has spoken and a journalist friend, Gina Smith, has written the words down. He recently sat in this same booth for what he reckons to have been 50 days straight while he and Smith went through the text. I think of all the Hickory Pit ribs that represents.

So what does Steve Jobs, four years younger and at high school when the two first met, make of Wozniak's rendition of this slice of Valley history? 'From what I understand, he read it and thought it made him look like an asshole,' says Wozniak.

I can see Jobs's point. Wozniak's book, *iWoz: From Computer Geek to Cult Icon*, tells the story of how, after those sleepless nights wiring up *Breakout* – one of the first hit video games – Jobs, the salesman, gave him half of the $700 he said Atari had paid for the work. Only it turns out Atari actually paid several thousand dollars, and he claims Jobs had short-changed his friend.

Nor does Wozniak go out of his way to seem overly careful of his friend's feelings. 'Steve can be annoying to people,' he says as he reminisces about the decade the two men spent at Apple, before both left in 1985. 'And he can be obnoxious. He would walk into meetings and just say, "Forget it. It's all a bunch of junk. You're not doing it," and walk out, and, "You're all idiots."'

Lest Wozniak be misunderstood, it should be noted that he speaks with an engineer's frankness, even naivety. He has complained of being quoted out of context before, though that seems only natural given the guileless barbs he throws out.

He says of the book, trying to right the balance, 'I'm sure I said some very good things about Steve Jobs, I can't remember.' For the record, he did – but not enough to outweigh the jibes.

The waitress has come back with iced tea refills three times and we can't put off ordering food any longer. This is not the sort of place you come if you are concerned about your cholesterol. I flirt with the idea of ordering the full rack of ribs with all the trimmings, lose my nerve and opt instead for the junior rack. Wozniak asks for a slice of key lime pie, seems genuinely disappointed when it turns out there is none, and settles for cherry.

When you listen to Wozniak talk, it quickly becomes clear that he is like an ageing rock star – eager to relive the glory days. For the first hour and more, in mind-numbing detail, he races through the electronics projects of his youth, all the resistors, flashing light bulbs and soldered wires of school projects dating back to age 11.

He is an engineer's engineer, a man who sees the twists and turns in the history of computing as the direct and sole result of engineering choices made by men such as him. Ask any business-school student how it was that Apple squandered its early lead in personal computing, and you will be told that it was because of a business decision not to license its technology to other computer makers. Microsoft, producing software for the 'open' IBM PC, won the day. Wozniak, though, can focus only on the engineering shortcomings of the machines that followed his own pristine creation, the Apple II.

In this version of events, his machine marked the high point of a golden age in electronics. It was a time when a single person, inspired by nothing more than a desire to produce the best work he possibly could, was able to change the course of computing history. It took only three months of work. If one person could do that, why wouldn't the following years bring a flowering of technology?

'We just envisioned all these computers where the human was more important than the technology,' he says. This has left a trail of bugs, badly designed products and machines that don't make allowances for their all-too-fallible users, he maintains. 'I'm absolutely convinced that Apple, just like the rest of the world, has lost that formula.'

What went wrong? In Wozniak's somewhat simplistic world-view, the Engineer was replaced by the Businessman. The causes of the weaknesses that crept into the personal computer business? 'A lack of good, solid testing. A lack of good caring. Just basically the way the business is run.'

The food has arrived and the ribs are surprisingly good. The sides – oak-roasted corn and wood-smoked beans – are pretty much inedible. I look enviously at the thick wedge of cherry pie.

Wozniak warms to his theme. In this story, the engineer is the lone hero, the creator. This is 'the person who's coming up with all the ideas just sitting down and programming it and getting it to work and show off and adding in the little touches they think of'.

In this idealized world – which is still the world that inspires many of the engineers drawn to Silicon Valley – this hero-engineer is also the artist.

'It's gotta be a part of me,' says Wozniak. 'It's an art. When it's gotta be a part of me, I'm gonna make it as perfect as can possibly be. I remember doing the floppy disk board [for the Apple II] when I laid it out myself, little pieces of tape where the metal traces on the PC board will go. I'm laying it out for two weeks every night till four in the morning. And when I got done, I realized that if I had designed the circuit a different way I would have five holes through the board instead of eight. So I took everything apart and redid it. The user doesn't see the holes. But it mattered to me. It's a part of me. It's like my own body is the device.

'There was a window in time when things did work that way.'

This smacks of self-mythologizing. Yet if this is a hallucination it is a common one in Silicon Valley, which still thrives on the dream that a lone engineer with a good idea can change the course of the world – in part because Wozniak himself helped to prove that it was true. Money may dictate the way that giant industries such as personal computing are built, but it can do nothing to stop the next hero-engineer from having his dream.

'The intent to try new things and find them is sort of built into the human being and the human brain,' says Wozniak. 'It's just part of our own innate curiosity. Thinking up a new idea that could really radically [make things] better can happen anywhere, and it doesn't necessarily happen because I'm gonna put some money down to some bright engineers and they're gonna come up with it.'

That mantle has now passed to the Google generation. For Wozniak himself, nothing else has ever come close to that early glimpse of engineering perfection. While Jobs later returned to Apple and launched a second act, Wozniak's later efforts – a company that built unified remote-control devices for the living room, and one that tried to create wireless electronic tags that people could use to keep track of pets or personal items – fizzled.

He professes satisfaction from the years spent as a concert promoter, philanthropist and (for eight years) teaching 10-year-olds, yet still clearly hankers for a place back at the centre of the personal-computing revolution he helped launch.

'I would love to have some involvement [at Apple]. But I don't think Steve would like it,' he says, before conceding that his knowledge of computer system design is no longer current. It is hard to avoid the feeling that, however indelibly the two men's pasts are linked, Wozniak is now like one of those old school friends or faintly embarrassing relatives that sometimes turn up; someone to be tolerated with a forced smile.

Of a recent business venture, he says: 'One friend sort of suggested, "Hey, you should put Steve on your board or something like that." The answer came back very quickly, "No."' Jobs was invited to write a foreword for the book but refused.

It is 4pm and lunchtime is long past. Wozniak, a self-confessed gadget freak, goes to the back of the Hickory Pit to retrieve his Segway – the self-balancing two-wheel electrical transporter that was once seen by its Silicon Valley backers as the machine that would revolutionize transportation. Instead, it has become little more than a curiosity.

It's nowhere near sunset yet, but as Wozniak prepares for the ride west on this oddball piece of machinery, it feels like it should be.

The Hickory Pit
San Jose

....

1 x junior rack of ribs
2 x cherry crunch pie
2 x coffee
1 x iced tea

....

Total $25.67

Fashion and Lifestyle

Eden Collinsworth

Ms Behaviour

The US entrepreneur is urging Chinese businessmen to increase their 'likability', forgo Confucius and instead take lessons on western etiquette. But why should they listen to a foreigner who barely speaks their language?

By Jonathan Ford

E ntrepreneurs, it is said, dream of selling a toothbrush to every Chinaman. My lunch companion is different. She dreams of selling them manners.

Eden Collinsworth plans to set up a finishing school in China, bringing deportment, etiquette and the essentials of civilized behaviour to the new generation of young thrusters. Stage one in her masterplan to teach one-third of the world how to eat soup without slurping, to give and receive compliments and to 'disagree agreeably' is her new book *The Tao of Increasing Your Likability*, launched at the end of this month. It is in Chinese – though I have been allowed to look at a translation – and the publisher is one of China's biggest private-sector players. Some powerful businessmen in the Middle Kingdom have clearly been charmed by Collinsworth's own command of the social graces. As for her, she hopes to make a great deal of money. Or, to quote from an email she sends me some days after our lunch: 'Simply put, the point of what I am doing in China isn't just teaching manners, it's pursuing a business opportunity.'

Collinsworth makes an unlikely emerging-market pioneer. An editor and one-time senior executive of the Hearst publishing empire, until

recently she lived the life of a New York socialite, flitting elegantly between gallery openings and charity dinners.

Her last job was running the EastWest Institute, a New York-based international think-tank specializing in conflict resolution. There she mixed with statesmen, policy-makers and do-gooding celebrities, haring between New York, Brussels and Moscow while discussing the latest thinking on arms control and cyber-security.

Then, at the age of 58, she jacked it all in to seek her fortune in China. A little more than a year later, Collinsworth is living out of a suitcase in Beijing where – despite speaking barely a word of Mandarin – she has set out to become a sort of Martha Stewart, laying down the law on deportment and manners.

Running late on my way to our lunch at Caffè Caldesi, a small Italian restaurant just north of Oxford Street in London, I recall with alarm that a whole section of Collinsworth's book is devoted to the importance of punctuality. 'There is an expression in America, "Time is money,"' it starts forbiddingly.

Collinsworth shrugs off my apologies, and even compliments me for emailing ahead to warn of possible lateness. 'In terms of deportment, you did just fine,' she assures me. I feel inordinately pleased with myself, like a child who has been patted on the head.

Tall, elegant and sporting a startling shock of copper-coloured hair, Collinsworth styles herself more like one of Dorothy Parker's co-conspirators at the Algonquin hotel in the 1920s than a boardroom operator from today's Beijing.

I am longing to skip the niceties and plunge in with a blunt question about what she thinks she is doing but first we have to order. 'This is such a pleasure for me,' she says languidly as we scan the menu. 'Just to have an inclusive role in deciding what to eat.' At the business dinners she attends in China, Collinsworth rarely gets to choose.

Not only does this mean she has to devour a profusion of dishes, clearly an ordeal for the X-ray-thin Collinsworth; it also exposes her to the risk of eating animal bits she would rather not think about, let alone consume. She still winces at the memory of ducklings' tongues, which are 'rather like the rubbers on the tips of pencils that you used to eat at school'.

The menu here contains no such excitements and Collinsworth

chooses the lemon sole while I go for the *saltimbocca alla romana*. We order wine even though Collinsworth declares herself to have a feather-light head ('even ginseng sends me practically into a coma'). She asks for a glass of Pinot Grigio, while I have a deliciously inky Malvasia Nera Salento.

Collinsworth's book is basically a primer of modern western business etiquette – the latest in a long tradition stretching from Castiglione's *The Courtier* right up to Lucy Kellaway's 'Dear Lucy' column in this newspaper. There are sections on table manners or greeting someone ('The proper handshake between men should be brief. There should be strength and warmth in the clasp. You should look at the person whose hand you are taking').

Although there is a fair amount of high tech – email manners, phone manners – much of the advice has a faintly sepia-tinted feel. For instance, when a woman holds her hand out to greet a man, Collinsworth advises, she should relax her arm and fingers 'because it is customary among Europeans for the man to lift her hand and bow slightly'. There is a chapter on rudeness which advises against 'spitting on the sidewalk, belching at the table or blowing your nose on anything other than a handkerchief'. Other traits singled out for admonition include treating 'a salesperson, waiter or waitress as someone who is beneath you' and 'not picking up after your dog on the sidewalk'.

Are the Chinese really going to buy into this stuff? I muse. After all, they have got pretty far without fretting about dog mess and the hurt feelings of underlings. And aren't those who care about fish forks and handshakes already sending their children to expensive schools in England or Ivy League US universities where you learn western mores through direct emulation?

Collinsworth assures me that the interest is there. As part of her research she went round Chinese universities quizzing the young. 'Students understand that as China opens up to the world, they are going to deal more and more with westerners,' she says. 'They absolutely want to receive this information.'

Good deportment, she claims, is a way to avoid the social pitfalls that come from the Chinese not understanding western culture and vice versa. Collinsworth cites an example from her own experience. She struggled to set up a business meeting with a Chinese publisher because he didn't want to set a precise time ('the whole afternoon was fine by him') while she wouldn't attend without one. The publisher was irritated by the misunderstanding; so was she.

'Getting it right is just a way to make sure you make the sale and boost the bottom line,' she says.

I am interested to know what questions the Chinese she has met want answered. 'Surprising ones,' says Collinsworth. One subject was gay marriage. 'To them it's a complete abstraction but they wanted to know what I thought,' she says. And how did she answer? 'Carefully.'

The book is aimed not at chief executives but at the many millions of young graduates who have grown up in the sprawl of China's new cities – first-generation products of its epic urbanization. Collinsworth has a theory that the rapid transition from rural to urban life has led to what she calls a 'social disconnect' among the urban young. While they know all about the latest communication technologies, mobiles, social media and so on, they lack 'the comfort and confidence to interact, even within their own age group'. They know how to act but not how to be.

Her book, she thinks, will help them deal with each other as well as with westerners. After all, manners are not ultimately an east–west thing, as she points out: 'It has to do with . . . I suppose I am sounding ridiculously female, but it has to do with kindness, recognizing, being sensitive to someone else's background.'

Which is all lovely, of course, but why should the Chinese take lessons in sensitivity to background from a westerner who barely speaks their language? 'I am not marketing the idea of western culture as in any way superior,' she insists.

The idea came from her son Gilliam. He spent two years in China while studying Mandarin at London University's School of Oriental and African Studies, where he is still finishing a degree. He introduced her to Beijing life and attended every meeting with her Chinese publishers. It was a role reversal. 'I became utterly dependent on him, which was kind of strange,' she says.

She admits that it has been unsettling moving from her comfortable New York existence to modern Beijing. When I ask if she could imagine staying there permanently, she shudders. 'It would drive me mad,' she says, adding that China's capital can seem like 'something out of a Philip K. Dick novel – or from *Blade Runner*. You see the sun come up every morning and it looks like the moon.' The dust and pollution has even deprived her of her daily jog. 'It's like the air has got shards of something in it,' she says.

The daughter of a Southern businessman and a Czech-born pianist, Collinsworth always possessed self-belief. After starting as a publisher's receptionist in 1970s New York, she rose rapidly through the ranks and was by the early 1980s running a publishing house, Arbor House, editing the likes of Elmore Leonard, Anthony Burgess and Richard Nixon.

Then, in 1990, she dropped that life and headed west to set up a magazine in Los Angeles, a Californian version of *Vanity Fair*. *Buzz* almost failed before it got going, when advertising dried up in the recession. 'I was sitting in an empty office – almost everything had been repossessed by the bailiffs – when I got the call to say that we were going to be rescued,' she says. Although the magazine survived and attracted a following, it finally closed eight years later.

But a Californian start-up seems as child's play compared with what she has taken on now. Collinsworth's strategy has been to write the book to establish herself as an authority on deportment before launching the school. This has the merit of minimizing the ever-present threat of intellectual property infringement. 'You can copy the programme but you can't copy me,' she says, fixing me with her grey-green eyes.

I am on my best behaviour so I nod obediently but those she needs to attract to make her business fly – a convention of spare-parts manufacturers from Hunan, say – might wonder what's in it for them. Collinsworth is convinced they will flock to her because what she offers – a way to achieve better communication with westerners – is good business. It will help Chinese companies to find a more creative way of doing things, she believes, something that requires a different way of thinking – a sense of empathy. 'They have to get away from the Confucian method of rote learning if they are going to innovate,' she says.

Collinsworth is still picking at her fish and the waiter is hovering. It dawns on me that pudding is out of the question. I bet a Chinese tycoon would have gone ahead and ordered a double helping of tiramisu but I am too feebly western to dare.

We have moved on to the political sensitivities of doing business in China. Collinsworth explains how her book has been vetted by 'the Information Office'. I am surprised the censors could find anything to object to. But no, they had two complaints. One was the word 'Muslims', which set off immediate alarm bells. 'It's as though you move into a no-fly zone of irrational anxiety,' she says. The other concern was an endorsement on the back from a public figure who had in the past supported the idea of democracy. 'So I spoke to her and she said, "I am surprised that they would be bothered but if there's a problem of course take me off."'

I am struck by her readiness to kowtow. 'It's foreign to me but I can't have it both ways,' she explains briskly. 'If I want to work with a Chinese publisher in China, writing a book for mainland Chinese, it would be unworldly of me to do anything else. It's a deportment book.'

When we talk about the Bo Xilai case and the uncertainties for the foreigner doing business in China, she suspects Neil Heywood, the British businessman who died mysteriously in a Chongqing hotel room, to have been the author of his own misfortune. 'He was clearly in way over his head,' she says. But how do you know when you are in over your own head in China? I ask. 'I think you know it when someone is poisoning you.'

The lunch reaches its conclusion. Collinsworth dabs her lips with a napkin as the waiter brings the bill. She thanks me politely, and takes her leave, anxious not to be late for her next meeting. It is only when the waiter moves to take away her plate that I realize how deftly she has given the impression of lunching, without actually eating or drinking anything at all.

Caffè Caldesi
118 Marylebone Lane,
London W1

....

saltimbocca alla romana
£19
sogliola alla mugnaia
£22.50
glass of Malvasia Nera
Salento   £6
glass of Pinot Grigio
Banfi   £7.30
latte   £2.60
double espresso   £2.60
....
Total (incl. service) £67.50

Domenico Dolce and Stefano Gabbana

'We are in each other's minds'

Over a detox meal at their gilded HQ in Milan, the Italian designers talk about dogs, dessert and destiny

By Vanessa Friedman

During fashion show season, which is any time between January's men's wear shows and this weekend, when their women's wear collection is shown in Milan, Domenico Dolce and Stefano Gabbana don't go out to lunch. This is not, in case you're wondering, an initiative reflecting the current austerity programme in Italy – Dolce and Gabbana actually own a restaurant in Milan called, pointedly, Gold. But during super-busy periods, the design duo – famous for turning Sicilian widow's weeds into objects of high-fashion fetishization, and for persuading celebrities such as Scarlett Johansson and Kylie Minogue to shoehorn themselves into said confections of corsetry and black lace – rarely leave their office once they arrive, at 9am, from their respective apartments in a building across the street (Dolce lives on the fifth floor, Gabbana on the sixth).

In other words, if you want to talk to them, you go to them, which is not as bad as it might sound. As Gabbana explained, when I invited them to lunch, 'The office is our prison. But it is a nice prison.' 'It's a golden prison,' added Dolce. He was not speaking entirely metaphorically.

Arriving at the general reception (pretty standard, featuring a woman behind a high desk), I am quickly escorted to a more private reception area. It is an eye-boggling combination of deep-burgundy velvet settees, leopard-print walls and assorted enormous paintings. These include an

oil of the designers and their three Labradors – one chocolate, one blond, one black – and the Italian pop artist Giuseppe Veneziano's depiction of an enormous classical Madonna with the head of Madonna Ciccone and two putti – with the heads of Dolce and Gabbana – playing at her feet. It is, frankly, a little disconcerting. Still, Dante Ferretti couldn't have made a better film set if he'd tried. As Dolce and Gabbana design, so do they live.

'Vanessa!' Gabbana enters, stage left, smile on his tan face, wearing artfully ripped Dolce & Gabbana blue jeans, an odd assortment of keys jangling from a watch fob on his pinstriped vest. 'Vanessa!' Dolce enters next: shorter, bald, with black-rimmed glasses perched on his head, wearing a grey sweater and jeans.

Dolce, 53, and Gabbana, 49, met in 1980 when both were assistants at a fashion atelier in Milan, and became Dolce & Gabbana in 1982. From the start, their inspiration was to tap into the romantic nostalgia people feel for the *Dolce Vita* clichés of Italy – Sophia Loren, pasta, Sicily – and to translate them, without irony but with great enthusiasm, into a modern aesthetic (one 2009 ad campaign featured Madonna in a kitchen cooking pasta). The clothes may have a complicated construction but their appeal is straightforward. Like many other Italian brands, they are, at least superficially, about sex. But where Gucci historically channelled hedonistic sex, and Versace aggressive sex, D&G's domain is happy sex: the wow-check-out-my-cleavage-I-can't-believe-it! sort of sex.

The two designers have been together professionally for 30 years and they were also involved personally for 23 of those but broke up in 2005. They know it is tempting to try to make sense of their partnership, to say one is a tailor and one a dressmaker, or one a sketcher and one a draper. Dolce says, 'I go to Pilates three times a week in the morning and recently I was in the dressing room and a teacher came in – which wasn't really nice, because I don't want to talk to the teacher when I am dressing – and he says, "So, how does it work: are you a tailor and he is more VIP? Or – wait, I know – are you like Bertelli and he is Miuccia Prada?"'

'Bertelli and Prada? Hah!' Gabbana snorts. The reference is to the division of business and design responsibilities that exists at another famous Italian fashion house, between the designer Miuccia Prada and her husband, and Prada chairman Patrizio Bertelli.

Instead, the way Dolce explains it: 'We are in each other's minds.' Certainly, by this stage in their lives together, they are a double act to rival Laurel and Hardy, Hope and Crosby, or Oscar and Felix from *The Odd Couple*. Dolce is quieter, more practical; Gabbana, the chattier one. He says Dolce is 'Sicilian – he came north to find "the new", and he's all the time looking forward'; he himself is Milanese, 'so I love tradition. It's very hard for me to let go of the past.' Gabbana talks not just with his hands but with his arms and occasionally also his shoulders. If Dolce uses any props to illustrate or underline his words, it's his eyeglasses.

Watching them in action, you know you are seeing a performance but to complain seems churlish. For those familiar with their runway shows, it provokes an interesting sense of déjà vu. Though their collections are full of push-up corsetry and crystals, the Dolce & Gabbana business is actually built on tailoring, white shirts and trouser suits. But while very profitable, this stuff is not particularly stimulating to look at. So, instead, the two men provide a show.

As we stroll to the dining room, situated across a wide hall with an enormous Venetian chandelier at one end, the routine continues. I mention that I have just come from the Paris couture shows and was disappointed by them.

'Today people think style is a handbag,' says Dolce, mournfully.

'But you don't change your style by changing your bag,' says Gabbana. 'You change it with your clothes.'

Dolce: 'In history, in ancient Egypt, did Cleopatra change her bag?'

Gabbana: 'It's clothes that change with the times. In 10 years, who is going to remember the bags? They will remember the clothes.'

Dolce: 'The fashion system has killed fashion.'

The patter pauses as we enter another room, with another enormous chandelier – gilt this time – and equally feral wallpaper, in tiger stripes. Gabbana's dogs are about to have lunch, too. The designer heads through a door and reappears with three dog bowls that he places in a corner. Gabbana loves Labradors. He has had Labs for 17 years, since Anna Dello Russo, the Italian fashion editor and blogging celebrity, gave him one as a Christmas present. 'They are the nicest dogs,' he says. 'So friendly to people.'

A waiter appears and hands Gabbana a piece of paper. He looks at it and hands it to me with a flourish. 'This is your menu,' he announces.

Unfortunately, it is in Italian, which I can only guess at, so he elaborates: 'I am on a detox, so what I get, you get. Madonna told me about it once when I was in New York, and now I do it twice a year. Ten days, all vegetables and protein.'

'I don't detox,' says Dolce. 'I like to cook. I cook Sicilian food: over the weekend I made a bolognese and roast for 15 people. I cook and wash, cook and wash. When I am done, the kitchen is like a mirror.'

A tureen of soup – carrot, with seaweed and bulgar – is brought in by a waiter in a white coat. As the guest, I am served first. I mention this, because it will become an issue later. 'This is good,' says Dolce.

'Mmm,' says Gabbana.

'Cheese?' says Dolce, proffering some shaved dairy products in a silver bowl. Gabbana gives him a look.

This is one of the last meals they will have in their current headquarters: they are moving to a new building next to the old Metropol theatre, a classic, mirrored venue they bought a few years ago and transformed for their runway shows. Renovations have been going on for three years, pausing briefly during the onset of Italy's financial crisis. The two men say they approve, generally, of what Mario Monti's government is doing to address the country's fiscal woes. This despite the fact they are facing a trial over a charge of alleged tax evasion ('We know we did nothing wrong,' says Gabbana. 'These things just take a long time'), and have been affected by a new law that means no establishment may accept cash over €1,000. 'We lost so much money in the sales,' says Gabbana. 'People come, they want to buy with cash, we tell them, "No, we need a charge card," and they leave without anything.'

'It's the right thing to do, though,' says Dolce. 'Think of all the manicurists who have been taking cash and not paying the right taxes. OK, one, on its own, it's nothing. But all of them together . . .'

'This is one of the ways we have changed the most since the beginning,' says Gabbana. 'We have learnt there is a time for everything.'

'Before we wanted everything immediately: fast, fast, fast,' agrees Dolce, having some more soup. 'We were like a machine. Well, I am still like a machine. But now my machine can wait.'

Dolce designed the new building (architecture is his domain) but Gabbana has not yet been inside. 'He won't let me in,' he says, waving a hand at Dolce. They will share an office, as they do now.

'About three or four years ago, I thought, "I am exhausted by seeing you all the time!"' says Gabbana. 'I mean, this is the conversation: he says, "I want yellow." But I want blue. And then he says, "This shirt is giving me a headache," and, of course, I have to say, "It's my fault?" and then he says—'

'No, it's not your fault,' smiles Dolce.

'So I said I wanted my own office in the next place. But then, in the end, we have one big room.'

A waiter brings a tray of steamed fish, seaweed, broccoli rabe and fennel. I take some – normally I like just one course at lunch but I was taught that when you are a guest in someone's house, you eat what you are served and this is Italy, where meals matter – but when the waiter gets to Dolce and Gabbana, they wave him away.

'I ate too much soup,' says Dolce.

'Me too,' says Gabbana. 'That was very filling.' I look at the food on my plate and feel a bit silly. I am the only one eating, which in the fashion world is pretty weird. Still, this means the designers can continue their dialogue without worrying about food coming out of their mouths, so maybe they have an ulterior motive. Either way, they have manipulated the scene effectively to their own advantage.

'The worst time for us was when we broke up but kept working together,' says Gabbana. 'We thought about splitting up, but no. And the truth is, everything is exactly the same. But no sex!'

'No sex,' agrees Dolce.

'I can't work without him,' says Gabbana. 'Maybe one day there will be a Dolce collection and a Gabbana collection—'

'No. Never,' says Dolce. 'This is my destiny.'

'Never say never,' scolds Gabbana.

This is also what both say when the subject of an initial public offering comes up. It is conventional fashion business wisdom that, to be competitive globally, Italian family-run companies must either turn to big groups (Bulgari has just been bought by LVMH), go public (Ferragamo) or take private equity investment (Moncler). Dolce & Gabbana – with revenues in 2011 of €1.1bn – is widely viewed as an attractive candidate for any of the above. 'When people ask if we are going public, we think, "Why?"' says Gabbana. 'For about six months, banks kept coming to talk to us.'

'But we don't want the money,' says Dolce. 'Tomorrow we could change our minds if we needed it to expand but, at the moment, we don't. We do need to grow a bit more. We have a lot of plans.'

Though they closed their younger, more accessible D&G line in September, they tell me it was to stop causing confusion with their main line, not for financial reasons. They want to open 30 stores in China over the next two years, as well as others in São Paulo and New York. They have also become something of a mini-publishing house, producing coffee-table books in conjunction with publishers such as Rizzoli and Taschen. Their dream is to be a '*maison*, like Chanel. But maybe we need to die first,' says Gabbana.

'And then Karl [Lagerfeld] could come in and do the collections!' says Dolce.

The waiter is back, this time with a glass-domed plate piled high with little Sicilian desserts. 'Oh!' moans Dolce. 'I love cakes.'

'Sugar is like a drug. If I have one bite, I need to eat it all,' says Gabbana. 'I can eat an entire panettone in one sitting.'

Dolce & Gabbana HQ
7 Via San Damiano,
Milan 20122

carrot and bulgar soup
steamed turbot, sautéed
fennel, broccoli rabe and
seaweed
Sicilian pastries and
mixed berries
bottled water
espresso

Total gratis

And, yet, neither touches the pastries. When we finish coffee and the designers mount the wide, curving staircase to their atelier and I am escorted out into the Milanese sunshine, I remember those sweets, sitting under the glass dome, and consider the fact that, no matter how much face-making and sighing Dolce and Gabbana did to indicate their desires, no matter how tempted they claimed to be, they stayed in absolute control. After all, you don't eat the props, do you?

Tamara Mellon

Head over heels

At the Four Seasons in New York, the founder
of Jimmy Choo talks about posing naked,
understanding private equity and her plans
for a lifestyle brand

By Vanessa Friedman

At the beginning of my lunch with Tamara Mellon, the 43-year-old founder and present chief creative officer of Jimmy Choo, the maître d' put us in the wrong room at the Four Seasons. Or, to be fair, he put me in the wrong room. There are two: the Grill Room, which is small and woody and near the bar, and the Pool Room, which is a much grander space in the back, set around a large burbling fountain. Fashion people tend to like the Grill Room; bankers and captains of industry tend to like the Pool Room. Mellon's uncle-in-law, Jay Mellon, for example, the Mellon family patriarch, likes the Pool Room, and that's where he takes her when they have lunch. Which may be why the maître d' assumed she wanted to sit there when we met.

But as anyone who reads both the tabloid and the broadsheet press knows, when it comes to Tamara Mellon, you should never assume anything. So five minutes after I start drinking my Pellegrino in the Pool Room, a rather flustered waiter appears and apologetically takes me back to the Grill Room.

Where I find Mellon, on a banquette, snuggled up under the arm of financier Nat Rothschild, giggling. She is wearing a leopard-print silk sheath dress and towering black Jimmy Choo booties, which look familiar from a YouTube video I had seen of the walk-in closet in her gigantic Fifth Avenue apartment (which she bought from Warner chief executive

Edgar Bronfman Jr, as detailed by blogger the Real Estalker, for $20m), including her hundreds of pairs of Choos.

In other words, she looks just like the sort of trophy wife you might expect to see sitting with an international mover and shaker in a quintessential uptown New York restaurant – except she is neither a wife (she was very publicly divorced from Matthew Mellon in 2003, complete with acrimonious court case and allegations of computer hacking, but they are now friends), nor anyone's trophy. On the contrary, these days she is busy collecting trophies of her own.

Earlier this autumn, for example, Mellon was in London receiving her OBE from the Queen for services to British fashion. Jimmy Choo has 115 stores in 32 countries, and has been valued at close to £500m. Then, the week before we meet, she was named as one of David Cameron's new global trade envoys, along with fellow accessory supremo Anya Hindmarch and Sir Anthony Bamford of JCB, among others.

'I was surprised,' she admits as we take our leave of Rothschild (who has his own lunch guests) and move to our table. Not so much, she continues, because unlike Hindmarch and Sir Anthony, she hasn't been very involved in Conservative party politics (though she did meet George Osborne in 2006 when they sat together on a council for British enterprise) but because of, 'Well, who I am.'

For instance, I say, because when you google 'Tamara Mellon', one of the first things that comes up is a profile in *Interview* magazine, published earlier this year, which was accompanied by a Terry Richardson portrait of her naked, lying on a couch with her head thrown back, smoking a cigarette and holding a cat over her nether regions?

'Yes!' she laughs, completely ignoring the menu. 'I could not believe the *Daily Mail* used [the trade envoy appointment] as an occasion to reprint that picture – especially because Terry holds the rights, so I thought I was safe, because he'd never sell it. But they just took it! Now he's made them take it down, and it's off the *Interview* website, but still.'

Did you really not think that would get out? I ask. Could Mellon, who has had numerous newspapers print paparazzi shots of her snatched while (one example) sunbathing topless on holiday with a former boyfriend, Christian Slater, really be that naive?

'It has such a niche audience, *Interview*,' she shrugs. 'It's such a specific thing. I really didn't.' And despite my obvious incredulity, she opens up her blue eyes and rolls them at herself and insists she really was that uncynical. And I kind of believe her.

Besides, the prime minister and his gang don't appear to mind – at least they haven't said anything to her – and neither did TowerBrook, the private equity company that currently owns Jimmy Choo, when the story was first published. 'It went over very well, apparently,' laughs Mellon, as though she can't quite believe it herself. After all, normally, if a member of a global company's C-suite were to pose naked, the resulting outcry would involve not only questions of propriety but probably shrieks about questionable judgement and requests to step down. That's what I would think, anyway. But then I – like the maître d' – would be mistaken. Besides – 'We should order!' Mellon cries.

It's been 20 minutes since we moved tables, and a waiter is hovering. I thought she just wasn't hungry. 'I'd like the tuna carpaccio and the Dover sole,' she says, which is a main course more than anticipated (as expected, however, there is no wine involved, only Diet Coke; this is New York, after all, and she's been sober for 'about 15 years'). I ask for the tuna, and tack on some soup to keep her company. Mellon may be skinny, but she eats: the day after we meet, which happens to also be Thanksgiving, she is planning to have lunch with the retired couturier Valentino Garavani, followed by Thanksgiving dinner with her ex-husband's family.

She has effectively been absorbed into the Mellon clan; they are one of the reasons she moved from London to New York in 2008: so that her eight-year-old daughter, Araminta, could be closer to her father and his tribe. Although Mellon was close to her own father, Vidal Sassoon co-founder Tommy Yeardye (he was her earliest champion, giving her $150,000 to start Jimmy Choo), she has called her mother, Ann, 'a sociopath', and since her father's death in 2004 no longer speaks to her, or her two younger brothers.

Living in New York also helps Mellon to avoid the paparazzi. And the United States is one of Jimmy Choo's biggest markets.

'I knew, from the start, that we needed to be in the US because of the buying power here,' she says as the tuna is deposited in front of us. 'You can't be global without America, and I always wanted to be global. It normally takes a British brand 20 years to get across the ocean, but we opened three stores in America between our second and third years in business, and we were able to do it because of what we did by coming to the Oscars and having the shoe suite.' In what has now become an annual tradition, Mellon famously set up shop in the Peninsula Hotel the week before the academy awards and hand-dyed shoes to match celebrities' gowns, one of the first brands to exploit the power of the red carpet.

'But we were only able to do it because at that time my father was my investor. Can you imagine saying to a banker, "I want to spend all this money and give the shoes for free"? They'd say, "You're crazy," and refuse. But when he worked with Vidal Sassoon, he had him cutting hair on stage in Japan, so he understood.'

Her father taught Mellon, she says, 'to trust my instincts. I think that's my biggest strength. People who are over-educated become risk-averse.' Given that Mellon did not go to university, this is not an unexpected statement. She elaborates: 'Money guys can look back at what you've sold and come up with a plan for future growth, but they can't pick the product that will put the numbers on the paper. I can do that, and my job is to make them understand that.'

She speaks from experience. In 2001, deciding that they wanted to buy out Jimmy Choo, the eponymous cobbler of the business whose dream (nice shoes for a few nice women) had diverged from Mellon's (global domination led by fashion-hungry trend-setters), Mellon and her father began to look for outside investment. They sold a 51 per cent stake of the company to private equity firm Phoenix Equity Partners, who held on to it until 2004, when they sold it to Lion Capital, who held on to it for three years, and then sold it to TowerBrook (Mellon has retained 17 per cent). This makes Jimmy Choo the most successful fashion/private equity story in the industry, not just in the UK but globally: though private equity has had a millennial flirtation with fashion, few funds have been able to make the unpredictable style cycles work with their traditional strategy of holding a company for three to five years. The global private equity firm TPG, for example, held on to the Swiss shoe and leather goods maker Bally for nine years after it struggled to restructure the brand following its purchase in 1999.

'It's the numbers,' Mellon says now. 'You make your numbers, and they're happy. So even though the private equity guys might not understand what you're doing – and what I do is very intangible to them – they start to trust you.'

Still, she admits as the Dover sole appears, it's exhausting. 'Just as you get to know one board, they sell you, and you have to start all over again.' You have to, for example, start again with explaining things such as the importance of 'hair and make-up', she says, 'which they just don't get'. You have to teach them the danger of underestimating, or making assumptions, about the creative side.

'I was young, and didn't really understand what private equity was when we sold the first time,' she continues. 'In retrospect, I wish I had been my own private equity firm and just gone to the bank and asked them to lend me the money I needed.'

Today, however, 'I couldn't buy the whole company now if I wanted,' even though she's worth about £102m, and she does want. Instead, TowerBrook, entering the end of its three-year cycle, is in the midst of a 'strategic evaluation', where they are trying to decide what happens next: whether they sell to another private equity firm, or take Jimmy Choo public, or hold on to the brand. Mellon won't commit to any scenario, though she does say that, having been on the Revlon board since 2008, she has seen at first hand the difficulties being a public company entails. Whatever happens, she hopes the owners will commit to a long-term strategy that she is currently devising.

The Four Seasons
99 East 52nd Street, Manhattan

....

3 x soda water	$13.50
1 x crudités	$10
2 x tuna carpaccio	$50
1 x consommé	$16
1 x Dover sole	$65
1 x coffee	$6
1 x cappuccino	$6

....

Total (incl. tax and service)	$181.29

'I think it takes 30 years to build a luxury brand,' she says, eating half her fish and then asking for coffee, 'so we're part-way through. And there's so much I want to do. I think we can become a lifestyle brand, because one thing doing the collaboration last year with [high-street retail chain] H&M showed us was that consumers would accept any product from us: we did men's wear, we did women's wear, we did jewellery. And I want to do all of that.'

She means this literally: a perfume will launch next year, followed by men's shoes, followed by children's wear, watches, jewellery, homeware, and so on. Perhaps as a security strategy during the next phase of the brand, she is the 'face' of the perfume, and will appear in the advertising campaign (clothed) with her head thrown back to expose her neck. It's not the only self-exposure she is considering.

For, as we walk out, Mellon mentions she would like to write a book. An autobiography. 'There's been so much nonsense said about me, I figure I should just get it out,' she says. All of it? I ask. The naked truth?

'All of it,' she smiles. Then she mentions she knows a filmmaker who told her if she ever did tell her story, he'd like to make the movie.

Who?

Before you guess Guy Ritchie or Matthew Vaughn, know this: the answer is Peter Morgan, author of high-minded talk fests *Frost/Nixon* and *The Queen*.

Twiggy

'My eyes were a work of art, I can tell ya'

The *FT* found Twiggy to be a model celebrity, despite a life which makes strange reading

By Lucy Kellaway

I am eating lunch with a woman so famous that her picture has been put in a rocket and sent into space, and what are we talking about? We are discussing dressmaking tips, in particular the importance of pressing each seam as you go along.

I had not expected to find Twiggy Lawson, as she is now known, quite so down to earth. For a start, her choice of restaurant was not promising. We were to meet at San Lorenzo's, which was the favourite lunch place of Diana, Princess of Wales, and is frequented by the super-rich and the super-thin. There was also the matter of the photograph. Twiggy's PR had warned that she was particular about who took her picture, and the *FT*'s photographer would not be acceptable.

Yet the woman who came down the stairs to meet me showed no signs of being tiresome. Dressed in a simple black trouser suit and ageing white T-shirt, she looked relatively normal against the Di-lookalikes around us. In easy confidential manner, she started telling me about her daughter's A-levels, about how she had left her purse at home, and wasn't going to be able to go to Peter Jones after lunch to buy an anniversary present for her husband, Leigh Lawson.

If it hadn't been for her face – still ridiculously recognizable after three decades – I could almost have been having lunch with the woman next door.

She glanced at the menu, a handwritten sheet bizarrely attached with

Blue Tac to a raffia place-mat. 'I'll probably have something light – a spinach and avocado salad. They do a lovely chicken on a griddle with mashed potato, but I couldn't eat that much at lunch.'

So I ordered the chicken, and she chose the salad, with water to drink.

''Ello!' she suddenly called out, the old Neasden accent still in evidence. A small, stout Italian woman came up to the table and kissed her warmly. 'This is Mara, who runs this marvellous restaurant.' Mara picked up the copy of Twiggy's autobiography from the seat beside me, and stroked the picture on the front cover.

'When I first met her she was just 16 and sat at that table over there,' Mara told me. 'She was wearing a fox.'

'No, I think it was a raccoon,' interrupted Twiggy, as if it were essential to get these details right. 'I got it in Portobello Road. Or was I wearing the Ossie Clark?'

'I had never seen anything so beautiful in my entire life,' Mara crooned, while Twiggy gushed back, 'Oh, you are so sweet.'

'Mara's hysterical,' Twiggy whispered after the patron had gone. 'If she doesn't like people she won't let them in.' She gave a shriek of laughter, surprisingly loud: 'Argh! Ha! Ha!'

Twiggy tells me how close Mara was to Princess Diana. 'She'll be badly missed. We were on holiday when we heard the news. I only met her once, but we came back because we wanted to be here. For days we just walked around unable to concentrate.'

I muttered something about Twiggy having had her own hounding from the press, but she protested.

'It was nothing like that. I tasted it a little bit in the 1960s in New York. I was so young and little I thought I would get squashed. I was six and a half stone. Argh! Ha! Ha!'

Why has she suddenly decided to write an autobiography? I asked. 'I didn't write it myself,' she corrected me. 'I can't write at all. I sing, I dance, I sew, I act. That's enough.' She says this in a funny voice in order to suggest that she is not boasting. 'Penelope [the ghost writer] and me spent hours and hours talking. I did get sick of me own voice and me life after six months of it.'

Her life makes strange reading. In her version she was happy to be famous, and equally happy to be no longer so. When she visited Los Angeles at the age of 17, Sonny and Cher gave a party for her and everybody was there, desperate to catch a glimpse of the world's first supermodel.

Now she is lucky to get parts in TV dramas and minor plays. She has never been remotely self-destructive, never taken any drugs. 'I think it was because I had a normal background and a normal mum and dad,' she explained; an odd assertion given that her mum was in and out of mental hospitals throughout her childhood.

'And maybe because I was so young it went over my head. I don't spend hours analysing it and thinking about it. I'm a wife, a mum, an actress. I'm talking about the past now because my book is coming out. But otherwise, you get up, make breakfast. I never think, "Wow! That was an amazing life I had." If you did, there would be something very, very wrong with you.'

But surely there is something very wrong with most celebrities?

'Two of our best friends are Paul and Linda McCartney. I don't know if you've met him?' she asked, as if that were likely. 'But think about what they have lived through. And he is so normal and their kids are so wonderful. We know some famous people who are normal and some famous people who are a pain. But then, I know a lot of ordinary people who are a pain. So in the end, it's the people, isn't it? I think. I don't know. Can't answer that question.'

She puts a couple of spinach leaves in her mouth and calls for some bread. I had finished mine, which was neither as special as she had promised, nor as large.

Twiggy's size has been a political issue from the outset: she was the first waif model, the first to be blamed for anorexia. 'They always come back to me about that,' she says, sighing.

'In the end, you have to blame the mags. I didn't go to them saying, "I am the look of the sixties." I was the person who happened to be chosen.' In the old days, she used to eat whatever she liked. 'All the rubbish. But if I ate that now, I'd be flabby. I don't like feeling like that. I go to the gym and Leigh and I play tennis.'

We started talking about modern models, the drugs they take and the pressure they are under. 'Do you know the models today can't do make-up?' she asked, as if expecting me to be shocked. 'My eyes were a work of art, I can tell ya. They took me an hour and a half. You had to be fully made up by the time you arrived at the studio at eight or nine in the morning, and that meant getting up early.'

A second menu was brought, which she did not even glance at. 'I'm going to have a decaff cappuccino, but they have wonderful puds if you want one.' So I ordered a pudding, which she watched me eat, while she talked about clothes.

I ask if the black suit she is wearing is something special. 'No, it's Wallis,' she said, mentioning the middle-of-the-road high-street chain. 'I love the long jacket. And I love trousers. I always hated my legs because they were so skinny. I do not go and buy expensive designer clothes. I'm the greatest bargain hunter in the world.'

This took us round to dressmaking, and her sewing tips. I found myself happier talking about paper patterns than when the subject shifted to her family. 'Leigh and I are very much in love and do not like being apart,' she says.

She tells me that her stepson is 'gorgeous', and that she and her daughter are inseparable. 'She's lovely. She's got a much better figure than I ever had!'

I asked for the bill, which, at £50, would have been cheap were it not for the fact that we had had practically nothing to eat or drink. Twiggy reflected that it is wine that bumps up the cost of meals. 'A nice bottle of Chablis in a supermarket – you are talking £4.99. In a restaurant, you'd pay at least £19.'

On the way out Mara cuddled Twiggy again, and extended a hand towards me. I held out my hand to be shaken, only to find her reaching for my pregnant belly and kissing it. It is not hard to see why Princess Diana, with her 'touchy-feely' leanings, loved this place.

Outside, in Beauchamp Place, Twiggy pecked me on the cheek, and headed home to get her wallet.

Food

Jennifer Paterson

Why one never eats food that wobbles

The *FT* meets the cook who became a cult figure thanks to the *Two Fat Ladies* TV programme

By Nigel Spivey

One fat lady knew just where she wanted to be taken to lunch. But first, find your fat lady. Her telephone answering service is a resident uncle, ancient and adamantly deaf. I bellowed hard for Jennifer Paterson.

Uncle put up stout resistance. I listened as he finally shuffled off to find his 70-year-old niece and tell her that there was a certain Knife Tidy, or Idle Slithey, in search of her. Then she was there, with the unmistakably abraded diction of the Woodbine addict. 'Dear boy. How divine. We must go to Marco.'

Some 3.5m devotees in Britain followed the *Two Fat Ladies* cookery programme, which made cult figures out of Jennifer Paterson and her accomplice Clarissa Dickson Wright (whom the uncle knows only as Agrippa). It may or may not comfort them to be told that Jennifer – the one who straddled a 900cc Triumph Thunderbird motorbike – was not acting in that show. She was nothing but herself.

This I realized almost as soon as she stomped into The Restaurant at the Hyde Park Hotel where Marco Pierre White is king. Loading a waiter with her crash helmet and other clobber, she called for a vodka on the rocks, and tapped out a Woodbine. 'Yum yum!' she declared. 'I'm going to adore this. Marco is simply the best chef in town. And he knows it, the scamp.'

'Hallo darling.' Marco duly bounced out of the kitchen. His aspect of a diabolic cherub seems timeless. Jennifer patted his girth. 'Look at you. You used to be so thin, it pained me. Have you given up smoking, heavenly boy?'

Another vodka was summoned. I winced. A single vodka is double figures at Marco's place. Meanwhile Marco, like some playground swaggerer, was boasting about his fishing exploits and his fossil collection. Soon enough he was also boasting that his restaurant was London's most expensive. Officially. 'Now, my lovelies,' he said. 'What are you going to eat? Do you like pigeon?' he asked me.

'Not passionately,' I said. He shook his curls. 'Milk-fed pigeon. Never even beaten its wings. Snuggled in a parcel with foie gras. Go on,' he said, rising. 'I'll sort you out.'

We were cautiously happy to be sorted out. This is a chef who does not believe in giving people what they can replicate at home. And such bonhomie betokened an experience. Jennifer wondered if it also meant an experience on the house. Less persuaded by this hope, I furtively chose the cheapest rosso on Marco's mostly three-figure wine list. 'Usually,' rasped Jennifer, 'I carry my own drinks with me. One's always given wine at parties, when what one wants is a proper drink.'

'You mean vodka.'

'Of course. Oooh, now look. What have we here?'

We saw no more of Marco. His messages to us were borne out on silver trays by legion emissaries. And they were superb statements of culinary bravado. Most of Jennifer's utterances were simply rhapsodic reactions. *What a treat. How adorable. How absolutely adorable. Oh, I do adore that.*Passim. Sensing that their transcription might make her seem simply a senior Sloane Ranger, or the pair of us disgustingly carnal, I struggled to excavate a life history before the cult status set in.

One day she was beetling about on her moped in search of the original recipe for Bakewell tart, a producer spotted her, matched her with another eccentric, and there they were: the two large ladies, hooting away in the kitchen, and getting fan mail from the likes of Sir Alec Guinness.

Meagre scraps came. Jennifer Paterson is a creature of today. Her yesterdays can be very briefly summarized. A childhood in Sicily, where, she declared, her father had to be rescued from worshipping goats on a mountain-top. 'Really?' I interrupted. 'Well, it was something of that sort. Vair peculiar. I say, is that a dollop of caviar there? How outrageously delicious.'

Then a spot of au-pairing in Portugal. Then a stint in Benghazi, nannying for a colonel. Where she learnt to cook on a Baby Belling. ('Not easy for a gal. I'd come back from the souk with quivering lumps of meat. No idea it had to hang.') A turn in Harrods; matron at a school; a spell with the *Candid Camera* team; various chaperone posts. And more cooking – for the Ugandan embassy; then for the *Spectator*, the British weekly magazine, in the days when a weekly six-hour lunch was editorial policy.

'Vair strange thing. Only the upper classes will work as domestics now. Everyone else regards it as demeaning. They're silly. I'd far rather cook for a living than sit in an office for a living, wouldn't you?'

Suddenly she shrieked. 'The wireless!' And at the same moment, her main course was unveiled. She flung down her serviette, and bustled to a phone behind a screen. This is what happens when you are a cult figure. The nation needs you to speak. We all heard her booming away. 'I'm in Marco Pierre White's . . . the most exquisite dish of pig's trotter has just been set before me . . . stuffed with sweetbreads . . . yes, divine.' A waiter came and remodelled her serviette into a lotus flower. Soon she was back.

'What was that about?'

'Some ridiculous programme. *Can Big Be Beautiful*, they wanted to know.'

'Of course it can.'

'Now how,' said Jennifer, plumping down to business again, 'can a beastly pig have such a tender little trotter? Isn't this a miracle? Yes, of course it can. These twig-like waifs are just invented by poofs, to model their clothes. Get girls to look like little boys, you see – little boys in drag.'

Pigeon and pig's trotter dispatched, an interim pudding arrived. Tiny creme caramel. 'Ah, at last,' said Jennifer. 'Something I shall refuse. I never eat things that wobble.' She lit another Woodbine, and beamed indulgently.

'Clarissa,' she said, 'Clarissa believes that it was the Victorians who ruined our cooking. We used to be the best. The Puritans spoiled it all. Food became fuel, catering done with a grudge. You know. Clarissa is a

Roman Catholic, like me. That's why we have such fun together. But don't you think – ooh, look,' as a second dessert materialized, non-wobbly – 'don't you think this is all perfectly wonderful – so long as one doesn't do it too often?'

It was, in fact, her first visit here – her first taste, indeed, of Marco Pierre White's mature skill. And she was the best of all possible guests – funny, opinionated, gossipy and well-connected (herself). But even between cult chefs, it seems, there is no such thing as a free lunch. At her insistence, I showed her the bill: £220. I escorted her out to find her moped, and she gave me a kiss. 'My dear,' she said, 'remember the Prodigal Son. Seize the day.'

Marco Pierre White

A chef out of his kitchen

He is part cherub, part volcano. But no one is assassinated and there are only three flickers of temper

By Michael Thompson-Noel

My scallops are being served with awesome precision. The dish is immaculate, the service terrific. I glance at the waiter but he is carrying out his task with so much concentration that he cannot be distracted.

The reason for this is the identity of my guest, who is watching the serving of the scallops with such brooding intensity that I feel I have strayed into an Aztec ceremony.

This is Marco Pierre White, the best-known, most lauded of all English chefs – still only 32, born in Leeds, half Italian, beefy, tousle-haired, charismatic and tempestuous: able to pass, in an eye-blink, from cherubic to volcanic. Or so the folklore says. By accident or design, my guest has attracted some of the most enviable publicity in the history of cooking.

The words used to describe him pop up all the time. Volatile. Flamboyant. Firebrand. *Enfant terrible*. Profane genius. Wild man. Wild child. Sulphurous. Rudest chef in London. The Apollo of the Aga. There have been wives, mistresses, children, dust-ups and bust-ups.

Over the years, the image that has been created is one of danger, decadence and theatricality. That is not bad going for a celebrity-chef, though the decadence has been exaggerated. White says he has never tasted alcohol or tried narcotics, and that two years ago he gave up 'smoking, gambling and marriage'.

There are those who must imagine that to enter one of Marco White's restaurants is to stand a good chance of being grabbed by the chef-proprietor and flung into the street for some imagined slight or lapse in table manners. But when I asked him how many customers he had expelled from his restaurants in the whole of his career, the answer was only two.

We are sitting in one of White's two restaurants, The Canteen at London's Chelsea Harbour, which has its own chef and one Michelin star. White owns a one-third stake. Another co-owner is actor Michael Caine. White's other establishment is The Restaurant at the Forte-managed Hyde Park Hotel, Knightsbridge, London, where he has two Michelin stars. He won his first Michelin star at the age of 25, his second at 27 – the youngest British two-star chef.

Our lunch was going well. No one had been assassinated, apart from (absent) rivals. There had been comedy to start with. Neither of us realized that the other had arrived. White had gone to the bar, I to the table. At 1.40pm the manager asked if I would like a newspaper to read, to help pass the time. Three minutes later the mistake was realized, and White and I shook hands.

He looked concussed with anger. But no one was to blame, and he was soon transferring food from his plate to mine. A large part of White's charm derives from his candour. His working-class Yorkshire childhood lurks just beneath the surface. I asked him where his extreme physicality and pugnacity came from.

He said, 'I have to break everything I touch. It's just something I've always done. Maybe it's a positive or maybe it's a negative, or maybe it's related to my need to progress professionally. Originally my aggression could be attributed to a lack of social skills – and shyness.

'Am I an arsehole? Some people say so. Some people rubbish me and my work, but who are these people? You don't get two Michelin stars if you are only an arsehole. There is more to it than that. Here is an example. One of the things I believe in in my restaurants is value for money –affordable, Michelin-class food. Here in The Canteen, all starters are £6.50 and all mains £10.50. People can afford that. That's why The Canteen turns over £70,000 a week.

'I want to achieve that sort of value for money at The Restaurant. It's too easy to rip the customers off. A lot of that goes on. The way I'll make my money is in the long run. The last thing I'm ever going to do is jeopardize what I've got already.'

White trained with the best chefs in Britain – above all, with Albert Roux, former mastermind at Le Gavroche, the first London restaurant to win three Michelin stars. 'I am an offspring of all the great (English-based) chefs,' says White, naming others who guided him.

'I was lucky. I appeared at the right time. I worked long hours, won my first Michelin star, attracted a few tarts – suddenly I became Marco Pierre White. But as a cook gets older his cooking gets simpler, and as I get older I have become more of a recluse. I spend a lot more time in my restaurants than I used to. I don't remember the last time I went to a nightclub, a dinner party or an event. I only deal now with a few old friends in the profession. I have my girlfriend, my two children – and fishing.'

Fishing looms large in a conversation with White. He hunts down macho fish: pike, barbel, grayling, tench and trout. He says his best pike weighed 32lb. A monster. Did he cook it? Not for the first time, a guile-less little question produced contradictory answers from the master-chef. 'Nah,' he said. 'I never kill the fish. I couldn't kill anything. I love nature too much – bird-watching, everything.'

Later, however, he said he liked shooting. 'The sort of customers I get, some of them invite me to shoot. I love it. I used to be a poacher. That was my first job. I went shooting on a private estate not long ago and this huge cock pheasant came strutting along the ground. It would not get up. It would not fly. So I blasted it on the ground.'

One of White's attractions is his hatred of taxi-drivers. I told him that I shared it. 'They're fascists,' I said, 'completely rotten people, the same the world over.'

'Yah,' agreed the chef. 'You've got it: fascists. I don't own a flashy car. Don't actually own a car 'cause I don't even drive. But my girlfriend's got an off-roader, the biggest you can buy, which I'm fitting out with bumper-guards and really major spotlights in case any taxi-drivers want to take us on.'

During lunch, White showed a flicker of temperament on only three occasions. He was irritated that the butter on our table was softer than it should have been, but said nothing. However, he told a waiter to go and tell someone in the kitchen to stop banging – 'I did not come here today to listen to his noise' – and remonstrated with another waiter for serving me cold milk with my coffee.

'He asked for black coffee,' White told the waiter, 'but if you're going to give him milk, make sure it's hot. Cold milk kills the flavour.' The waiter rushed away. White said to me, 'Now he's going frantic. Bet he thinks I'm an arsehole.'

On the strength of a single lunch, I formed the impression that Marco White is a lot cleverer than widely realized. I suspect that people see his Italian side, the charisma and machismo, and forget the Yorkshire half – gall, grit, gumption.

At 3.30, I said I would pay the bill, giving him a chance to read the six-page fax that a waiter had handed him.

'Nah,' said White. 'Forget it.'

'I'm supposed to pay,' I said. 'That's the idea. We choose the guest. The guest chooses the restaurant. We pay the bill.'

'Nah,' growled White.

'OK,' I said. 'The food was great. No doubt I'll return in my own capacity. Then I can pay for myself.'

'Yeah,' said the big man. 'In your own capacity. That's the bill you slip through the *FT*.'

The thought had never occurred to me.

'There you go,' he said, laughing loudly. 'You've found the real Marco White.'

Poachers and Gamekeepers

Martin McGuinness

Sinn Féin's hard man with a soft face

The newly elected MP for Ulster-Mid is hard to fathom – except when he talks about fishing

By Kieran Cooke

Martin McGuinness's right-hand man walks across the bar and introduces himself as Dominic. With his black blazer and grey trousers I had assumed he was the head waiter. The image of Sinn Féin, political wing of the IRA, has changed. Gone are the donkey jackets and jeans. It's more Armani than bargain basement these days.

In comes the newly elected MP for Ulster-Mid. At 47, he is slightly stooped in the shoulder but is built like a retired rugby player. McGuinness, a teetotaller, orders an apple juice. Dominic has a lemonade. I join the party and order mineral water.

We slide into things gently. 'Is it true you're a keen fisherman?' I ask.

'That's an understatement,' says McGuinness. He leans forward confidentially. 'Do you know I have written an ode to the sea trout?' I say I'd like to see it.

We are sitting in the bar of the Trinity Hotel in Londonderry. A party of US tourists in bright colours passes the door. So too do two army Land Rovers, with soldiers and machine-guns poking out of the top. The threatening and the humdrum live side by side in Northern Ireland. The tourists reach for their cameras.

For a time the conversation meanders around rivers and streams. McGuinness is worried about the growing problem of sea lice and the effect on the trout population. But the fishing talk is soon at an end.

McGuinness is first and foremost a product of Northern Ireland's 'Troubles'.

In 1972, when he was only 21, McGuinness was part of an IRA (Irish Republican Army) delegation that travelled to London for talks with the British government.

He has associated with leading IRA members and carried coffins at IRA funerals. In the early 1970s he was jailed in the Irish Republic, convicted for being a member of the IRA. He has never been convicted of terrorist offences in Northern Ireland. He is admired but also feared – described as a hard man with a soft face.

McGuinness looks around: he was born and bred in the nearby Bogside area. Everyone knows him. There are nods and handshakes.

'Your face is familiar,' McGuinness says to me. Indeed, we had met before. The last occasion was on a miserable March afternoon in 1988 at a cemetery in West Belfast. Three IRA terrorists shot dead by SAS soldiers in Gibraltar were being buried and I was there to cover the story.

As the first coffin was being lowered into the ground a loyalist terrorist threw hand grenades and started shooting. Lying on the ground, I saw the face of Gerry Adams a few feet away, his glasses askew.

McGuinness was up on his feet, directing operations.

Adams is considered to be the brains behind Sinn Féin. McGuinness has always had the reputation of a man of action – he is said to be regarded as good officer material by some in the British Army.

The food arrives. Dominic has ordered roast beef, McGuinness chicken casserole and I have the fish. People in Northern Ireland are not known for a healthy diet. McGuinness upends the salt cellar on his chicken. The conversation becomes serious.

He says the British government is now putting forward very different proposals on the peace process. 'If it had done that 18 months ago then so many deaths could have been avoided.' He lists each recent incident, from Canary Wharf to the murders last month by the IRA of two Royal Ulster Constabulary (RUC) men.

'You seem always to blame someone else for the murders and bombings,' I say. 'Don't you ever take responsibility?'

'We are all part of the problem,' says McGuinness. 'At least the IRA admitted responsibility for the deaths of those two policemen. It's something the British Army and RUC never do.'

So does that make it all right? I ask. People can be murdered but, as long as you admit it, everything is fine? I find my voice has risen. My fish is getting cold.

McGuinness is totally calm. 'I'm not justifying what happened to those policemen or other tragic events but you've got to understand the feelings of neglect and exclusion of people in the nationalist community. It's to do with levels of hurt and anger.'

McGuinness claims reporting of events in Northern Ireland is often selective. The deaths of the two policemen last month were met with a lot of media hysteria, he says.

A wafer-thin man comes up to shake the hand of the chief Sinn Féin negotiator. 'This here is a player of the uilleann pipes,' says McGuinness. The man looks embarrassed. 'I taught him to play the tin whistle when we were in Crumlin Road jail together in 1976.'

But I want to get back to talking about the man from the Bogside. Why has so little been written about him?

'The two greatest influences on my life have been the British Army and the RUC,' says McGuinness. There is a slight smile. The eyes twinkle.

I bring up the question of credibility. Who am I talking to? The IRA or Sinn Féin? Surely they are one and the same thing.

McGuinness is unruffled. 'You might never trust me,' he says. 'I might never trust you. But we have to find a way forward. We have to break the cycle. And I vehemently refute your allegation that the leadership of the IRA and Sinn Féin are interconnected.

'I don't speak for the IRA. People try to demonize Gerry Adams and me, to marginalize us. That's the road to nowhere and to more confrontation. Look at the election results. Look at how many people voted for Sinn Féin. They voted for our analysis of what's happening. You can't turn them into second-class citizens by denying them a voice.'

We have finished eating. I look over McGuinness's shoulder. Who is watching us? Is he concerned for his safety?

'It's something I don't get up in the morning worrying about. I'm careful, not foolish. I can still go off trout fishing alone.'

I ask if he ever regrets becoming so involved in events. 'Sometimes I want to grab my fly rod and just go away but I'm a republican first and foremost. What motivates me now is that I can help bring about a settlement.'

He talks of taking risks for peace. I wonder where the threats come from – the loyalists or his own side.

Is the reason he does not condemn the IRA that, if he did so, he would be killed by an IRA bullet in the morning?

There is a slight pause. 'Ritualistic condemnations are pointless,' he says. 'I go beyond condemning by the work I'm doing. Look at the way the unionist politicians condemn the killing of nationalists. I can't believe they are sincere. Their condemnations are not worth tuppence to me or to most people in the nationalist community.'

We have coffee. I say I can't understand what Sinn Féin and the IRA are about. To most people in both the north and south of Ireland the idea of unity is irrelevant. They just want to get on with their lives in peace. 'The southerners don't want you. You are trouble,' I venture.

McGuinness points to recent Sinn Féin election successes on both sides of the border. People in the south have shown their support. Even in Britain he finds many people agree with him. 'What is going on has caught the world's imagination.'

I say we must live on different planets. Most people I meet, in Ireland or Britain, just wish Northern Ireland and its problems would go away.

The photographer arrives. Dominic tells me McGuinness hates photos. The waitress jokes with him. No doubt about it: the Sinn Féin man is a charmer. His answers are as practised as those of an old-style politburo official.

But after two hours' conversation I can't say I feel any more optimistic about the future of Northern Ireland.

The day this article was published, the IRA declared a ceasefire.

General Rosso José Serrano

A seat at the traffickers' table

The *FT* is invited to the office of the
world's best policeman but finds that
success has its price

By Adam Thomson

Would lunch at police headquarters be all right? It's for
security reasons, you understand.' Oh dear. Over-
cooked vegetables and indigestible carbohydrates
sprang to mind. I felt queasy.

But what were the options? Insisting on a civilian venue for a meeting
with General Rosso José Serrano, Colombia's top cop, recently selected
as the world's best policeman by US attorney-general Janet Reno and a
panel of international judges, would have meant lunch for 17: the two
of us plus 15 heavily armed, moustachioed, barrel-chested bodyguards.
I doubted my credit card could keep up with their appetites.

'Yes, OK, the headquarters,' I conceded. The headquarters are in an
uninteresting administrative district of Bogotá, close to the centre.

Serrano, having led one of the largest raids on drug lords in Colombia
just a few days before, looked sprightly and focused. So how did it go?
I asked.

'It was perfect, right down to the last detail. We captured all the
31 drug traffickers we had set out to get. Before we struck, I told myself
that even if we had got half of them, it would have been a resounding
success,' he says.

The operation, dubbed 'Millennium', was indeed a marvel of preparation and timing. More than a year of meticulous planning with local and
international authorities, including the CIA and FBI, had dismantled

the country's largest drug syndicate, responsible for exporting 30 tons of pure cocaine to the US every month.

'The ringleaders are as important as any drug traffickers Colombia has produced,' he said, ushering me into his office.

Operation Millennium was the latest in a series of arrests that Serrano, director of the national police force, has led against organized crime – particularly against drug trafficking – which has turned him into a national folk hero.

In the early 1990s, he masterminded an operation which toppled the infamous Medellín drugs cartel. And in 1996, he captured all the leaders of the Cali Cartel, responsible for exporting an estimated 80 per cent of Colombia's cocaine production, the largest in the world.

But Serrano's fame as the world's most successful hunter of drugs barons was secured in 1993 when, as head of Colombia's anti-narcotics police, he helped corner Pablo Escobar, the most famous and ruthless of the country's traffickers. Escobar never made it to prison: after Serrano's men found him by intercepting a telephone conversation, he died in a hail of bullets as he tried to flee across tiled roof tops.

'More than joy, I felt immense relief that day,' he said. 'Escobar was one of the most wanted criminals in the world at that time. He ordered the assassination of the three leading candidates for the 1990 presidential elections, two bombing campaigns which killed hundreds of innocent people, and the blowing up of a passenger flight in which 107 people died.'

We were sitting at a round table in Serrano's office that had been covered for the occasion with a white linen cloth. A glass of water and a small plate garnished with a napkin lay on the table. It looked improvised.

Did Serrano feel he was fighting a losing battle in the war against drugs, given the constant emergence of new cartels?

'New cartels do spring up, but if we didn't do anything there would be at least five Pablo Escobars today. It is the same with our crop-spraying campaigns. Illicit crops have more than quadrupled in the last few years, but if we didn't spray at all we would now have 500,000 hectares of coca instead of 100,000.

'Having said that, you have to admit that Colombian ingenuity knows no limits. The other day, we discovered a shipment of cocaine hidden in the stems of roses which had been hollowed out.

'The problem is that we are the ones who have volunteered the lives and the money to fight drugs so far. Until the international community begins to collaborate more, it is difficult to see the end of production in Colombia.'

We had been talking for more than 45 minutes, and there was no sign of waiter or food. I broached the subject by asking whether he always ate at this table.

'Never. This is where I chat with the people I arrest. All of the biggest drug traffickers have sat in that chair where you are sitting now. I take their handcuffs off, give them a glass of water and talk with them. It is something I started doing during the arrests of the Cali cartel.'

I looked over at the glass of water before me and began to feel my shirt collar tighten. Still no sign of lunch.

'I always post some of my men by the window to stop them from jumping. You can never tell what they'll do.' He had not taken the same precaution with me.

'The idea of talking to them on a one-to-one basis is to get into their minds. The thing is that they are all very shallow. They are uneducated, drink too much and spend their time with different women. There is never any desire for self-improvement.

'Take Pablo Escobar. He had all the money in the world, and he died rich. What for?'

Serrano's strong, earthy values were showing through: peasant values rooted in the era before the drugs economy eroded large chunks of the country's social fabric. He is – as a local phrase goes – a man who calls things by their true name.

Surely, though, the Rodríguez Orejuela brothers – leaders of the Cali cartel and considered more shrewd and calculating than the confrontational Escobar – were more philosophical about life. After all, Miguel Rodríguez was known as The Chessplayer.

'No, they're all the same. They just throw away their money on stupidities.'

He was right. I had visited Escobar's country residence several years before – a 7,000–hectare playground filled with life-sized models of dinosaurs, a private zoo complete with rhinos, elephants and a Tibetan yak, and solid gold fittings in the bathrooms.

Finally, a waiter appeared with a silver tray. It was another bad sign.

Too much pomp in Colombia invariably means the food will be disappointing. He delivered a salad of diced vegetables and a small metal vessel containing a typical broth made with rice. It was surprisingly good.

Serrano's uniform, an unfortunate palette of institutional greens, was moulded to his body like a second skin. Did he ever wear anything else?

'I don't even have any civilian clothes,' he admitted. 'I went to London recently and had to buy some shirts and trousers specially for the trip.'

The waiter returned almost immediately, armed with a tall glass of fresh passion-fruit juice and yet another silver platter, this time prawns in a creamy garlic sauce on a bed of iceberg lettuce. On the side, there were some fried and salted Creole potatoes, cherry-sized, round and yellow. The portly Serrano was struggling with the main course.

I asked whether hunting the world's most dangerous criminals made him fear for his life.

'Both my family and I are heavily protected. But being a policeman here is dangerous.'

Serrano talked of the days when Escobar placed a $2,000 price tag on every policeman's head. As a result, the city of Medellín lost 500 officers in 1989 alone.

'I've been to more funerals than anyone else on Earth. One day there were 15 coffins lined up in the chapel. They hardly fitted in. It's uncomfortable having so much security, but ultimately you either get used to it or you get killed.'

So just how many bodyguards did he need to ensure his own safety? I asked.

'About 50, including the ones at the house.'

I tried to look unfazed. It would have been quite an escort to be accommodated by any restaurant. Yes, the police headquarters had definitely been the sensible choice.

Ksenia Sobchak

The party girl's over

The TV host who has transformed herself from Russia's Kim Kardashian to an activist tells the *FT* about Putin, politics and her part in the country's protest movement

By Courtney Weaver

We are nearing the end of our two-course supper at Moscow's swanky Tverbul restaurant when my guest, socialite and TV host Ksenia Sobchak, has an urgent request: she needs to borrow my phone.

This is strange for two reasons. The first is that Sobchak's iPhone is lying right in front of us on the table. The second is that it is working. I know this because for the past hour she has been on it constantly, using it to send half a dozen tweets, to answer three phone calls and to take a photograph of me, the interviewer, for posterity.

But Sobchak is insistent: she must have my phone. She has recently joined the ranks of Russia's nascent opposition movement and her every conversation is, she says, being clocked by Russia's security service. 'They are listening to me,' she insists, leaning in conspiratorially.

I solemnly hand over my phone, ears pricked for insights into the country's biggest anti-government protests in 15 years, the subsequent backlash from authorities and the secret strategy of the opposition.

She dials. A pause. Then: 'Thank you so much for the flowers!' Sobchak gushes into the receiver. What follows is a five-minute conversation about horticulture.

The 30-year-old Sobchak is a woman of many iterations. The daughter of Anatoly Sobchak, a perestroika-era political reformer and early mentor to Vladimir Putin, she grew up with connections to the Kremlin elite. In her teens and early twenties she was the rich kid who rolled up to Moscow club openings in BMWs, wearing sable and chinchilla.

In her mid-twenties, the socialite aimed for notoriety. She shook her barely clothed derrière in music videos, posed for Russian *Playboy* and hosted a foul-mouthed, sex-mad reality TV series called *Dom-2*. The nadir was a reality show about her life, called *Blonde in Chocolate*, when she was filmed drunk and falling out of a bejewelled mini dress as three security men escorted her to bed by the wrists and ankles. 'I went to bed fine,' she says calmly in an overlaid interview, 'why are you asking?'

These days Sobchak wants people to take her seriously. Since last December, when irregularities in parliamentary elections sparked mass protests in Moscow, she has refashioned herself as a political activist and journalist. She has come out on to the street against Putin, who despite fierce opposition was re-elected for a third term as president in March. She now hosts two surprisingly hard-hitting interview programmes, grilling opposition members and Kremlin associates.

Needless to say, some have been sceptical of Sobchak's transformation. The first time the star spoke at an opposition protest, she was booed by the audience, with many believing she had been sent by the Kremlin to guide the protesters into dialogue with the state. Others have accused her of joining the protest movement just because it is fashionable, noting that she would not face the same repercussions as, say, the members of punk band Pussy Riot, who recently received a two-year jail sentence for a 30-second anti-Putin concert in a Moscow church.

Sobchak is adamant that the new version of herself is 100 per cent real. So what if she was never politically active before the December protests? As she points out, neither were most of the 100,000 other Muscovites who took to the street last winter. She even claims she has more to lose than them, given her prestigious position.

While all this may be true, the new Sobchak is not immediately evident from her choice of restaurant, a place she happens to co-own. Socialites in long flowing skirts sip cocktails, flatscreen televisions are showing a channel called Fashion TV and a trio of model-thin hostesses stands guard.

Having arrived 40 minutes late for our 8pm supper, she first makes a circle of the restaurant, doing the requisite round of smiles and air kisses. The fur and jewels are gone, replaced by a hipster's uniform of jeans, lumberjack shirt and Buddy Holly glasses. The only things not sacrificed to the makeover are her perfectly coiffed blonde hair and, apparently, her diet. Before our meeting, her assistant emailed to ask if the eating part of Lunch with the *FT* was 'binding'.

When Sobchak reaches our table, she flags down a waiter and orders herself a pot of tea and a mint-flavoured hookah. Next, she turns to me and asks curtly, in Russian, how long this is going to take. I remind her we are here to share a meal and she brightens considerably. 'Well, let's order something to eat!'

We settle on starters – cucumber and tomato salad for her, tuna tartare for me – and we both pick the sea bass, Sobchak's favourite, as entrée. I am anxious to pin down her apparent transformation from Russia's Kim Kardashian to its Christiane Amanpour. Is, I ask, the new Ksenia Sobchak for real?

'Why was I going around in rhinestones before, and am now wearing a plaid shirt and glasses?' she muses with mock seriousness. 'It's not a question of fashion. It's a question of time and yourself. The country changed, I grew up, life changed. It's normal.'

Yet for much of the country she represents a group that got filthy rich as the rest starved, and then rubbed it in their faces. In 2003, for example, talking to the *New York Times*, she bemoaned the need to shuttle between 'home, the car, the health club, entertainment' to avoid ordinary people. 'You go out on the street and it's dirty,' she explained. 'There are people and their envy. It's a lot of negative energy.'

Sobchak admits that, in retrospect, she would 'probably do differently' the previous 10 years of publicly chronicled partying and debauchery. But she is unapologetic about how she got to where she is. 'I wanted to become a star, of course. That was very important to me. I wanted to achieve something,' she says.

Did that have anything to do with being known for something besides her famous father, the first democratically elected mayor of St Petersburg? 'Probably.'

Sobchak's recent transition is further complicated by her family background. In the 1990s, her father appointed the future president Putin as his deputy, essentially paving the way for the latter's political career. Anatoly was once spoken of as a future president himself, and events surrounding his sudden death in 2000 are still disputed. However, Sobchak and her mother, Lyudmila, a pro-Kremlin MP, have retained close ties with Putin, with some media reports claiming that Putin is Sobchak's godfather – something she denies.

For sceptics, it is one of the absurdities of Russia's 'revolution of the satisfied' that anti-government protests in Moscow are being championed by a rich, Kremlin-connected socialite. Yet the reasons she cites for joining the movement, such as wanting a vibrant civil society to develop in Russia, are hard to fault. She declares that fighting for honest regional elections and calling for an early Moscow mayoral vote will be her main objectives in the autumn.

Despite all this, Sobchak insists she is not one of the movement's leaders. 'To present me as the main face of the opposition movement is completely incorrect,' she says. 'I'm not a person who is "against Putin". I'm just a person who is standing up for a fair society, for free elections. If Putin can do this, I think it would be the ideal scenario for everyone because there won't be any revolution or any protests.'

It is this type of assertion, with its suggestion that Sobchak is willing to enjoy the political limelight while still trying to retain special immunity, that riles other protesters.

I ask her a question that has been bugging Kremlinologists this past year: is it possible for Putin to change? 'Maybe yes, maybe no. But it doesn't mean we shouldn't try. And it doesn't depend on me.'

At this point, her mobile rings. She spends the next five minutes simultaneously discussing the details of an upcoming magazine party at Tverbul and stabbing at her tomato and cucumber salad, which has arrived along with my tuna tartare.

The salad and the phone call finished, we move on to murkier matters, specifically a police raid on Sobchak's apartment in early June. Newspaper accounts of the events that morning read like an extract from a Jackie Collins novel. At 8am on a Monday, a bleary-eyed Sobchak wearing only a negligee opened the door to about 20 armed policemen (she thought it was the cleaning lady). Inside the apartment, the police found not only her boyfriend, opposition leader Ilya Yashin, but more than €1m in cash, reportedly divided into 121 different envelopes.

The cash has understandably raised some questions, which Sobchak has answered to varying degrees of satisfaction. Tonight she says, 'In a country where there is so much instability, I believed it was advisable to keep my cash at home. I think it's the only way to feel safe here.'

But why so many envelopes? 'I'm not going to answer that question because I have my own tactics,' she replies cryptically. 'Yes, there were envelopes, but not as many as they said and not with those sums of money. It was quite a lot of money but what's the problem with keeping money in envelopes? What else are you supposed to keep it in – socks?'

I am briefly entertained by the thought of Sobchak keeping her money in a hundred cashmere socks, when, taking a long drag from her hookah, she accidentally drops the pipe and shatters her teacup.

'Bring me a new cup, will you please?' she asks the waiter, without batting an eyelid. A new cup is immediately fetched and, soon after, our sea bass arrives, white and tender, with grilled tomatoes and rocket salad on the side.

As we navigate the bones, Sobchak more deftly than I, we delve further into her recent police encounter, which appears to have taken her unawares.

Did she really not think that, after becoming a prominent figure in the opposition movement, she would be exposed to any number of charges, fictitious or otherwise?

'I didn't kill someone or call for a siege on the Kremlin,' she counters.

But this doesn't mean they can't arrest you, I say. Take Mikhail Khodorkovsky, the tycoon imprisoned on tax evasion charges in 2003 – shortly after speaking out against Putin – and who is due to stay in jail until 2017.

Sobchak disagrees. 'Khodorkovsky absolutely broke the law,' she claims. But, she admits, 'he is not sitting in jail for the reason they arrested him'.

Many believe she will prove no more than a fair-weather friend to the protest movement. While most protesters end their public pronouncements with chants of 'We will win!' she is more measured. 'There is a big possibility that if the political leaders don't find a forum for joining together, the political will of the movement will drain out,' she says bluntly.

The movement, which has coalesced around a ragtag group of activists, among them the blogger Alexei Navalny and radical leftist Sergei

Udaltsov, has planned its first big rally since June for 15 September, a protest that will incorporate new grievances, such as the Pussy Riot jailing, and will focus on regional elections. At the same time pressure is being applied to various protesters, including Navalny and Gennady Gudkov, an opposition Duma deputy, both of whom face criminal charges for business dealings. Navalny, Udaltsov and Sobchak are also being questioned over their involvement in a May protest that turned violent – the pretext for the police raiding the apartments of Sobchak and others.

When Sobchak speaks about how the past six months have strained her relationship with her politician mother she goes suddenly quiet.

'She is in a difficult situation,' she finally begins. 'On the one hand, she is my mother. On the other hand, she is a person who is loyal to the system.'

Would her father, I ask, support the regime in its current state? She looks as if she might cry. 'No, I think he would definitely not be able to be part of this system.'

She is more upbeat when it comes to her own fate, almost naively so given the circumstances. 'I've studied a lot of psychology. I'm religious. With situations that you have no power over, there is no point in worrying about one thing or another,' she says simply. 'Why think about things that you can't control?' It seems like the statement of someone who has grown accustomed to thinking that when one teacup is broken, a new one will appear.

Her phone rings again. It is Yashin – the Che Guevara to her Eva Perón. She has a request: she does not want me to write about their relationship. 'Everything about me has already been written, published, smeared everywhere. Enough is enough,' she says.

Supper with a serious financial publication seems an odd place to

Tverbul

24 Tverskoy Bulvar,
Moscow

....

cucumber and tomato
salad   Rbs390
tuna tartare   Rbs750
2 x steamed sea bass
                              Rbs2,400
strawberry lemonade
                              Rbs380
tea   Rbs600
mint hookah gratis

....

Total   Rbs4,520 (£90)

make such a declaration, but I decide to let it slide. Instead, I mumble that it must be hard having all these famous relationships and famous boyfriends. I am thinking not just of Yashin but of the Moscow official with whom she turned up at her first protest and whom she later dumped; as well as of a handsome Russian-American businessman who was, briefly, her fiancé.

Sobchak gently corrects me. 'I don't think they were that famous until they started going out with me,' she says sweetly.

A few minutes later we get the bill and after a minute of back-and-forth, Sobchak agrees to let the *FT* pay at her restaurant. She is, thanks to the raid, down €1m, after all.

She gathers her things to go. When I remain sitting, she asks if I am planning to stay. I remind her that I am still waiting for my card. 'Oh! I'll wait!' she says.

Thirty seconds later I can tell she is getting restless, and tell her again to go ahead. This time she agrees.

'You're a really pretty girl!' she exclaims, apropos of nothing.

It is her parting political shot, and she is off into the Moscow sunset. For Sobchak, the show goes on.

Politics

Bao Tong

'Tanks were roaring and bullets flying'

20 years on from the Tiananmen massacre, the former Communist party official is still under house arrest

By Jamil Anderlini

When China's ubiquitous state security agents want to intimidate a dissident or political activist for the first time, they usually come knocking in the middle of the night with an invitation for 'a cup of tea'. Once the tea is served in some secret location, the agents explain that if their guest continues publicly to criticize Communist party rule, the likely consequences range from unemployment to long prison sentences or even 'disappearance' for them, their family and friends.

So it seems somehow fitting that Bao Tong, the most senior Communist party official to be jailed as a consequence of the 1989 Tiananmen Square pro-democracy protests, should have invited me to tea at his apartment in the west of Beijing.

It was 20 years ago next week, on 3 and 4 June 1989, that the People's Liberation Army opened fire on unarmed demonstrators, killing hundreds, perhaps thousands, of peaceful student protesters and bystanders. As the anniversary of the bloody crackdown approaches, Bao, now 77, remains under house arrest, his apartment watched around the clock and his movements tightly restricted by state security officers. I'd originally invited him for lunch at a restaurant but, as he patiently explained, under the terms of his house arrest it would be more convenient to meet in his home.

He greets me at the door with a wry smile, jet-black hair and a lithe frame wrapped in a Princeton University sweatshirt. It is hard to believe that he spent six years of his life doing hard labour during the Cultural Revolution and then, from 1989, another seven years in solitary confinement in the notorious Qincheng political prison. When I mention the sinister-looking men at the entrance to his apartment block who asked me to explain why I've come to see him, his face cracks into a sly grin.

'I'm contributing to the country by stimulating domestic demand, increasing employment and helping solve the financial crisis,' he says. He speaks Mandarin with the soft consonants of a southerner and the confidence characteristic of a senior party cadre. 'You only saw three people down there but if I want to go out I'm followed by three groups – one on foot, one in cars and one on motorbikes. Just think – it takes more than 30 people to keep an eye on me so if the government decided to monitor all 1.3bn people in China we could solve the unemployment problem for the whole world!'

While this kind of gallows humour and the satirical use of communist propaganda slogans is common on the anonymous internet, I have never heard a senior Chinese official, even a retired one, talk like this in public.

Bao Tong was born in 1932 in Shanghai, where his father was a clerk in an enamel factory. The young Bao was influenced by two uncles, prominent left-wing intellectuals: one became a professor at Oxford University; the other became famous for a hunger strike aimed at convincing the government of the day to fight the Japanese.

At high school in Shanghai, Bao met his future wife, Jiang Zongcao, an active member of the communist underground who was kicked out of a string of schools for organizing demonstrations. She convinced him to join the Communist party in 1949, the year it came to power following a bloody civil war. Comrade Bao quickly worked his way up through the communist bureaucracy, but then in 1969, during the Cultural Revolution, he was denounced and sent to do hard labour at a re-education farm in Manchuria.

After the Cultural Revolution ended in 1976, many previously persecuted officials were politically rehabilitated and Bao was assigned to senior government positions. During the 1980s, he worked as a top aide to premier Zhao Ziyang, a liberal reformer who helped usher in a period of political and economic openness in the 1980s, and in 1987 was appointed to the Communist party's central committee. He served as the minister in charge of political reform and as political secretary to the standing committee of the Politburo, the five-man group that ran the country at that time.

One of the first things I notice in his spartan, dimly lit apartment is a large photograph on his bookshelf of Zhao. Only two weeks ago, Zhao's secret memoir, *Prisoner of the State,* was published in Hong Kong – a rare first-hand account of Chinese elite politics. Over the next hour, Bao gives me his own blow-by-blow account of the secret and increasingly intense power struggle that raged during the seven weeks of upheaval that ended with tanks rolling down the Avenue of Eternal Peace in Beijing.

He begins with his verdict: the man who bears full and sole responsibility for ordering the People's Liberation Army to turn their guns on the people is Deng Xiaoping, the Communist party elder who controlled the leadership from behind the scenes until his death in 1997. Most historians regard Deng as the father of modern China: the architect of its economic reform and opening to the world. But in 1989 his only official title was chairman of the Central Military Commission.

'Most of the students weren't trying to depose Deng Xiaoping; they were hoping he would carry out reforms,' Bao says. 'The problem was Deng felt threatened and he called in the troops. This is how the tragedy happened, a true tragedy in Chinese history.' Zhao, explains Bao, felt the students' demands for democracy and an end to corruption were exactly what the Communist party itself claimed to stand for, and that a conciliatory approach would be the best way to end the protests.

This difference of approach ultimately proved critical. But Zhao's struggle to avoid sending in the troops ended on 17 May 1989 when, after a state visit to China by then Soviet leader Mikhail Gorbachev, Zhao's colleagues in the Politburo forced him to resign. In the middle of the night on 18 May, Zhao made his final, tearful, public appearance in Tiananmen Square, urging students to give up their struggle and return to class.

In a famous photograph from that night, Wen Jiabao, now premier of China, can be seen standing next to Zhao as he addresses the demonstrators. Bao won't be drawn on whether Wen was a Zhao sympathizer, as some historians suggest. 'Who knows if he supported Zhao? Only he knows.'

His caution reminds me that every word we're speaking is being recorded and I glance around the room involuntarily, as if I might be able to spot one of the bugs. This line of questioning is not going to do me or my host any good, so I return to 1989 and the days after Zhao's resignation.

'Many people thought Zhao Ziyang was conspiring to launch a coup against Deng Xiaoping,' Bao says. 'In fact, he and I did hatch a "conspiracy" [on the day Zhao was forced to resign], which was to sing the praises of Deng Xiaoping.' Zhao believed he could avert a massacre by appealing for calm, explaining to the masses why Deng was in charge, despite holding no formal government or Communist party positions.

Bao was implicated – and later punished – for his alliance with the discredited Zhao. I ask if he regrets not having tried to plot a real coup with Zhao at that point. 'Some people said Zhao Ziyang could copy Yeltsin and climb up on to a tank, but that,' says Bao, 'was impossible: no single soldier would listen to Zhao, they didn't know him at all. They listened to their officers, the officers listened to the generals and the generals listened to Deng Xiaoping.' As Mao Zedong famously said, political power grows out of the barrel of a gun.

Bao describes the night the old men, women and children of Beijing took Thermos flasks to the soldiers and begged them not to enter the city; how ordinary citizens built barricades in the streets to protect the students and how the tanks and troops stormed the city. 'The tanks were roaring and the bullets were flying into people's homes. In my building, the son-in-law of a government minister was killed as he was pouring a cup of tea in his living room.'

I look down at the untouched porcelain teacup on the table in front of me. I've been so engrossed I haven't taken one sip and now I'm not sure if it's my cup or his. Bao's vivid description belies the fact he was not in Beijing that night and was not able to piece together the whole story until years later, with the help of smuggled western media cuttings.

On 28 May 1989, Bao himself was arrested and taken to Qincheng, China's main political prison since the 1950s. There he became number 8901 – the first prisoner to enter Qincheng in the year 1989 – and was put in a 6m by 6m cement cell with only a stiff wooden board propped on two sawhorses for a bed. 'I lay down on the board and went to sleep. People ask me why I wasn't terrified. Before that moment I didn't know when they would come for me, but now I didn't need to worry any more.'

There was no door to his cell but a guard sat at a table propped across the entrance; two soldiers stood to attention behind him. The seated guard's job was to record the prisoner's every action in a notebook 24 hours a day, one entry a minute, for seven years. Bao chuckles at the frustrating boredom of the job assigned to his captors – '20.00 hours – prisoner 8901 sleeping; 20.01 hours – prisoner 8901 sleeping; 20.02 hours – prisoner 8901 sleeping, and so on.'

In 1996 Bao was finally released from prison and placed under house arrest. His jaw tightens slightly as he describes the hardships his family has endured as a result of their relationship. His Princeton-educated son Bao Pu, 42, is a US citizen and the publisher of Zhao's memoirs in Hong Kong. He is barred from entering China to visit his elderly parents.

But it is Bao Tong's wife who has suffered the most. He describes the day Zhao Ziyang died in 2005. He and his wife wanted to pay their respects, but were blocked by people guarding the door of the lift in their apartment block, threatening them not to go out. 'I explained that it was illegal for them to stop me from going.' The men instead shoved his elderly wife to the ground, breaking her hip. She spent more than two months in hospital. 'The Chinese Communist party is just like the Mafia,' says Bao. 'If the Mafia boss thinks you might betray him, he will just kill you or throw you into prison for as long as he likes. This is not how a political party or a government should behave.'

For all he and his family have endured, Bao considers himself lucky, compared to those even now imprisoned for supposed crimes related to the 1989 demonstrations, or to those who died in the crackdown or in the brutal witch-hunt that followed.

According to Bao, his tormentors' niggling fear is that one day this old revolutionary insider might either be rehabilitated and return as a top Communist official or become a figurehead for a new wave of activism. Bao says he still receives a measure of protection from old friends in senior government positions. 'I should count myself lucky and express my thanks with the popular slogan: "My eternal gratitude to the Communist party and to Chairman Mao!"'

It is in this ironic humour that one senses the real threat to the current leaders in China, even two decades after the Tiananmen massacre and 12 years after the death of Deng Xiaoping. Bao mocks their slogans and denigrates their demigods, but he is, after all, one of them. If he were to be allowed to air his views, they fear the whole authoritarian edifice could start to crumble.

'China has almost erased the memory of Tiananmen by making it illegal to talk about what happened. But there are miniature Tiananmens in China every day, in counties and villages where people try to show their discontent and the government sends 500 policemen to put them down. This is democracy and law with Chinese characteristics.

'The first sentence of the Chinese national anthem goes like this: "Arise! All those who refuse to be slaves." I believe there will be real democracy in China sooner or later, as long as there are people who want to be treated equally and have their rights respected.

'It will rely on our own efforts, it will depend on when we, the Chinese people, are willing to stand up and protect our own rights.'

The tea is now cold and the table has been set for lunch. Bao's family is waiting in the other room for me to leave. Even shaking the hand of a foreign journalist could expose them to criticism from the authorities and, after all they've been through, I don't want to be another source of inconvenience. As I leave the lift, I turn my video camera on the security agent sitting at the desk in the lobby.

Bao Tong's apartment
West Beijing, China
....

Tea gratis
....

He yells at me to turn it off and I leave the compound in a hurry, 30 pairs of eyes boring a hole in my back.

A few days after this interview, Bao Tong was invited on a tour of a scenic reserve in southern China by the Public Security Ministry. According to his son, he left of his own volition in the company of his security agent entourage last Monday and will not return until 7 June, when the sensitive anniversary has passed.

Fernando Henrique Cardoso

Brazil's philosopher king

The world may be in love with his successor, but the former Brazilian president is credited with putting the 'B' in Bric

By Jonathan Wheatley

The sun slanting through the open sash windows, the cool white blinds and tablecloths stirred by the gentle breeze, the whitewashed walls and the pale wooden floorboards make Carlota seem as though it might be in one of Brazil's torrid, northern plantation provinces – or on some hilltop in the south of France. In fact, the restaurant is on the edge of Higienópolis, a hilly residential neighbourhood in bustling São Paulo, the largest metropolis in the Americas.

It is also the preferred local of Fernando Henrique Cardoso, the former Marxist intellectual colloquially known as FHC, who went on to slay hyperinflation and then twice became president of Brazil, from 1995 to 2002. Few people can claim to have been a philosopher king, let alone to have put the 'B' in Bric – the now commonplace acronym, coined in 2001 by Goldman Sachs's chief economist, that groups Brazil, Russia, India and China. And, although both the world and Brazil have fallen in love with FHC's successor, President Luiz Inácio Lula da Silva, Cardoso is the man widely credited, at least abroad, with laying the foundations for a boom that has caught many off guard both by its speed and by where it has come from.

I am a quarter of an hour early for lunch: São Paulo's chaotic traffic is famously unpredictable. It is hard mentally to grasp a city of this size – the second biggest in the world, by some counts, with a greater urban population of about 20m. It is even harder to grasp the vastness

of Brazil and the surrounding continent. I remembered a previous time I'd met Cardoso, in this same restaurant, when he had told me how, occasionally, he would exploit that vastness to get away from the strictures and stresses of being president. He'd board a single-engine water plane, be flown several hours over jungle treetops that looked like broccoli, and land at a remote fishing spot in an upper tributary of the Amazon. There he would while away a couple of days in swimming shorts, meditatively gazing at the water with just a rod, his wife Ruth and a single security man for company.

'Once, after our boat had floated downstream for a few hours, I noticed the flash of binoculars in the tree canopy. After a while a patrol boat came up to us, with a Bolivian corporal in charge. I'd left Brazil without knowing it,' Cardoso recalled. 'I asked the corporal to patch a message through to the president – I was good friends with the Bolivian president at the time. I left a message saying that I was sorry to have invaded his country, especially as I was only wearing underpants.'

Bang on time, Cardoso appears in the archway leading to our dining room. In a grey summer suit and blue shirt and tie, he is a slim man with walnut-coloured skin (as he once said, his ancestry has 'one foot in the kitchen', a reference to Brazilian slavery in the 19th century), and looks far younger than he should at nearly 80. He smiles when he sees me.

Although a senior senator for many years, Cardoso only properly emerged on the national scene in 1992 as one of a new breed of serious, well-intentioned Brazilian leaders. Back then, he became known in Brazil as the man who introduced the 'Real Plan' – a package of economic reforms that stopped the country's repeating cycle of boom and bust, and chronically high inflation (over the prior decade, inflation averaged 732 per cent a year). To the rest of the world, however, Cardoso was better known as a sociologist and the author of *Dependency and Development* (1969), a book that influenced a generation of Latin American thinkers while advocating economic policies that turned out to be the opposite of those that he successfully implemented while president.

I rise to let Cardoso into the corner seat. He jokes with the waiters that this way his back is covered, but it also makes him visible and several times during the meal he exchanges greetings with other diners. The former president has been driven here today but often walks alone from his apartment two streets away. He declines an offer of wine – one glass an evening is his limit now, and he has given up his beloved whisky – and we ask for sparkling water and the menus. For a few minutes we chat about England and his time as a visiting professor at Clare College, Cambridge, in the mid-1970s. 'They've given me an honorary PhD now,' he says, with a self-deprecating smile, before adding: 'I seem to get them from everywhere these days.' (He has more than 20, including honorifics from the universities of Oxford, London, Notre Dame, Rutgers, Jerusalem and Moscow.)

We discuss why Brazil should have developed an image in the eyes of the world as an exotic, lazy, tropical paradise, associated with football, carnival, samba – and not much else. 'Because of slavery and because it was once a European monarchy in a tropical country, it was much easier for outsiders to stick to preconceived ideas than to do any analysis,' he says. But, by the 19th century, abetted by waves of immigration, Brazil already had a strong export sector. And by the 1940s, it had really taken off.

The big change came with the Second World War when, after flirting with Nazi Germany, Brazil joined forces with the Allies. 'Intellectually, Brazil had previously looked to France; economically, to Great Britain,' says Cardoso. 'Now the focus moved to the United States.'

Along with the US investment Brazil secured in return for its support – CSN, the Brazilian steelmaker built with US money, is still going strong – the war delivered an automatic defence from imported goods. Brazil became a closed economy, withdrawing into itself in the same way that other big countries with huge land masses such as Russia and China have done.

The country's post-war boom and industrialization were led by powerful, centralized governments, at first civilian and democratic, and then, from the mid-1960s to mid-1980s, under military rule, until democracy was re-established in 1988.

Under democracy, Cardoso says, fingering the menu, it was no longer possible to ignore the demands of Brazil's growing population. 'Under the military in the 1970s, growth was seven per cent a year,' he says. 'But education, health, infant mortality were all getting worse. Under democracy, you have to meet those needs.'

By now the waiters are getting impatient for our order. I'm

disappointed he doesn't want a starter – one of Carlota's specialities is a selection of wonderful appetizers but it is for two people, so I pass. Cardoso orders ravioli de gruyère, while I choose grilled lamb fillets with ratatouille and goat's cheese agnolotti.

But the transition to democracy, he says, was chaotic, and culminated in a world-class bout of hyperinflation in 1990, which 'only strengthened outsiders' preconceived ideas: as well as being exotic, Brazil was not a serious country'.

Then Cardoso describes in a low voice, almost as an aside, his emergence as a policy-maker. After Itmar Franco became president in 1992, 'I [as finance minister] managed to secure inflation and we began the reform of the state. From then, all the social indicators began to improve, sometimes by more or less, and improvement has accelerated under Lula, but the beginning was there . . . Anyway, from then on Brazil began to believe more in itself.'

This is the Brazil that the world has come to know recently. It is a country of soccer and samba and an immensely charming president ('I love this guy,' as Barack Obama once said of Lula: 'he's the most popular politician on earth'). It is also a country of giant companies such as JBS, the world's biggest meat producer, and Petrobras, which this week launched the globe's largest ever share issue, worth almost $70bn, to exploit oil reserves that are larger even than those of Kuwait or Russia.

We pause for the arrival of our food. Cardoso says his ravioli is good. My lamb, though, is a bit disappointing.

So now that Brazil has found self-belief, what next? I ask.

'The big thing is quality,' he begins. 'We've spent all our lives worrying about quantity – whether GDP grows or not. Now the question is quality. What kind of education is this? The main reason children skip school is no longer economic. It's because they've lost interest. There's no point. The quality of teaching is awful.

'We need a new wave of reforms,' Cardoso continues. 'How will we increase productivity to compete? That means fiscal reform, lower taxes, investment in human capital and infrastructure.'

To many, this is known as 'the Brazil cost' – the challenge of getting things done in a country where the state is so inefficient that Brazil ranks only 129th out of 183 countries in the World Bank's annual 'Doing Business' survey. I ask why there appears to be no popular appeal for reforms that might change this. 'During my time there was popular appeal. There was a lot of discussion,' he replies.

There was indeed. 'Flexibilization' was the word in the late 1990s, when monopolies were broken, large sectors of the economy privatized, the banking sector was recapitalized and other reforms begun, such as of state pensions.

'The discussion stopped,' FHC continues. 'In a way, Lula has anaesthetized Brazil. We have forgotten that Brazil needs to keep advancing. What I managed to do moved the country forward. But then it stopped. Just stopped.'

Cardoso starts to talk about the election on 3 October. But when he mentions his own party, frustration enters his voice for the first time. 'The opposition got it wrong. We allowed the mythification of Lula. But Lula is no revolutionary. He rose from the working class and behaves as if he's part of the old conservative elite.'

I suggest we already know who will win the election, still three and a half weeks away at our lunch. 'Yes,' he admits – Dilma Rousseff, Lula's anointed candidate from his Workers Party. (Lula himself is outlawed from running for a third consecutive term, otherwise he would walk it.)

What will that mean for Brazil? 'It will prevent us from developing more quickly. But it won't take Brazil backwards. Society is too strong for that.'

If so, I ask, why do Brazilians complain so little, given rising crime, high violence and persistent inequality? Cardoso thinks this is changing.

He describes field trips as a sociologist he once made into *favelas* and factories, when the poor would step aside out of respect for the men in suits and ties. 'Not today,' he says. 'People used to be afraid even to talk to you. Not now. There's a bad side, of course, in the violence, but there's a good side too. They're thinking, "What is this guy doing here, who doesn't belong?" They're not submissive any more.'

Our puddings arrive: guava soufflé with cream-cheese sauce, a Carlota speciality and absolutely delicious. Cardoso's driver is hovering in the archway, worried he will be late for his next appointment. But FHC is in no hurry and we order coffee. He talks about his packed schedule – this is his third meeting of the day and he has one an hour for the rest of the afternoon – but when I suggest retirement he laughs and says that's not possible, though he would like to slow down a little.

He talks about his work with the Latin American Commission on Drugs and Democracy and with the Elders, a group of statesmen and women assembled by Nelson Mandela to tackle some of the world's problems. 'You can't imagine the amount of work involved,' he says. 'Jimmy Carter [one of the group] has a physical and mental stubbornness you wouldn't believe.' Over coffee we chat about his friendship of many years with Bill Clinton, and he tells me he is also friends with Richard Branson ('very intelligent, and totally crazy. Looks like a Viking and wants to go to the moon') and Peter Gabriel ('he's the more intelligent – full of ideas and messages'). Bill Gates, introduced to him by Clinton, FHC reports sadly, is 'not a sympathetic man. The others are, very. But he's not.'

As we prepare to leave, I ask Cardoso what he thinks history will make of Lula. 'I think he will be remembered for growth and continuity, and for putting more emphasis on social spending. He's a Lech Wałęsa who worked out.'

And of his own importance? 'I did the reforms. Lula surfed the wave.'

Carlota
Rua Sergipe 753,
Higienópolis, São Paulo

....

1 × lamb fillets with ratatouille and goat's cheese agnolotti	R$51
1 × ravioli de gruyère	R$42
2 x guava soufflé with cream-cheese sauce	R$36
2 x espresso	R$8
4 x sparkling water	R$16
2 x cover charge	R$22

....

Total (including service)	R$193 (£72)

Jimmy Carter

Out of office reply

The ex-president is criticized as much for his term in office as he is praised for his promotion of human rights. But he says that he at least didn't start wars or condone torture

By Andrew Ward

J immy Carter is the man who brought informality to US politics by walking to the White House from his inauguration ceremony and addressing the nation in a woollen cardigan. So it should not have surprised me when the former president emerged from his home, in Plains, Georgia, wearing a grey shower-proof jacket, heavy checked shirt and blue jeans, with a rash of white stubble across his face.

The 81-year-old looks at my dark suit, shirt and tie with an expression that seems to combine amusement and derision, as if to ask why anyone would come to Plains dressed so pompously.

Carter and his wife Rosalynn occupy a modest, single-storey home, in two acres of woodland on the edge of Plains, a small southern farming town where they were both born and raised. A Secret Service outpost at the front gate provides the only hint of the residents' identity.

We are to have lunch at Pharjac Grille, one of the town's three restaurants, a two-minute drive away. Rosalynn, dressed almost as unpretentiously as her husband in a fawn sweater, explains she will be joining us to eat but must leave early.

The three of us squeeze into the back of a sports utility vehicle, with me nestled between the former president and first lady. In the front are two Secret Service agents.

My sartorial misjudgement becomes even more glaring when we

arrive at the restaurant, a small and homely diner with bottles of Heinz ketchup and a basket of paper napkins on each table. The Carters appear to know all the half-dozen diners and are greeted warmly, without deference.

'This is Mr Andrew Ward from England,' announces the former president, as if seeking to explain my strange attire. 'He's here to do a story.'

Part of the 'story' is well known – a peanut farmer from rural Georgia rises through state politics to the governor's mansion in Atlanta and then, against all odds, to the White House. The story would be impressive enough if it ended there. But some of his greatest achievements have come since leaving office.

Two years after losing to Ronald Reagan in 1980, he founded the Carter Center, a non-profit organization dedicated to promoting peace, human rights and health around the world. Today, the centre is active in 65 countries – half in Africa – monitoring elections, brokering peace deals, training farmers and tackling disease. In 2002, his efforts were rewarded with the Nobel Peace Prize.

It is hard to square such accomplishments with the elderly man bantering with diners in Pharjac Grille. Here, 'Mr Jimmy' is respected as much for the 160 years his family has lived in Plains, and the weekly Bible classes he teaches at a local Baptist church, as for his exploits in Washington or Africa. When I learn that the lunch crowd includes the town mayor and a pastor, it strikes me that, in Plains terms, Carter may be only the third-most important person in the room.

We eventually take our seats in a small cubicle, my knees jousting with those of the former president under the narrow table. The Secret Service agents keep watch nearby, perhaps pondering how a career associated with glamour and excitement has brought them here.

'We're probably going to eat kind of light,' says Carter, eventually ordering a green tomato soup, while his wife opts for chilli soup. I choose traditional southern fried chicken and a selection of local pulse vegetables, recommended by Rosalynn. 'If you want something country then you need some fried chicken,' she says.

Gradually the conversation shifts from a who's who of Plains society to weightier matters. I ask Carter how he feels about the frequent description of him as 'America's best ex-president' – a back-handed compliment used to praise his work with the Carter Center while dismissing his presidency as a failure.

Carter grunts a rueful laugh, understanding that this is my polite way of asking about history's dim view of his time in the White House.

'Well, yes,' he says, accepting the partial praise. 'But without any degradation of my presidency. You cannot separate the two because there wouldn't be a Carter Center had I not been president.'

His wife is more insistent. 'He was a good president,' she says firmly. 'He got more legislation passed – 77 per cent – than any president, except Johnson and Kennedy.'

Critics portray the Carter years as a period of malaise for a country still shell-shocked by defeat in Vietnam and the Watergate scandal. Inflation surged at home while overseas the Soviet invasion of Afghanistan and the Iranian hostage crisis made the US look impotent.

Carter, however, makes no apologies for his restrained use of American power. 'I kept our nation at peace,' he says, as if there is no greater success a president can achieve. 'We never dropped a bomb, we never launched a missile.'

Some advisers urged military action when Iranian militants seized 66 US hostages in 1979. But Carter stands by his patient handling of the crisis, which ended with the hostages' release on the day he left office. 'I could have destroyed Iran,' he says. 'But it would have resulted in the death of tens of thousands of Iranians and they would almost certainly have assassinated our hostages so I think to resolve the crisis peacefully was the right thing.'

Carter's faith in peaceful diplomacy could hardly be further removed from current US foreign policy. It is no secret that he has a low opinion of George W. Bush. But it is still shocking to hear a former occupant of the Oval Office talk so scathingly about a successor. He accuses Bush of making a 'radical departure' from the principles of multilateral co-operation and respect for international law followed by previous presidents.

'We started a war in Iraq that was unjustified and based on a false premise, we've tortured prisoners in secret camps [and] we've refused to co-operate with the rest of the world on global warming,' he says. 'All these things are startlingly different ideas from what George Bush Snr or Ronald Reagan or Bill Clinton or Gerald Ford or Dwight Eisenhower practised.'

Nothing troubles Carter more than the Bush administration's attitude towards torture. He says it is 'beyond dispute' that some of the coercive techniques used to question prisoners in the war on terror amount to torture, despite White House claims to the contrary.

'The nuances of trying to define what torture is in order to justify what we have done and what we would like to continue to do are embarrassing to people who believe in human rights,' he says. 'When the US does this it makes it easier for abusers in other countries to perpetrate the same crimes.'

While there is no doubting the authenticity of his anger, Carter's criticism of Bush has the feel of a well-practised spiel. Seeking to steer the conversation on to fresher territory, I ask him about his party's chances of reclaiming the White House in 2008. To do so, I suggest, the Democrats will have to find a way of reconnecting with the kind of rural, southern voters that surround us in Pharjac Grille.

'It's going to be difficult in the south,' he concedes. 'The Democrats are going to have to show a compatibility with deeply religious people. We have about 630 people in Plains and about eight churches and they are heavily attended.'

He says the party can win back so-called 'value voters' provided it picks the right presidential candidate. Who might that be? 'I have my own thoughts,' he says. 'But not to be shared.'

Rosalynn has by now left and the increasing brevity of her husband's answers indicates our time is up. Before we part, he invites me back to their home to see the workshop where he paints and makes furniture – skills learned at Plains High School in classes designed to equip boys to be farmers or craftsmen. In the centre of the room is an intricately crafted wooden cabinet made for a Carter Center fundraising auction.

How long does he expect to continue such an active life? 'Probably not very much longer,' he says, laughing at the morbid implication of the question. Among his remaining objectives: to complete the eradication of guinea-worm disease in Africa and river blindness in Latin America – two parasitic diseases the Carter Center has helped bring under control.

Carter gives me my cue to leave by mentioning several telephone calls he has to make. Anxious not to miss the opportunity, I fish a copy of his latest book, *Our Endangered Values*, out of my bag and ask him to sign it. Only as I hand it over do I notice the red sticker on the front declaring '40 per cent off' and the dog-eared page showing how little I had read.

'I get the same amount per book so I'm glad you got a good deal,' he says, promising rather pointedly not to lose my page.

Pharjac Grille
Plains, Georgia

....

1 x green tomato soup and salad
1 x chilli soup and salad
1 x southern fried chicken
1 x southern-style vegetables (black-eyed peas, butter beans, cabbage)
3 x iced tea

....

Total $ 24.77

As I drive out of Plains, past the peanut silos Carter once owned, it strikes me that I did not tip the waitress in Pharjac Grille – a serious omission in the US where waiting staff draw a large part of their income from gratuities. Returning to rectify the mistake, I find Pharis Short, the owner, clearing up after the lunchtime rush.

With everyone gone, I ask how Carter's views compare with those of her average customer. She confirms what I suspected: that most broadly support President Bush and the war in Iraq, while illegal Mexican immigration and jobs losses to China are bigger concerns than guinea worm in Africa. But swimming against local opinion is not something new for Carter. During his farming days in segregation-era Plains, he refused to join the town's whites-only business council, sparking a boycott of his products.

Perhaps the most surprising thing about Carter is not that he became president but that he did so with such a progressive brand of politics. 'Not everyone agrees with Jimmy,' says Pharis. 'But everyone respects him.'

Helen Clark

Premier league

Once known as something of a control freak, the New Zealand prime minister has proved remarkably adept at leading her country's coalition government

By Beverley Doole

V ery sorry but the PM is running about half an hour late. She's seeing the Queen. Please sit tight.' That's not the sort of text message I usually get at 3pm on a Friday. And I don't mind in the least sitting tight in the elegant surroundings of London's Sofitel St James hotel, on the corner of Pall Mall, waiting for Helen Clark, the prime minister of New Zealand.

The hotel's Rose Lounge couldn't really be called anything else. It is a vision of pink and green, with chintz upholstery and twee lampshades. It is rather like the sitting room of a prim aunt.

I look wistfully at the silver cake-stands being delivered to the other tables, each tier promising tuile biscuits, dainty cakes and finger sandwiches. I hope Clark hasn't filled up on Battenberg cake with the Queen. Thirty minutes pass. I reach for a book from the shelf – *Tiaras: A History of Splendour*. That couldn't be less appropriate for the down-to-earth, straight-talking leader of the furthest nation of the Commonwealth. I quickly put it back in case she catches me.

Forty-five minutes pass. A man who pronounces Bev as 'Biv' approaches and shakes my hand. He is Clark's press secretary and assures me the PM isn't far away – she's just freshening up in her room. And finally, a few minutes later, a tall, athletic figure walks confidently past the tables of ladies who take tea and businessmen who are talking golf, without a blink of recognition from any of them.

Dressed in a tailored black suit and black boots, Helen Clark smiles, apologizes for the delay, and makes herself comfortable in the rather upright chairs. Despite the newly applied make-up she looks tired, which is perfectly understandable for someone who flew across the world the day before and doesn't appear to have stopped since. But she is too professional to flag – she gives me another encouraging smile and scans the afternoon tea menu. 'Orange-blossom tea – that sounds good.' Tea? Just tea? Can't I tempt you to some sandwiches or cake? 'No, no thank you. A pot of tea will be fine.' We order orange-blossom tea for two, and I silently curse the caterers at Buckingham Palace.

Although Clark's face isn't familiar to the other guests in the Rose Lounge, her deep and measured voice may well be. In the run-up to the invasion of Iraq in 2003 she seemed to be regarded by Radio 4's programme producers as the political voice of reason. New Zealand – unlike its closest neighbour and ally, Australia – did not join the war in Iraq. Clark said she felt that the case for war had not been made – she wanted a UN security council resolution as a basic condition.

She strongly advocates an independent foreign policy for New Zealand, placing her Labour government a long way from the traditional New Zealand position of total loyalty to the motherland. At the start of the Second World War, the then prime minister Michael Savage declared of England: 'Where she goes, we go. Where she stands, we stand.'

Clark, who is 56, says the greatest influence on her in terms of war was being part of the Vietnam generation and knowing that it was wrong. 'You have to be very careful about decisions where you commit other people's children to go and fight a war. Vietnam was not a just cause. And nor was Iraq. They are value judgements, but they happen to be my values.'

Yet Clark has been a driving force behind the unveiling of the New Zealand memorial at Hyde Park Corner, to commemorate those who died fighting for their country. 'There's been a lot of unfinished business for New Zealand soldiers – traditionally they came home from war and everybody shut the door on it, they never talked about it again. But I have a great interest in heritage and I think you have to properly commemorate significant events in a country's history.'

She describes the memorial – 16 slanting bronze 'standards' in formation that could be troops on parade, or Maori performing a haka, or a cricketer leaning forward to play a defensive stroke – as a work of art: 'It is a beautiful and creative design. The patterns on each standard are highly symbolic of the people who make up New Zealand, the literature, the birds, the shoreline, the forest. It's a statement about New Zealand today.'

When Clark became prime minister in 1999 she also took on the portfolio of minister of arts, culture and heritage. She believes these are the areas that forge New Zealand's identity and can help it get noticed on the world stage. 'We are a country of four million people. We are geographically remote, so we have to find ways of saying "Look at me" as a country.' Not a natural show-off, she laughs, almost apologetically. But this philosophy is one of the reasons her government has increased funding to creative industries such as film. 'Film is an iconic industry and if your country is producing great movies then that has a cachet about it. *The Lord of the Rings* has given New Zealand fantastic publicity in the past seven or eight years, and it was followed by *King Kong* and *The Chronicles of Narnia*, also made by New Zealanders.

'The other way to get international attention is to host very large events, such as the America's Cup, and then leverage off that. We're now looked on as world-leading yacht designers, and builders of super yachts and marine technology. The film industry also enables you to showcase your technology and digital solutions, so New Zealand becomes a place where you'd be interested in buying very sophisticated goods. In other words, we're trying to shake that chocolate-box image of 1950s sheep and mountains.'

By now our tea has been poured from the inevitably rose-speckled teapot into our china cups. I am reminded of David Lange, a previous Labour prime minister, who in 1988 famously announced it was time for the country to have 'a cup of tea', meaning a pause in the free-market frenzy of reforms unleashed by his finance minister, Roger Douglas. At that stage Clark had been housing minister, struggling to keep state houses (provided at affordable rents for people on low incomes) from being sold off or rented out at market rates. Now, as prime minister, she is able to introduce a range of left-leaning policies, with social justice at its core. 'I had to bring our Labour party back from the lurch to the right.' She says her administration is more consistent with the first Labour government, elected in 1935 and renowned for creating the country's welfare state and providing free healthcare and a universal pension.

However, some ideas pioneered in New Zealand in the 1980s have migrated to the UK – such as giving the Bank of England the independence to set interest rates and so keep inflation under control. And the country continues to be a social laboratory for Britain. The call by the Conservative leader David Cameron for a points-based system to ensure immigrants have the skills the country needs mirrors the New Zealand experience. And Tony Blair's government has been studying the KiwiSaver scheme where employees receive NZ$1,000 (£345) from the government if they start saving regularly to top up their state-provided pension.

One idea the UK has not adopted is proportional representation, yet Clark is proving adept at leading a coalition government after winning her third term in office in September 2005. 'On 41 per cent of the vote [Labour] have a minority of seats. So we govern through relationships and understandings with other parties, and that requires a particular style. You can't be an autocratic "it's got to be done my way or the highway" kind of leader, because people won't deal with you.'

She says that being a woman, and having women in senior positions in her government, suits this system. 'I think the style I've developed – that you've got to work things through with people, try to get a result everyone can live with – is very appropriate for this style of politics.'

Perhaps Clark is mellowing after seven years in the top job: in the past she has been described (by friends, colleagues and the media) as a control freak, 'the minister for everything'. She does admit to being self-sufficient, something that comes from her upbringing as the oldest of four daughters on an isolated North Island farm. 'The way I grew up means that I'm very self-contained. And you need that to operate in politics. If you allowed yourself to feel every sling and insult and bit of unpleasantness you'd be a nervous wreck.'

And there were other benefits to her early family life: 'Because there were no brothers, the girls got to do the things the boys would have done on the farm. So it's probably quite emancipating not having brothers. I got to drive the tractor,' she chuckles.

Is there a mood in New Zealand to be similarly emancipated from the monarchy? Clark almost sighs – I suspect she is asked this question by every journalist she meets in Britain. 'Nothing's going to change fast,' she says. 'My view's always been that the relationship between New Zealand and the monarchy will change, but it will be another generation away. The family link with Britain for most people is, say for my generation, more likely to be a grandparent than a parent. For my nieces' generation it will be a great-grandparent, so the links start to attenuate a bit – most New Zealanders now are pretty firmly rooted in their country. Over time I think people will say, "Well, isn't it time that somebody like our governor-general was the head of state?"'

As for her own future, she has every intention of contesting the next election, for her fourth term. Retirement is not on the agenda, but it holds no fears. 'I've got plenty of skiing I'd like to do, trekking I'd like to do, books I'd like to read, plays I'd like to go to.' These are interests she shares with her husband, Peter Davis, who is professor of sociology at Auckland University.

My tea has gone cold, but at least Clark finished her cup. She stands up, shakes my hand and heads upstairs to her room – she reckons she's got time for some sleep before her evening schedule kicks off.

The Rose Lounge

Sofitel St James,
London SW1

....

1 x pot of orange-
blossom tea

....

Total   £10.13

....

Saif Gaddafi

The son also rises

When your father is Colonel Gaddafi, it's only
natural to conduct hostage negotiations
and rear tigers during your studies.
Now Saif Gaddafi is ready to bring the
west and al-Qaeda to the table

By Roula Khalaf

F our months after I first suggested a lunch in London with Saif
al-Islam al-Gaddafi, I received a telephone call from a person
close to him. The son and potential heir of the maverick Libyan leader, a doctorate student in London, had settled on a
faraway destination: he wanted to dine in Tripoli. A few days later I am
sitting on a red velvet sofa, surrounded by walls of colourful Moroccan
tiles, in Saif's 'farm', a luxurious Moorish-style villa on the main highway
between the airport and Tripoli. A tall young man with a boyish look and
a shaved head is facing me; he is dressed in a traditional white tunic over
tight black trousers, the top covered with an embroidered vest.

No one is sure what role Saif, second-eldest son to the colonel, plays
in Libya. He is often credited with helping to persuade his father to
resolve the Lockerbie crisis and to give up his weapons of mass destruction. Though he holds no official position, he's the man to see if you want
something done in Libya – a meeting with the leader or a business deal.
His own take on this is that he is an accidental mediator: 'I get credit
because I lived in London during that time (of Lockerbie and the weapons) so it was easy for the west to contact me and easy for me to contact
my father.'

The 'facilitator', as one businessman describes him, is as eccentric as

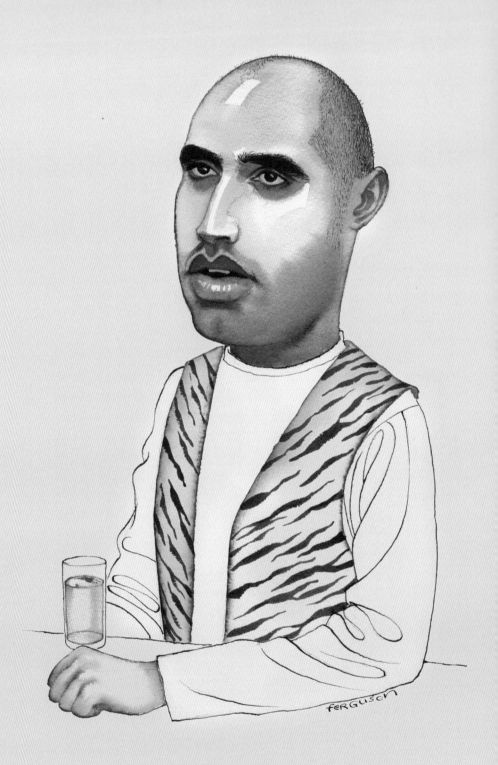

his father – a sort of new-age Gaddafi. He likes to shock with his behaviour and to provoke with his words. He's unpredictable: outrageous one moment and pragmatic the next. He tells me he is just back from a jungle, where he celebrated his 32nd birthday. 'I was invited to go to the end of Russia, to a remote place, a jungle, with birds, deer, no roads, nothing. I saw hot springs, active volcanoes.'

Saif has been studying at the London School of Economics, so our conversation is mostly in English; he speaks it well. But from time to time we switch into Arabic, our mother tongue, particularly when one of us wants to emphasize a point. He is the oldest son of the colonel's second wife, Safiya, and he has seven siblings. His eldest brother Mohamed (son of Gaddafi's first wife Fatiha) runs the telecommunications sector in Libya. Then there's the footballer Saadi, who loves the limelight and has played with Perugia, a team in Italy's Serie A league. There's also Aisha, a law student who is looking for a political role and recently offered to be part of Saddam Hussein's defence team.

Lunch, such as it is, takes place in front of a television screen, tuned to the pan-Arab al-Jazeera channel. Saif sits back and gazes into the distance as if posing for a picture. It's an instant reminder of his father, depicted in portraits all over Libya with his head tilted upwards, staring into space. We are served sweet mint tea in small glasses, as is the custom in North Africa. There's a huge basket of fruit on the table and small plates with melon and watermelon cut in cubes. But the *pièce de résistance* are the dates, sweet and juicy. Saif gulps a glass of buttermilk while I sip a fruit juice. 'It's the poor man's meal,' he quips.

This 'poor man' raises tigers as pets. He urges me not to leave without visiting his small private zoo, in the garden outside. I later meet three tigers, including a rare white breed. Saif took one of his tigers to Vienna when he went to study for a Masters in Business Administration a few years back. The MBA was squeezed between his architectural studies and the doctorate he's still pursuing in London. Along the way he also became a painter. He won't say who inspires him. 'I remember the style but not all the names. It's called the complex style; mixing techniques within one painting: surrealism, collage and realism.' He has exhibited his paintings in several European capitals.

Saif's doctorate is in 'governance and non-governmental organizations'. There is no such thing as a non-government organization in

Libya. But the Gaddafi International Foundation for Charity Associations likes to act as one and it has been the vehicle through which Saif has pursued his political ambitions.

The foundation has helped to improve Libya's image by raising human rights issues, visiting prisons and inviting Amnesty International to Libya. But it was tremendously annoyed when Amnesty later issued a report accusing Tripoli of continuing to jail and torture political prisoners and timed its publication to coincide with Colonel Gaddafi's arrival in Brussels on his first visit to Europe in 15 years. 'Amnesty accepted that it had come under pressure [from European political circles] to release the report during the visit. But torture is part of history, it's finished. There are no such practices any more. We brought them [Amnesty] here to speak about facts and the achievements in human rights.'

A week after the colonel's European trip a Libyan court handed down the death sentence to six Bulgarian medical workers who had been accused of infecting hundreds of children with the HIV virus at a Benghazi hospital. Human rights organizations and European governments were outraged and consider the case to be fabricated. Saif insists the judgment must be respected, even if his foundation is against capital punishment. The case is now on appeal and there is still hope that Gaddafi will intervene and perhaps pardon the Bulgarians.

Saif tells me he wants to see political reforms in Libya, that *The Green Book*, his father's quirky prescriptions of how a country should be run, has not been well applied, and that it would produce a democracy if it were. But he admits that Libya is a bit lost, as it tries to be accepted again by the rest of the world. 'We haven't taken the final decision about where we want to go. Now we are without an identity.' He pauses, thinking about what he's just said. He jots down notes on a yellow Post-it Note pad. 'Yes, we're at a crossroads. We got lost and we don't have a passport yet.'

The foundation's other hat is 'conflict resolution'. It has been involved in negotiations for the release of hostages held by rebel groups in the Philippines and in Algeria, a process that sometimes involves paying a ransom to the kidnappers. 'We accomplished miracles in that foundation, to free hostages in the Philippines or Algeria, which a lot of people had failed to do. One of the key reasons is good timing and negotiating skills. I do the negotiations myself, even if it doesn't appear like that sometimes.'

I tell him some people have suggested that such activities could be construed as a continuation of the same unsavoury support for rebel groups that led to Libya's isolation. Those who criticize the foundation, he says, are simply envious of its success. But he adds nonchalantly: 'We can do this [negotiate] because we have something in common. We're all rebels. It's the history of my family.'

One of the people associated with the foundation is now in a Saudi jail, captured after the Saudis allegedly uncovered a bizarre Libyan plot to assassinate Crown Prince Abdullah, the de facto Saudi ruler. The Saudis have taken these allegations very seriously and the Americans are investigating. But Saif dismisses the whole story as a joke. 'It's not professional of me to send someone to wait in a hotel to assassinate the crown prince. It's a made-up story but not well made up.'

We talk about America and the rather positive outlook he has towards the US. He says the US is a big shopping centre. 'You pick things you want and leave the rest. They have oil companies with their big dollars to invest so you bring them. They have MIT and one of my dreams is to bring it here for a joint programme with a Libyan university. Americans can help you to bring democracy and have a free press. At the same time, sometimes they're ugly, like in Iraq or Palestine, so you reject them. It's a big dinosaur. It's not easy to say America is good or bad.'

I tell him that it strikes me that welcoming the US project to reform the Arab world marks him out as something of an Arab neo-conservative. He is miffed and quickly reminds me of his radical side: he considered the attack on the Pentagon on 11 September not to have been a terrorist act. He also says the killing of Italian soldiers in Iraq is an attack on a military target. 'But I'm against killing all the Jews and saying they're all our enemies. I have my own way.'

Saif al-Islam al-Gaddafi's farm
Tripoli

sweet mint tea
basket of fruit
melon and watermelon cubes
dates
1 x glass of buttermilk
1 x fruit juice

Saif believes that if elections were held in the Arab world, those associated with al-Qaeda and Osama bin Laden would win. 'I challenge governments to hold free elections and see if bin Laden wins.' Dealing with al-Qaeda, he says, requires a political, not military, solution. He ends our modest lunch by offering himself as a mediator. 'I'd do it. Why not? I've negotiated with groups in the Philippines, in Algeria.'

Paul Kagame

'We don't go out begging'

Some see the Rwandan president as the country's saviour; others as a bloodstained tyrant

By William Wallis

P aul Kagame, 53, has been president of Rwanda for the past decade and vice-president – and de facto leader – for seven years before that. But for all the power and years of command he appears as lean and austere as he was as the 36-year-old guerrilla commander of the Rwandan Patriotic Front, a rebel army that fought an end to the 20th century's swiftest act of mass murder – the killing between April and July 1994 of some 800,000 Tutsis and Hutu sympathizers.

In the years since, we have met a number of times but this is our first lunch: the president is visiting London and suggests meeting at the Wyndham Grand in Chelsea Harbour, an expensive but unremarkable hotel not known for its restaurant. Our meal is to be prepared by a chef travelling with the presidential party. Kagame's aides assure me in advance that this is not out of fear of being poisoned. Rather, they explain, it is for organizational reasons – feeding the entourage and past experience with the vagaries of hotel catering – and I half believe them. Kagame's administration, which has approached development with the same single-mindedness as it approached guerrilla warfare, is nothing if not well organized.

The country that Kagame took over had collapsed, its institutions and people abandoned or destroyed during the genocide. In the ensuing years his government has overseen the return of millions of Rwandans

displaced by conflict; hundreds of thousands of genocide crimes have been tried by village committees.

And, with the help of international aid, on which the government still depends for nearly 50 per cent of its budget, Rwanda has seen some of the highest growth rates in Africa. Yet no African leader divides opinion as sharply as Kagame does or inspires such contrasting caricatures: on the one hand, the visionary statesman, forging prosperity out of ruin and courageously tackling continental taboos; on the other, the bloodstained tyrant. He is accused of war crimes and human rights abuses at least as often as he is celebrated with honorary doctorates and global leadership awards.

The polemics are fuelled by Kagame's mixed record. Unlike many of his African peers, he has relentlessly pursued results in his bid to transform an inward-looking mountain nation into a regional centre for services, agro-processing, tourism and transport. But he has also been given extraordinary licence to repress dissent, and the prosperity of elites in Kigali derives at least partly from the plunder of minerals from the Democratic Republic of Congo during Rwanda's serial invasions of its neighbour.

According to United Nations reports, tens of thousands of Rwandans and Congolese died at the hands of Kagame's army as he established authority and secured his country's borders in the face of continuing threats to surviving Tutsis. Political opponents and journalists still end up in exile, jail or, in some cases, six foot under.

Yet Kagame can count among his international supporters the likes of Tony Blair, Rick Warren, the evangelical US pastor, and Howard Schultz of Starbucks among other influential figures in the west. Members of his fan club tend to overlook the more troubling aspects of his rule or support the notion that he has done what was necessary to restore security and lay the foundations for development.

In the anonymous, faintly ascetic meeting room at the Wyndham Grand, where we are about to be served carrot and tomato soup, Kagame says, 'I have no regrets about being who I am, and being what I am in my country for my people. No regrets at all.' The round table where we are to eat, bedecked with white cloth and silver cutlery, is something of an oasis in a desert of empty carpet.

The wider global setting is more compelling: Kagame, though

relaxed, is not a man for small talk and our conversation moves quickly to the conflict in Ivory Coast, revolutions sweeping the Arab world and the ramifications of both for sub-Saharan Africa. 'These are not problems that just emerged yesterday: they are problems which people were not paying attention to because it suited their own interests not to,' he says of the corruption, social injustice and repression that fuelled the Arab uprisings.

Such a statement might raise an eyebrow among his detractors, coming as it does from a head of state who has yet to allow a strong opponent to rival him, and who in 2001 locked up his predecessor Pasteur Bizimungu, when he formed an opposition party. But the attention Kagame has focused on developing Rwanda's essentially peasant economy has fostered the shoots of a remarkable recovery for anyone bothered to observe it closely. Few of Kagame's detractors do, something he finds infuriating.

Fiercely defensive of the moral high ground, he is not shy of playing on western guilt at having failed Rwanda in its hour of need. 'I don't think anybody out there in the media, UN, human rights organizations, has any moral right whatsoever to level any accusations against me or against Rwanda. Because, when it came to the problems facing Rwanda, and the Congo, they were all useless,' he says, quietly emptying his soup bowl.

Weary of the problems associated with being a recipient of international aid – from the patronizing, bullying tactics of donor nations to the often fickle nature of their policies in Africa – Kagame has developed an acute sensitivity to western mendacity and double standards. He also has a strong sense of irony. So it is with a wry laugh that he suggests that the historic focus of western governments on stability over freedom and good governance in the Arab world has had its comeuppance. 'They have to face the reality now I think. They just can't ignore it . . .'

If there is a broader lesson from the Arab Spring for countries south of the Sahara, he continues, it is in what happens to those in office who do not pay attention to the interests of their people. 'You can be up there, talked about, appreciated all over the world, with people singing a lot of songs about you. But if you don't measure up and you are not really connected with your people . . . it will explode in your face, no question about it.'

Next on the menu chosen for us by his chef is steak, with beans, green peppers, rice and potatoes. It looks fortifying, so I introduce an awkward comparison. Bahrain, ruled by a Sunni minority distrustful of a majority Shia population now in open revolt, could, I suggest, be compared to Rwanda, with its administration dominated by a minority – ethnic Tutsis, who make up around 14 per cent of the population and were victims of the 1994 genocide. Not unlike Bahrain's ruling elite, Rwanda's fears real democracy would lead to majority rule and that this would invite chaos given the history of extremism among majority Hutus.

Kagame reacts sharply to the comparison. For one, he is not a monarch, he says, like King Hamad bin Isa al-Khalifa. But, I murmur, you were elected by a remarkable 93 per cent of votes only last year, facing no real opposition.

'In Rwanda there is a constitution. There are term limits; there is a parliament, there are elections. Somebody who makes that comparison, I will just say is ignorant,' he insists, defending the near unanimous result of last year's polls as a vote for stability in the context of the country's peculiarly bloody history.

Yet international concern is, if anything, mounting over whether the peace and economic growth Kagame has established is sustainable alongside a political system that remains rigidly controlled.

He continues with a tactic often deployed by African heads of state but which in this instance seems somewhat disingenuous: to harp on the exaggerated expectations made of developing nations by the west and the west's failure often to meet the same exacting standards. 'Why isn't the majority in the developed world interpreted on the basis of race or colour or tribes? Why? You want to tell me that, in the United States, Barack Obama comes from which majority?' he asks.

We reach a point of agreement when we decide that had Rwanda been an oil-rich state like Libya it is unlikely that UN peacekeepers would have backed off when mass murder started as they did in 1994. We also agree that in the case of Ivory Coast, the elections that sparked this year's conflict were premature, symptomatic of the pressure applied on African nations to import political systems that are not always suited to local circumstance.

'Elections must be held. But when? You don't carry out elections anyhow, or under any conditions,' he says, pointing to the fact that Ivory

Coast was divided when the vote took place under UN supervision in November, with rebels in control of the north, and a government army in the south. 'It's as if elections or political processes were things worked out in a factory . . . They can't be made in the UK; they can't be made in America. No. If you force it, you end up with a problem.'

The waiters remove our empty plates, and replace them with bowls of fruit salad with oranges, pineapples and blackberries. We find another point of agreement: had we been almost anywhere in Africa, the fruit would have tasted a great deal sweeter. 'Pineapples are very bland here,' says Kagame. 'And the bananas are different.'

As coffee is served, I ask Kagame a question that intrigues me. He has skilfully courted the evangelical Christian community in the US, a factor that I am told helped swing the Bush administration to his side, after a frosty start. But is he himself a believer? 'Yes and no,' he says. 'I encourage believers to believe.'

The complicity of members of the Catholic Church in the Rwandan genocide partly inform this doubt. There were priests among the killers. 'I've seen religions make blunders. Let's look at what the Catholics did in Rwanda, which still disturbs me,' he says. 'You see the Catholics apologizing for child abuse by priests and bishops, and the Pope has gone out of the way to apologize to the Americans. Then he goes to Australia and does the same. But they will never apologize for their role in the Rwandan genocide.'

For all the blame he heaps on the outside world for turmoil past, he tailors much of his rhetoric these days to chime with the times. He is acutely conscious, for example, that Africa will only catch up if Africans themselves live up to the task. He singles out the leaderships in Ethiopia, Gabon and Burkina Faso as like-minded. 'People will patronize us but at the end of the day we have to remember it's our problem,' he says. 'Africa should not just wait to be exploited or influenced. No. We should be part of the conversation. We should raise ourselves to a level where there are certain terms we dictate in the conversation because we have a lot to offer.'

It is partly Rwanda's meagre resources, he continues, that has made it so imperative that it behave differently, that it root out petty corruption and improve the business climate if it is to compete. And it has, becoming one of the world's fastest reformers, rising to 66th out of

178 countries in the World Bank's ease of doing business rankings. 'We are landlocked, a very small country, in the middle somewhere. Some of our neighbours, they are richer than us, and they tend to attract people more than we do. So we have to strategically create uniqueness about us.'

Unique, too, is the ruling Rwandan Patriotic Front, which grew out of the rebel movement he led to power from exile in neighbouring Uganda. It is one of the best-endowed political movements in the world. Funds it controls own large stakes in key sectors of the Rwandan economy, including telecoms, banking, real estate and energy, as well as investments abroad that were launched when his movement was still in the bush. Kagame puts the RPF's wealth at several hundred million dollars. 'We don't go out begging. For example, we didn't have any money from Gaddafi for our elections . . . And the reason is really we want to maintain our independence all the time in everything we do.'

That is one of the paradoxes about Rwanda. The country has depended on foreign donors to rebuild in the wake of 1994. Yet it is focused, as much as any aid-dependent African country, on becoming self-reliant. And its leader, despite the debt he owes to many for-

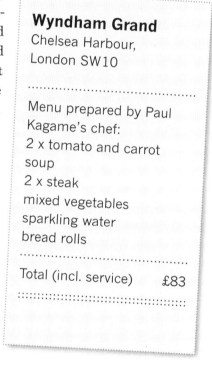

Wyndham Grand
Chelsea Harbour,
London SW10

....

Menu prepared by Paul Kagame's chef:
2 x tomato and carrot soup
2 x steak
mixed vegetables
sparkling water
bread rolls

....

Total (incl. service)   £83

eign allies, never appears anything but independent-minded. 'We've dealt with our problems very unconventionally and because we've had to do that,' he says – adding that this has often infuriated foreign partners who would like everything done their way – 'it's a struggle all the time.'

F. W. de Klerk

White man unburdened

Two decades ago, he stunned the world by moving to end apartheid. Over springbok carpaccio at his favourite Cape Town restaurant, the former president of South Africa discusses what brought him to that momentous decision

By Alec Russell

T he last white president of South Africa is deep into his reminiscences on the dying days of apartheid when a fruit fly, no doubt overcome by the day's intense 35°C heat, dives into my glass of crisp Cape Sauvignon. Unconsciously, I fish it out and make to have another sip. F. W. de Klerk is having none of it. He abandons the story of his once fraught relationship with Nelson Mandela, raises his hand and attracts the attention of the waitress.

For a moment, seen from afar, it could have been the quintessential apartheid tableau: black servant summoned by Afrikaner patriarch. But this is 21st-century Cape Town and, apart from on remote farms on the *veld*, that relationship is of the past. The waitress confidently looks de Klerk in the eye. There is none of the pre-emptive cringing that once marked such inter-racial encounters. It is, I reflect over a replacement glass of Sauvignon, a reminder of the revolutionary changes that my lunch guest set in motion almost exactly 20 years ago.

History is moving rather fast in South Africa. In June the country hosts football's World Cup, as if in ultimate endorsement of its post-apartheid progress. Yet on 2 February 1990, when the recently inaugurated state president de Klerk stood up to deliver the annual opening address to the

white-dominated parliament, such a prospect was unthinkable. The townships were in ferment; many apartheid laws were still on the books; and expectations of the balding, supposedly cautious Afrikaner were low.

How wrong conventional wisdom was. De Klerk's address drew a line under 350 years of white rule in Africa, a narrative that began in the 17th century with the arrival of the first settlers in the Cape. Yet only a handful of senior party members knew of his intentions.

Today, seated at his regular table in the white-washed premises of Aubergine, his favourite restaurant and just a five-minute walk from parliament, Frederik Willem de Klerk, or F. W. as he is universally known, smiles to recall his momentary mastery of spin. His hapless spokesman was dispatched to brief journalists to expect nothing special. Even his then wife, Marike, was in the dark. The first inkling she had that anything was up was when, as he took the salute outside parliament, he told her, 'After today South Africa will never again be the same.'

Having cannily played down expectations, de Klerk's address then turned history on its head: bans against the African National Congress and the Communist party were to be lifted after 30 years; ANC leader Nelson Mandela was to be freed from jail after 27 years; negotiations on a new South Africa would begin forthwith. De Klerk had calculated brilliantly. He became the toast of the world. Only a week later, with the release of Mandela, did the focus change.

Why did he do it? I open, as the waiter takes our order. Did he have no last-minute doubts? 'No,' he insists. 'I wasn't taking a chance. I believed I was doing the right thing. It was a rational decision. I thought it through properly . . . There was nothing opportunistic. It was no sudden impulse.'

But, I press, as he takes his first sip of a red Stellenbosch blend, was he not an arch conservative? Little about his background suggested he was the man to persuade his people to abandon power. He was, after all, a blue blood of the National Party that had governed since 1948. A forefather had come to South Africa in the late 17th century as a Huguenot fugitive from Europe. An uncle, J. G. Strijdom, had been prime minister, and his father, Jan, was a government minister and Senate president. After practising as a lawyer, F. W. entered parliament in 1969 and then the cabinet nine years later. What is more, he was from the strict Dopper branch of the Dutch Reformed Church, which for so long gave a theological underpinning to apartheid.

We misjudged him, he contends. He was 'a middle of the road man' who made conservative statements to keep the right on side. Also, he argues, he spent much of his career trying to reform apartheid. There is a whiff of selective history here. He did have a hand in the 1985 repeal of the Mixed Marriages Act, which barred marriage between different races and which his father, he points out, had put on the statute book in 1949. But the National Party's reforms were agonizingly slow and his argument reminds me of the claim of so many whites that they themselves never backed apartheid.

Yet de Klerk's address to parliament *was* remarkable. There was nothing inevitable about his decision to lift the ban on the ANC. Though the apartheid regime was economically and diplomatically under siege, it was far from defeated on the battlefield. There were many in the security forces, he says, who thought they should hold out. But he had looked into the future and, ultimately, seen only disaster if they dug in their heels. 'It had to end and we brought it to an end in a way which prevented upheaval.' Encouraged by the fall of the Berlin Wall, which took away the *rooi gevaar* (red danger), or fear of a communist takeover, de Klerk was emboldened to press ahead.

De Klerk does not encourage the romantic media line of granite Afrikaner having 'road to Damascus' experience and suddenly recognizing the evil of apartheid. It was a gradual process, he insists. By the mid-1980s he had 'reached the final conclusion' that apartheid was 'unjust towards the majority of the population'. That was rather late in the day, I suggest. He stresses the word 'final' and says his reappraisal of apartheid was a long process.

We choose springbok carpaccio for a starter. It is hard to imagine the Boers of yesteryear having much truck with this sort of cooking, let alone with 'rose geranium brioche' and 'cherry vinaigrette', and I reflect on the symbolism of de Klerk's choice of venue. In the early 19th century, this was the home of the first chief justice of the Cape. In decor and cuisine, Aubergine is a fusion of the contemporary and the traditional – scrubbed yellowwood tables offset by Africana art on the walls. De Klerk, too, is a blend of the old and the new. Indeed, that was the key to his success in leading his fractious tribe to cede power to the black majority.

In his heyday he was seldom seen without a cigarette. But he gave up a few years ago and now chews intensely on Nicorette gum. Otherwise he is, at 73, little changed from the dramatic years we are discussing, when his stocky physique, clipped English and heavy Afrikaans accent were staples on international news bulletins. Four years after his address, in May 1994 – following thousands of deaths in political violence, a joint Nobel Peace Prize with Mandela, the repeal of apartheid's laws and the negotiation of an interim constitution, not to mention his admission that South Africa had dismantled a secret atom bomb project – he did what had been unthinkable to his adamantine predecessors and handed over power to a black man.

As our main courses arrive – grilled Cape salmon for me, duck for him – I reflect on how astonishing it is for a politician to step down. Surely there must have been some emotion stirring within him on that chilly morning when Mandela took over? De Klerk, however, is not one to ham up his feelings. There is no foraging into his soul. A 'positive emotion' is all he will confess to feeling on that extraordinary day.

I suggest, mischievously, that 2 February 1990 was the high-water mark of his career. For a moment a trace of the old political warhorse returns. It is as though I am an impish young National Party MP challenging the great leader. His career has 'many, many other high points', he says, including the interim constitution in 1993 and the Nobel Prize in that same year.

But had he not initially wanted to retain some form of a minority veto for the whites before being worn down by ANC negotiators? He dismisses out of hand the argument of some National Party insiders that he had originally hoped to share power with the ANC long into the future. Yes, he made concessions but, he says, that is 'the essence of a true compromise'. It was vital they struck a deal when they did. 'How would South Africa have looked today if we had not signed the agreements which were reached? We would not have exported one case of wine this year. [Wine is now one of South Africa's healthiest export sectors.] We would have been totally isolated. South Africa would have been on a downward slope towards calamity and catastrophe. So the new South Africa, warts and all, is a much better place.'

Yet in the week before our lunch, the Afrikaans press buzzed with an angry debate over the post-apartheid settlement. Prominent Afrikaners on the left and right, who suspect the ANC of undermining the constitution and fear for the future of their language and their children, think de Klerk ceded too much and should have enshrined minority rights in the constitution. He shrugs off the critique and says the Afrikaners are as 'divided as ever. Not all Afrikaners feel the same, just as not all Scotsmen feel the same about independence for Scotland.'

What of Mandela, I ask, and their famously tetchy relationship? In the early 1990s Mandela regularly accused de Klerk of not caring about black lives, and even suggested that P. W. Botha, F. W.'s predecessor, was a more reliable interlocutor. Does Mandela, despite his saintly image, still have a very human and bitter streak?

'The charm is there,' says de Klerk. 'It's real and his commitment to reconciliation is above any doubt. He's one of the all-time greats. But he is like all of us a human being and I saw him at times also being unreasonable, unfair . . . Nobody's perfect.' He says he was 'deeply offended' by Mandela's intermittent tongue-lashings but now they have a good rapport. Mandela, who is 91, spoke at de Klerk's 70th birthday party three years ago and joked that given he'd had 27 years of contemplation in prison, while de Klerk was in the 'rough and tumble' of politics, they were about the same age.

De Klerk argues that the ANC's current affirmative action policy is too extreme and is unjust on whites. He also believes they have been trying to erode 'by stealth' some rights in the constitution. Yet, to his credit, he is a loyal ambassador for South Africa. He describes Jacob Zuma, the charismatic yet controversial new president, as 'a good communicator . . . astute and pragmatic'.

Briefly, we are distracted by a text message on my phone. De Klerk is as keen as I am for the news. An epic game of cricket is unfolding in Johannesburg, where Afrikaner fast bowlers are pummelling English batsmen on the way to victory in the final match of the recent Test series. More than a century after the Anglo-Boer war, Afrikaners still enjoy humbling the old colonial foe. De Klerk chuckles as the message heralds another South African triumph on the pitch.

As he polishes his legacy, de Klerk is enjoying life. He runs the Global Leadership Foundation, which advises developing states on good governance, and is a popular figure on the international lecture circuit. He was divorced from Marike in 1998 and, a week later, married Elita Georgiades, the former wife of a wealthy Greek businessman and an old friend of the de Klerks. The disclosure of the relationship titillated Afrikanerdom. Three years later Marike was murdered in her apartment, a victim of South Africa's appalling crime rate.

We drain our espressos and I venture further on to sensitive ground. The ANC accuses him of being evasive over responsibility for apartheid. Should he not have given a blanket apology for all the abuses carried out by the apartheid state? And what of the charge that he did not do enough to curb those security forces who were fostering violence? De Klerk repeats his familiar legalistic riposte, one which still enrages many in the ANC: the assassinations were aberrations carried out by rogue agents and not state policy.

So apartheid *was* wrong, I say as we push back our chairs. Even now this National Party scion chooses his words carefully. The idea of separate homelands for South Africa's black tribes – 'nation states', as he describes them – was 'morally defensible', he says. But it failed for three reasons: the whites were too selfish; as the economy grew so the races became intertwined – 'we became an omelette and you can never unscramble an omelette'; and the ANC did not want to accept division along tribal lines. 'In the end, because we failed we ended in the place which was totally morally unjustifiable.'

It is classic de Klerk. Most modern politicians would have concocted a more disingenuous response but he doggedly insists apartheid in its purest form just might have worked. At dinner that night, I ask my oldest South African friend, a liberal Afrikaner lawyer, about F. W. He was not an inspirational politician, the lawyer reflects. And yet, at a critical moment in his country's history, he conquered his fear of the unknown and acted in the best interests of his country and not of his party – and that, we agree, marks him out with greatness.

Aubergine
Barnet Street, Cape Town

....

2 x two-course lunch
R368

springbok carpaccio
salmon with a
Mediterranean crust
duck breast with crackling

glass of red wine   R49
glass of white wine   R50
2 x espresso   R36
sparkling water   R28

....

Total (incl. tax and
service)   R600 (£49)

Lord Lawson

The dessert trolley passed by unnoticed

The *FT* tries to tempt a slim former Chancellor of the Exchequer

By Lucy Kellaway

So there I was last Tuesday lunchtime at London's Savoy Grill, offering Lord Lawson some advice on cosmetic surgery.

The problem with losing five stone, he had admitted, is that his skin is now too big for him. 'It gradually adjusts but at my age it won't adjust totally. I haven't had anything done about it yet. I may or I may not, I haven't decided.'

I looked at the loose skin under his chin and counselled him against a cut and tuck. Just imagine the figure of fun he would become. Just think of the newspaper headlines. 'Perhaps you are right,' he said. 'I think I will take your advice.'

Had you told anyone 10 years ago that the then chancellor, famous for his arrogance and his fatness, would be reborn as a thin man, the author of a diet book, who meekly takes advice on personal matters from a journalist, you would not have believed it.

And you would have been right to be sceptical. In terms of bulk, Lawson is two-thirds the man he once was, but in terms of personality he has not changed one bit.

I had met him a year earlier at a dinner for writers of the *FT* Lex column and, on that occasion, he had seemed wearied by my attempts at small talk. He had also looked terrible, with skin yellow and crumpled like that of a tortoise; one could not say that the weight loss suited him.

Still, on Tuesday he was in excellent form and looking better; older but spry. 'My favourite thing is grouse, and there is no better grouse than at the Savoy Grill,' he said cheerfully.

In an attempt to provoke him, I ordered a fattening dish of fried fish cakes with potato ratatouille. But nothing doing: his full attention was fixed on the wine.

'Can I have something really good?' he asked. He had in mind a 1989 Chateau Kirwan at £37.10 a half-bottle; I asked how much the next one down was. There seemed to be a wine which he was prepared to drink at £23.65, but not wanting to seem mean, I told him that he would have to make the choice himself. 'Well, if it won't get you into trouble . . .'

'So tell me about yourself,' he said, once the waiter had been dispatched. I talked. He listened charmingly.

But before long we got down to the serious business of discussing diets, and *The Nigel Lawson Diet Book* in particular.

'Did you enjoy it, may I ask?' he inquired.

I muttered something about me not being his target audience, but said I admired its length, a mere 120 half-sized pages of which he had written 60 and his wife the rest. 'It is a limited subject and only requires a short book,' he said, commending to me some of the psychological tricks described in the book that make the discipline of a diet less difficult.

However, his most effective 'trick' seems to have been in marrying Thérèse Lawson. When he decided to diet he gave her a list of acceptable ingredients and she drew up some delicious menus. A typical dinner chez Lawson might be a rack of fat-trimmed lamb, roasted *à point* with ginger, a strongly flavoured jus, and steamed spinach with lemon. I remarked that the diet might work less well for those of us for whom a typical dinner is microwaved lasagne.

'The principles can be applied by anyone, but it may not taste quite so good,' he insisted.

Over our first courses – his a marinated salmon with an anything but innocent looking sauce – we got on to the ticklish matter of his changed appearance. 'People are extremely disconcerted,' he explained, 'because they have an image of me and if I don't conform to it they feel uncomfortable. You know inside you are the same – but there is a mismatch with other people, who think you must be different. I think that happens with the ageing process too.'

I was glad it was he who brought up ageing, so without seeming rude I could say that losing weight makes you look older.

He gave me a fixed look. 'At first I may have looked older, partly because my clothes didn't fit me,' he replied. However, so many people asked him if he was ill that he started to fret. 'I was worried, so I went to the doctor for a thorough health check.'

His grouse arrived and he was poured some wine. He gestured for a brief silence while he tasted it.

Does he expect his diet book to outsell *The View from Number 11*, his heavyweight political memoirs? I asked. 'Nobody in their right mind, first of all,' he said, easing himself into a lecture, 'judges the merit of relative books by how much they sell. My ambition with my memoirs was to write something that would be of lasting value. I would hope that it will still be read long after I'm dead. But I wrote this book because it was meeting what appears – to my surprise – to be a demand, and it was something I could do jointly with Thérèse.'

Still, how would he feel if this book was so successful that he went down in history as Nigel Lawson, the man who lost the weight?

'If I thought that was the only thing I'd be remembered for I'd feel disappointed.'

The waiter poured another half-inch of the wine into Lawson's glass.

'If you put the rest in the glass I can calibrate – co-ordinate – how much is left with the food.' The waiter was at a loss, so Lawson explained more directly that he wanted all the wine poured out. 'Thank you. Excellent.'

A trolley of desserts was wheeled past. 'A double espresso,' he said, as if he had been saying that all his life.

Still, he had had a good meal – rather better than mine – and the only things he had refused were bread, bread sauce and the dainty little crisps with the grouse.

So what is your next book going to be? I asked as I put my credit card on top of a bill for £114.55p.

'I don't want to say anything now,' he said in a tone familiar from years of fending off questions on BBC Radio 4's *Today* programme. 'I wouldn't want to tempt providence.'

The meal over, I took him to meet the photographer. 'I hate having my photograph taken,' he complained. Was that because he doesn't like how he looks? I asked.

No, it turns out that if you are Lord Lawson you can teach yourself to change the eating habits of a lifetime. But you can't teach yourself to hold a convincing smile.

Angela Merkel

New Europe, new divide

The chairwoman of the Christian Democratic Union has established herself as very different from most other leading German politicians. Preparing for a trip to the US this week, she talked to the *FT*

By Amity Shlaes

E veryone is talking about the New Europe these days, so I thought I might seek her out. Who is this creature who dares to diss Schröder, Fischer and Chirac?

In the end, I located her – or one of her kind – in an improbably Old European setting: a private breakfast room in downtown Berlin's Hotel Palace, the sort of sterile five-star place where the ghosts of the Elysée Treaty might commune. She appeared in the person of Angela Merkel, potential chancellor of Germany.

Merkel may be chairwoman of one of the stuffiest of Europe's political parties, the go-along, get-along Christian Democratic Union. But this season she has challenged the German establishment by throwing the support of her party behind the smaller nations that penned the 'New Europe' letter to President Bush. On a Washington visit later this month, Merkel plans to take a position decisively to the right of Germany's other big conservative leader, the preachy Edmund Stoiber of the Christian Social Union.

The Merkel rallying cry – 'dictators understand only the language of threat' – is so sharp, so inappropriate to the salon as to seem positively un-German.

When we met at the Palace, I reflected that the 48-year-old Merkel differed from most German alpha politicians in at least three ways. The first is that she is not a professional politician. She trained as a particle physicist, a job more serious and precise than any to be found in the marketing-obsessed Bundestag. The second is that she is an Easterner and lived plenty of adult years under the communists, even years when it still seemed at least possible that the Soviets would send their tanks rolling westward. In other words, her formative experience was the cold war. And she and her constituents in northern Stralsund and Rügen have had personal experience with a regime that is worse than anything the bad old US could possibly represent.

The third is that she is a woman, still not the norm for the top echelon of German politics. (In Germany, speechmakers from all parties but the Greens expand their chests like gorillas behind their podiums in order to maximize the breadth of their shoulders.) And while certainly pretty, Merkel does not sport the irradiated blonde look that tends to be mandatory for bright-eyed power women over the age of 35.

All these factors mean that the German political world tends to underestimate her as a competitor, or dismiss her as 'not cutting edge'. A non-blonde, non-young woman without a big power base can't win for the CDU and is just a quota choice, goes the received wisdom. Therefore, Stoiber had to be the 2002 chancellor candidate. Besides, Merkel's critics argue: the cold war and its rhetoric are so yesterday. But it also means that she is accustomed to criticism, and is therefore refreshingly unflappable.

This morning, in any case, it does not seem to bother her a bit that the federal chancellor and foreign minister Joschka Fischer are hard at work negotiating the twists and turns of the German Sonderweg (special path) not far from where she sits. By her second sip of orange juice, Merkel has already detailed differences between her position on the US and Chancellor Schröder's. These turn out to be wider than – to stick to the cold war imagery – the old Fulda Gap.

'If I had been the head of the government, I would have signed that initiative,' she says, referring to the letter published by leaders of eight countries airing their differences with German policy on Iraq.

'There are two lessons we have from history. The first is "no war". The second is "no special path for Germany."' And that means, she sums up,

'We always have to find solutions with our allies.' This is the opposite approach of Schröder and Fischer's UN blocking action.

'What's more,' she says, staring from beneath her fringe, 'Germany must ask: "What is in German interest?" It is not merely giving thanks to the US for history.' It is also aiding the US. Germans, she says, are completely convinced that if anything happens to them, the US will save them. 'They don't realize if we don't help America, America won't help us.'

Now she speeds up, and the salmon, sausages and swirls of smoked ham in front of her lie untouched. Germans, she says, have to think about the reality of their new life as a big nation. Freedom is fine. But 'we have not only rights, but also duties'.

There remains, however, the question of whether the 'Angela as Rebel' model will break down when it comes to economics. Chancellor Schröder has left the CDU and its Christian Social Union partner an enviable opportunity when it comes to taxes. Schröder's insistence that it is time to raise rates provoked national outrage, generating a pop hit, 'The Tax Song' ('Dog tax, tobacco tax – did you really believe more wasn't coming?'). It's a telling fact that the hit is also available in karaoke, so that the super-tax frustrated can belt out anti-tax solos to their heart's content.

Merkel, alas, does not seem eager to exploit her tax advantage. Rather, she posits that Germany cannot afford rate cuts because they will widen the deficit too much.

Merkel's stolid thesis reflects the extraordinary pro-tax consensus of the German political leadership: there is little difference here between Merkel, Schröder or Fischer. And without the tax card to play, Merkel is stuck arguing for labour market deregulation and programmes that would increase incentives to return to work. That's nice, but these steps are not sufficient to restore ailing Germany. Nor do they make great billboard copy.

Still, it is foreign policy that matters most this morning and here Merkel, with her unabashed embrace of the US, has established herself as a true radical and one of the minority.

This very week, Mike Moore's *Stupid White Men*, a parody-attack on the Bush administration, tops *Der Spiegel*'s non-fiction bestseller list. Moore's film, *Bowling for Columbine*, which confirms every prejudice about US society a German might dream up, is doing pretty darn well too. Many Germans, especially eastern Germans – a great number voted for Schröder last autumn – will think she's like Tony Blair. If he is the lapdog, she is the Schnauzer of the 'Amis'.

The Merkel position is not even uniformly popular within her own party. This is something her rivals will try to exploit. Their goal would be to bump her up to candidate for the ceremonial presidency post, while reserving the powerful chancellor job for themselves.

Still, while Merkel may be a national exception, she is not necessarily a regional one. It was the central European nations, after all, that joined Spain in signing the Bush letter. In central Europe, pro-American sentiment is strong, and not especially party-political. Thus, for example, in neighbouring Poland opinion polls show citizens supporting the US to the same numbers that Germans reject it.

Even as Merkel finishes up at the Hotel Palace, the Polish prime minister Leszek Miller (head not of the conservative but the post-communist party) is arriving in Washington to meet President Bush and show his support. Topic A of the meeting: relocating some of the US military to Polish bases from German ones. For both Poles and the US, this prospect is delicious: no more nasty demos at Ramstein or Frankfurt. Just peace and quiet near Krakow.

The atmosphere within Germany may be changing as well. Earlier this month, voters abandoned Schröder's Social Democrats in droves in two big state elections. Polls suggested the economy was the main factor behind their shift, but Schröder's explicit peace-at-any-price line did not carry his party either.

Public opinion will probably move toward the US the moment an Iraq war is launched. Much, of course, depends on what happens in Iraq. In other words, Germany remains both isolated and in play. Its foreign policy confronts challenges not only from outside, but, as Merkel proves, from within.

Queen Rania

A beauty battling for balance

Star status, world travel and controversy may have come with the job, but Queen Rania of Jordan would prefer to stay at home with her children

By Roula Khalaf

Queen Rania's chief of protocol greets me at the River Café and tells me she is stuck in the Hammersmith traffic. 'If she knew her way around, she would get out and walk,' he assures me.

When the grey Mercedes enters the driveway half an hour later, Jordan's tall, riveting beauty steps out. She apologizes as we make our way to a table in a shady corner of the garden.

She seems in a hurry and suggests we order promptly. 'I hope they have good desserts,' she says – a surprising remark given her tiny waist. Only nine months ago, she gave birth to daughter Selma, her third child. 'You lose weight quickly after the third child,' she explains. 'And I work out.'

I stare at her – as do many around us – as she studies the menu. Her white Céline trouser suit and small diamond-studded earrings seem fit for smart royalty. But the camouflage top is the taste of a fashion-conscious 30-year-old. A few lines are visible under her huge brown eyes; the shiny eye-shadow is definitely superfluous.

Rania, brought up in a middle-class Palestinian family, has won sudden stardom as the youngest queen in the world.

'Being the youngest queen doesn't mean anything,' she says, as she settles on a safe bet of mozzarella salad, grilled sea bass and sparkling mineral water. 'Being young is temporary.'

She maintains the same confident, no-nonsense style throughout the lunch, as she displays her two personalities – the queen who speaks seemingly well-rehearsed lines with a US accent and the more spontaneous working mother who attempts to juggle family life and a hectic job and peppers her talk with Arabic expressions.

As she nibbles on a piece of bread, she tells me that King Abdullah – 'my husband', as she refers to him – took the children that morning to buy toys (she does not mention that he was due to meet British prime minister Tony Blair that day).

The rest of the family met her in London for a short break, following a trip to the US, where Rania attended the congressional launch of a bill providing $155m to the US Agency for International Development for microfinance projects around the world.

Her star status and interest in microfinance, the main activity of a foundation she runs, have turned her into the unofficial spokeswoman for the industry – a role the Business Administration graduate from the American University in Cairo seems keen to highlight.

'In a country like ours where we have unemployment, where we want people to be more self-reliant and not count on the government to create jobs for them, microfinance can be part of a solution,' she says. 'It's also excellent for women. The majority of borrowers in Jordan are women and they gain confidence, become in control of their lives.'

There is, surprisingly, no hint of inexperience in her fast talk, even though she was thrust into the limelight in controversial and unexpected circumstances. The late King Hussein altered the course of the succession shortly before his death two years ago, removing his brother Hassan as crown prince and appointing Abdullah, his eldest son.

Also awkward was that her mother-in-law, the glamorous Noor, retained her title as queen – a move the late king insisted upon. 'There is no tension between us,' insists Rania, denying rumours of a family feud. 'It's very normal to have gossip about this. People come and go into positions. I understand this and she understands this – and I'm not a jealous person.'

Much of Rania's focus seems to be on helping push forward King Abdullah's agenda of modernizing a desert kingdom with a struggling economy. She travels around the country to open new computer centres in schools – one of her husband's key projects. And, like him, she is often abroad.

But while the couple may be toasted in the west as a model of modern leadership in the Arab world, they are criticized at home for spending too much time away. Some people ask whether the royal family is more concerned with its international image than Jordan's problems.

'When people see me and King Abdullah, they see Jordan,' says Rania. 'In this global community we live in, if you don't have your agenda on the world scene, you don't get the attention.' In fact, she adds, 'if you ask me what I hate most about my job, I'd say it's the travelling. I'd love to stay in Jordan, with my three kids, in my house.'

Perhaps because the king is untouchable, any disapproval of the royal couple has been targeted at Rania.

As we move on to the second course, I glance at her khaki handbag and ask how she feels when she is called the 'handbag' queen in the fancy salons of Amman, the Jordanian capital.

'Of course I shop, every woman shops, and everything in my wardrobe I bought because I need to be involved in every aspect of my life,' she says. 'Labels will come and go, but the most important thing is not to feel victimized. It just comes with the territory.'

It is easy to be a popular leader, she says. 'But those who follow public opinion all the time sometimes make the weakest leaders.'

Is this not a time when the monarchy in Jordan might want to make an effort to win popular approval for the sake of stability? Since the Palestinian uprising against Israel's occupation of the West Bank and Gaza Strip erupted last year, neighbouring Jordan has faced concerns of a spillover.

Most of the kingdom's population is of Palestinian origin and it complains of discrimination in politics and public service. Jordan's 1994 peace treaty with Israel – never favoured by the local population – has become increasingly difficult to defend.

The government has appeared to raise tensions through a ban on anti-Israeli demonstrations and a brief decision last month to restrict access to Palestinians from the occupied territories.

'People have the right to express themselves but we've had enough demonstrations. The trouble with them is that they're not peaceful and they turn into non-productive situations,' says Rania, toeing the official line. 'And if you're in the UK and you see demonstrations in Jordan, the tourists won't go.'

Jordan, she says, can only help the Palestinians in the territories if it is strong and stable.

While Rania's Palestinian origins were once thought an asset to the king, they have become controversial. During a soccer match last year, supporters of the Jordanian team called on the king to take a Jordanian wife.

Rania is unperturbed when the subject is brought up. 'When I came, people started saying that I'll bring the two people together, but I think the fact that I'm married to the king means that the two people are already together.

'Now we have an uprising and people are using me as a symbol of what's going on. There will always be some people who will say I'm not Palestinian enough and others who will say I'm not Jordanian enough, no matter what I do.'

As a chocolate cake with caramel ice-cream is placed before her – chocolate is 'one of my major vices' – we talk about Tulkarm, the West Bank town her family comes from and where her grandmothers now live under Israeli economic blockades.

She has not been there recently.

An aide approaches to remind her she is due at another appointment. Half the cake is left on the plate when she rises to leave.

That evening, she was to attend the dinner of the Osteoporosis Foundation of which she is the international patron. I learn later that it was the event where the Prince of Wales publicly kissed Camilla Parker Bowles for the first time. I am kissed, too – as she leaves, the queen places three kisses on my cheeks, as is the Arab tradition, and says she hopes we will keep in touch.

Donald Rumsfeld

'Are we better off now? You bet'

Intimidating? Mistaken? Repentant? Not me, says the controversial former US defense secretary over an austere lunch that takes in Saddam, score-settling and the Super Bowl

By Gideon Rachman

O n a silent Sunday afternoon in Washington DC, I am sitting at a table in the restaurant of the Mayflower Hotel, waiting to be joined by one of the most controversial men in recent American history. Donald Rumsfeld was defence secretary for George W. Bush and, along with the president himself, became the public face of the invasion of Iraq. He left office at the end of 2006, three years into the conflict, reviled both by opponents of the war and by many of its most ardent backers.

For the anti-war movement, Rumsfeld had become the face of a cruel and misconceived conflict. He was the man whose reaction to looting in Baghdad – 'stuff happens' – was regarded as the epitome of a callous disregard for the consequences of the invasion. But for many of the war's strongest advocates, Rumsfeld had become the scapegoat for everything that had gone wrong in the early years of the war. He was accused of pig-headedly refusing to send enough troops to fight the conflict and of neglecting the vital task of nation-building in Iraq.

Now, four years after his resignation, Rumsfeld is publishing his own account of events, entitled *Known and Unknown*. The Café Promenade, where we are meeting, is situated in the Mayflower, one of Washington's grandest hotels. This is no ordinary hotel café – it has marble pillars,

thick carpets and a huge chandelier. At 12.30, there are just three other diners in a room that could easily seat a hundred.

Rumsfeld arrives bang on time and greets me with a disconcertingly warm smile. He is dressed formally in a grey suit, pale blue shirt and striped tie. He sits down and swiftly asks me a question: 'Have you read the book? What was your reaction?'

I say that I have read most of the book on the flight over from London and that I had enjoyed it – particularly the early chapters about his life growing up in suburban Chicago and his memories of selling newspapers, carrying the news of the bombing of Pearl Harbor. Rumsfeld laughs with apparent pleasure – and points out that, at the age of 78, he has been alive for a third of the entire history of the United States. 'You multiply my age three times and it takes you back to 1776 . . . Isn't it amazing. It's a third of American history.' For 54 of those years he has been married to his wife Joyce and the couple have three children.

Until the final debacle of the Iraq war, Rumsfeld had a reputation as one of the most competent managers in Washington. Elected to Congress when he was still only 29, he served in top jobs under four different presidents – Nixon, Ford, Reagan and Bush. His two stints as secretary for defence – separated by a quarter of a century – have given him the distinction of being both the youngest and the oldest man ever to serve in the position.

At the Pentagon he was famous for working standing up, and he tells me that this is still his habit. His office houses his archive and the Rumsfeld Foundation, which among other things helps retired troops. I ask him what time he normally gets up and he replies, unsmilingly, 'I get up at 4.30 or 5 and exercise generally and read the paper in the sauna.' His way of life seems almost comically spartan. I suggest that perhaps we might order something to eat, and he seems genuinely surprised. 'You want something to eat?' A waiter is summoned. I order an avocado and bacon salad. Rumsfeld orders a cup of clam chowder and a glass of lemonade.

Rumsfeld also had a reputation for ferocity at the Pentagon. In his memoirs, he records Paul Bremer – the diplomat charged with the reconstruction of post-war Iraq – as complaining that many of Rumsfeld's civilian employees were terrified of him. I ask Rumsfeld if he thinks that was true and I get an aw-shucks smile. 'I've never heard anyone else say that, so I don't give it a lot of credence.'

I wonder aloud whether 'as a leader you have to be a bit intimidating'. But Rumsfeld demurs – 'Oh no, in fact you don't want to be. The truth is that I had tough jobs, a lot of them, and I'm comfortable taking tough decisions and I ask tough questions . . . and that isn't fun sometimes for people . . . But I've always been open to people coming back.'

Rumsfeld's book has certainly generated a lot of tough comeback from those who see it as an extended exercise in self-justification and score-settling. Unsurprisingly, Rumsfeld sees things differently. Sipping his lemonade, he says he has written 'a serious book of history that is rooted in the primary documents that I will have on the website [www. rumsfeld.com], and historians and interested readers, serious people, will be able to go in there and make their own judgements'.

When I invite him to discuss the fairly damning remarks in his book about former colleagues, such as Condoleezza Rice, whom he criticizes for avoiding tough choices as head of the National Security Council, Rumsfeld's instinct seems to be to back off. He tells me that Rice is a 'smart and able woman, let there be no doubt. A very accomplished person and a good person.'

Some antagonisms, however, are too open to disguise. Senator John McCain, the Republican candidate in the last presidential election, became one of the foremost critics of Rumsfeld's approach to the Iraq war. He is criticized in the book for having a 'hair-trigger temper and a propensity to fashion and shift his positions to appeal to the media'. McCain's reaction to these jibes has been to renew his criticisms of Rumsfeld and to remark: 'Thank God he was relieved of his duties.' I quote this back at Rumsfeld, who responds with a chilly smile: 'That's fairly typical of him . . . He was opportunistic. He spent his whole campaign attacking the Bush administration and he was not a good candidate.' So, had Rumsfeld, the life-long Republican, actually voted for McCain? He frowns: 'I did. It was not a happy choice.'

The inside-Washington score-settling will strike many of the people horrified by the Iraq war as supremely beside the point. For them, Rumsfeld is a guilty man because he presided over a 'war of choice' that led to hundreds of thousands of deaths. Unlike Robert McNamara, defence secretary during much of the Vietnam war, who was later very open about his regrets, Rumsfeld is unrepentant. In the book and in conversation, he presents the Iraq war as justified and ultimately successful. 'Is our country and region better off with Saddam Hussein gone?' he asks me briskly, before answering his own question. 'You bet.'

But, I point out, the justification for the war was Iraq's alleged work on weapons of mass destruction – and the WMD were never found. Let's say we had known there were no WMD, I ask, would it have still been justified to go to war? Rumsfeld's response strikes me as oddly circuitous and detached. 'Apparently. The Congress had passed regime change legislation in the 1990s and it passed overwhelmingly. Now you can't know what you would do. What you know now helps you in what you do in the future. It can't help you with what's been done in the past.'

But was the Iraq war really worth all the pain and suffering it has caused? Rumsfeld's tone becomes sharper: 'Have you ever visited one of the killing fields in Iraq where Saddam Hussein killed hundreds of thousands of people and the mass burials and the godawful prisons he had and the rape rooms?' he asks. 'I've got videos of what they did to their political opponents. They cut their tongues off.' As for the American troops who died – 'they had families, they had children and it's heartbreaking, there's no question about that . . . But what they did was they liberated millions of people.' Like Tony Blair, Rumsfeld is donating the profits from his book to help wounded troops. Unlike Blair, Rumsfeld's decision to do so has not provoked an angry reaction.

For all his efforts to take the long view and to present himself as a detached elder statesman, Rumsfeld is clearly still infuriated by coverage of the 'war on terror' and the events surrounding it. He complains that reports that prison guards in Guantánamo Bay had flushed a Koran down the toilet had caused riots and deaths – but then turned out to be untrue. The press had eventually apologized – 'If some portion of their story was incorrect, they're sorry . . . And, of course, the people they were sorry for were dead. Now everyone makes mistakes and that's fair, but there's no penalty for that.'

All this talk of making deadly mistakes and then paying no personal price for it rings a bell. It is, of course, exactly what infuriates some people about the sight of an elderly former defence secretary eating a comfortable Sunday lunch in a Washington hotel while the killing continues in Iraq and Afghanistan. As politely as I can, I say: 'Some would say, "Here's Rumsfeld, maybe he was wrong about the Iraq war." What's the comeback for you?'

Rumsfeld's tone remains even. The only faint sign of agitation as he replies is the furling, unfurling and scrunching of a napkin with his left hand. 'Well, I mean, there are plenty of people commenting on that about Afghanistan or Iraq or transformation, anything you do . . . That's quite a different thing than what I'm talking about.'

Throughout his career, Rumsfeld has consistently been a man who cares above all about protecting and extending American power. So I wonder if he has any regrets on that score. Does he think that Iraq and Afghanistan have left the US looking stronger or in some senses have they weakened America because the wars went on for so long? I am expecting another brisk dismissal. Instead, there is a long pause and Rumsfeld simply replies: 'Time will tell.'

My salad is long gone, so I suggest that perhaps we might have a coffee. I order a double espresso. Rumsfeld smiles at this indulgence and says: 'I don't need caffeine.' He has a decaf.

As we get ready to part, we resort to the standard topic for male banter – sport. The Super Bowl – the most important game of the American football season – is being played that night, and Rumsfeld asks if I will be supporting the Pittsburgh Steelers or the Green Bay Packers. I say I like the Steelers, because I have memories of watching them play some epic games against the Oakland Raiders, in my first visits to the United States in the 1970s. 'Oh nobody could support the Raiders,' he says, 'they're evil.' At this the retired boss of the Pentagon laughs heartily, and strolls back to his office and his archive of documents.

Café Promenade

Mayflower Hotel,
1127 Connecticut Ave NW,
Washington DC

....

cobb salad	$18
clam chowder	$9
lemonade	$4.50
iced water	
double espresso	$7
decaffeinated coffee	$4.50

....

Total (excl. service)	$43

Morgan Tsvangirai

'Mugabe is very humane'

Over 'sundowners' at his Harare home the prime minister of Zimbabwe talks about what working with a former enemy is really like

By Alec Russell

One moment all we can hear are the cicadas, the next the quiet Harare evening is broken by the sound of a rapidly accelerating engine. The security guard outside the Zimbabwean prime minister's residence turns quickly as a car appears at the end of the road. He peers through the gloaming and speaks urgently into his phone. Then he relaxes. It is the prime minister's spokesman, Luke. Paranoia? Probably. Then again, where else in the world can you arrive, having flown thousands of miles to speak to a prime minister, and yet be advised by government insiders that it may be best not to tell police or immigration the reason for your visit?

Luke is wiry, besuited and angry. He has spent much of the day in court, where dozens of activists were facing treason charges for having watched video footage of the Egyptian democracy protests. In Zimbabwe this is a capital offence. The activists' lawyer says they have been badly beaten in prison. It seems clear that if there is one person who definitely won't be popping round to join Luke's boss, Prime Minister Morgan Tsvangirai, and me tonight, it is his partner in government since 2009, that veteran African autocrat, President Robert Mugabe.

I wait in his garden, relishing the cool air after an afternoon rainstorm. In a continent where political power all too often leads to Croesan wealth, Tsvangirai's home in Strathaven, one of Harare's northern suburbs, has a modest feel – though I later learn he is having a big new house renovated in another part of the city. A colonial-style bungalow,

it is one of thousands of unassuming family homes favoured by mid-level civil servants in the days of white-run Rhodesia. Only a dilapidated sentry post inside the gate signifies the occupant's status. Clearly neither the Irish street names nor the road surfaces have been changed since independence in 1980.

I have come to see Tsvangirai over 'sundowners', that ritual of the African safari: the serving of drinks at the close of the day. My ambition of dinner at Meikles, the gloomy old colonial hotel in the centre of town, or maybe the Harare Club, has had to die. Dinner was at the last minute impossible in these frenetic times. It is not just that after two years of a relative truce between Mugabe's Zanu-PF, whose ruinous three decades in power had devastated the economy, and Tsvangirai's Movement for Democratic Change, Mugabe's thugs are intimidating voters again ahead of a possible mid-year snap election. Tsvangirai, a dogged battler through a decade in opposition, is facing increasing questions in the press, and not just the pro-Mugabe state media, about his private life – and, from some in his own party, suggestions that he is not up to the job of prime minister.

One of the prime minister's younger brothers emerges from the tin-roofed outhouse that is his private office. 'He is bearing up,' he says. 'But he needs support, spiritual and moral as well as political.'

When I first visited Tsvangirai's home three years ago, it was at an electrifying time, just days before the 2008 elections. As leader of the MDC opposition, the bluff ex-union leader seemed to have Mugabe on the run. We ate a snatched lunch of sandwiches on the campaign trail – which was probably all to the good, as if we had opted for a formal Lunch with the *FT* I would have needed a satchel of banknotes. Those were the days of 100,000 per cent inflation and billion-dollar notes, when the price of drinks could and did change between courses.

It is a sign of the times that you no longer need your calculators to go for lunch in Harare. Just over two years ago, shortly before the coalition government was sworn into office as part of a regional deal to end months of impasse, the Zimbabwe dollar was abolished in favour of the greenback. To the delight of business, the world's second-worst recorded hyperinflation in a century is over. (The worst, according to Steve Hanke at the Cato Institute, was Hungary in July 1946, not Weimar Germany.)

After a decade of freefall, the economy is at last growing. And yet Zimbabwe is far from out of the abyss.

As I settle back in Tsvangirai's office, my eye is caught by an old 2008 election poster leaning against the wall. It shows him smiling, relaxed, exuding vigour and fire. We begin by reminiscing about a barnstorming trip together to a Zanu-PF heartland when we met a rapturous welcome in a hitherto no-go zone for the MDC. He relaxes into his seat. On the table in front of him are an iPad and a copy of Tony Blair's recent memoir, *A Journey*. We share our experiences as Apple newcomers and trade impressions on the lessons of the former British prime minister. 'Politics is the same the world over,' Tsvangirai chuckles. Blair's relationship with Gordon Brown, his Chancellor of the Exchequer and successor as premier, was indeed poisonous. But they were as blood brothers when compared to Zimbabwe's president and PM.

He has spent most of the day at the Tuesday cabinet meeting. There he has to sit alongside Mugabe, whose supporters have spent a decade trying to crush the MDC. It must have been difficult, I say. He beams. 'It was very good, very productive . . . It's enlightening that everyone was serious about addressing the concerns.'

I raise my eyebrows. But are you not old enemies? Tsvangirai beams again. 'If you were to enter the room you would not know who was who, MDC or Zanu-PF. The seating is Zanu-PF, MDC, Zanu-PF, MDC . . . and he [Mugabe] and I direct. We really do consult when things get out of hand.'

The Zanu-PF lion lying down with the MDC sheep: it is a charming vision of reconciliation but utterly unconvincing. Mugabe may have celebrated his 87th birthday a week before my visit but all the talk in Harare is that he is running rings around his 59-year-old prime minister – just as he outmanoeuvred other rivals, such as Joshua Nkomo, once they decided to stop opposing him and instead to share power. So I am all but lost for words at Tsvangirai's Milquetoast reference to his and Mugabe's latest meeting – as, I have been told, was David Cameron when he was given a similarly bright-eyed and bushy-tailed account by Tsvangirai at Davos earlier this year.

I relay instead that I had lunch that day with an MDC-supporting Zimbabwean businessman who had said gloomily that if there were a free election the MDC would win 90 per cent of the vote – but that there would never be a free vote.

'No, no, no, that's rather pessimistic,' Tsvangirai insists. He cites the role of regional bodies, which will in theory police the next election. I point out the craven stance of most regional leaders towards Mugabe when he bullied his and his party's way to re-election in four elections between 2000 and 2008.

'I know people are sceptical because we have had so many experiences of violence at elections before,' he says. 'But I have never given up hope. People may want to see instant change, like instant coffee, but we have chosen the evolutionary path not the revolutionary path and evolution is sometimes disappointing because it is slow.'

An aide knocks on the door bearing a tray of drinks. The prime minister and I opt for Coke. Luke has a Sprite. These are clearly the tipples of choice in the coalition – I was to drink Coke with a Zanu-PF minister the following night. The days of gin and tonics on the prime ministerial *stoep* finished 30 years ago, with the end of white rule. We raise our glasses in a toast. At a time of crumbling dynasties elsewhere, I ask, why has there been no revolution in Zimbabwe? Surely MDC supporters think the coalition government was a mistake? His answer is clear: Zimbabwe had its war of independence, so better negotiations than war.

'We said back in 2005 we are going to drag Mugabe to the negotiating table for a transitional government, a new constitution and an election. That's the path we defined and I don't think we are off it . . . In the past two years it is a miracle what we have achieved.' Then again, he adds: 'I can't even predict what will happen tomorrow. Suppose people wake tomorrow and say they don't want this.'

So what are we to make of the 'old man'? I ask. Over a decade the boot-boys of Mugabe's Zanu-PF have killed hundreds of MDC supporters. Tsvangirai himself was viciously beaten four years ago, just a day after I had shared dinner with him. How does he judge Mugabe after seeing him so often at close quarters?

'I used to think he was callous and all that,' he says. 'But you know what? He's human after all. He's very humane. There is a split personality between Mugabe the [revolutionary] hero and Mugabe the villain . . .'

I fear I am going to struggle to elicit an insightful word about one of the world's more notorious leaders but he allows himself the tiniest bit of mischief-making at the president's expense. 'If you confront him, he tends to close his mind and to say "I'm not guilty of violence. I'm not guilty of this. I'm not guilty . . ."' He and Luke laugh. I am reminded of an account of a recent meeting when Tsvangirai and his ebullient finance minister, Tendai Biti, were supposed to have insisted that the cabinet had to discuss the upsurge in violence. Mugabe nodded sombrely and told them it should be aired later in the meeting – and then skipped out of the room before it could come up, pleading tiredness.

So, how is Mugabe's stamina? I ask – there is endless speculation that he has advanced prostate cancer. I recall how on meeting the president back in 1994 he answered questions with wit and verve. As for the cut and thrust of conversation, is he still as sharp as ever?

'Yes, when he's alert . . . not when he's sleeping . . .'

Does Mugabe sometimes doze off in cabinet? The prime minister clearly feels he has said enough and leaves my question hanging. We turn to more concrete matters. Mugabe is promoting a long-mooted law which will force foreign businesses to give a 51 per cent stake to 'indigenous' business people. Investors are appalled, fearing this is the equivalent of the forced expropriations of Zimbabwe's white-owned farms at the turn of the century. Tsvangirai is clear. Black Zimbabweans must be 'empowered' but not in this way. 'We don't support grabbing people's property. The 51 per cent figure was a mistake. Who is going to come [and invest] if we do this?'

He also argues cogently that the international sanctions on Mugabe and his elite should be removed, on the grounds that the president has seized on them as his most powerful political argument. As so often in his career, he has whipped up nationalism and is inflaming rallies with his claim that he is the victim of persecution by the imperialist west.

'We are in a vicious position. We want the sanctions removed but Zanu-PF is doing everything to ensure they are retained,' he says. He is less convincing, however, on the other great political scandal: the apparent theft by state officials of tens of millions of dollars in taxes from Zimbabwe's diamond fields. He pledges an audit and transparency. Fine words, I think, but who will bring the Zanu-PF culprits to book?

His mobile phone barely stops ringing. When one of his daughters calls, I am reminded of the reaction of a friend in Britain when she heard

I was going to see Tsvangirai. Her eyes filled with tears and she recalled how his wife Susan, mother of their six children, was killed in a car crash in March 2009, a month into the new government, and how just weeks later a three-year-old grandson died in the swimming pool in his garden. Tsvangirai seems almost surprised that I relay her response. He cannot be accused of Blairite or Clinton-style emoting. 'It had a big impact . . . but eventually you move on,' is all he says.

The sun has long since set. We repair to the washroom, which has the brightest lighting, for a photograph. The prime minister's golf clubs lean against the wall. They have become a leitmotif for his MDC critics, who mutter he spends more time playing golf than fighting the good fight. Some party insiders echo the assessment of a former US ambassador, published on WikiLeaks, that Tsvangirai has 'questionable judgement'. Then there is the speculation about his private life. On the day we meet, one of the local newspapers has as its front-page headline: 'Tsvangirai fathered my child'. The accusation was at first denied but there has since been an out-of-court settlement. There have been other allegations but he is talking about revolutions and tyranny and I don't interrupt.

In his office is another poster – this one of Nelson Mandela. The great statesman is smiling beneath the slogan: 'There is no easy walk to freedom'. Tsvangirai is no Mandela. A better analogy is Lech Wałęsa, the Polish union leader whose finest days were in opposition and who proved rather better at rousing rallies than the subtleties of government.

Morgan Tsvangirai's home
Strathaven, Harare

....

Coke $1
Sprite $1

....

(Return flight from
London to Harare   £950)

::

I have over the years had a clandestine breakfast with Tsvangirai, dinner in a Johannesburg ballroom and now drinks, but still no formal lunch. It would signal a fairytale ending to his career if that lunch were to occur in the presidential palace. But he is up against one of the canniest and most ruthless politicians of our time. The chances of this happening seem as remote as ever – and may never come.

Sports

Akebono Taro

Champion meal for a yokozuna

Taking sumo wrestler Akebono for bongo bongo soup, Hawaiian chicken salad, two plates of lemon butter veal, fried noodles, rice and . . .

By William Dawkins

The trouble with lunching with sumo wrestlers is keeping up. Akebono chose Trader Vic's in the Hotel New Otani, a favourite hang-out of Japan's biggest men. It is also the only place in Tokyo, he said, where he could get something like the home cooking of his birthplace, Hawaii.

I was surprised when he accepted the invitation. After all, Akebono Taro – the name means dawn boy – is a demi-god in Japan. Not only is he the first foreigner to have become a yokozuna, or grand champion, but he is also the tallest and heaviest yokozuna in history, at 6ft 8ins and 473lb. Perhaps it was human appetite – the chance to make a homely change from his usual lunch, sumo wrestlers' stew of meat and vegetables – that tempted?

So it was with awe that I rose to offer my business card to an ample hand extended from the sleeve of a powder-blue kimono. It was the first time during my stay in Japan that I ever had to look up to someone. I duly did, and was surprised again, this time by the calmness of that face, no trace of that murderous determination you see from Akebono in the ring.

The yokozuna settled himself on to a broad stool, more like a cushioned coffee table, reserved by Trader Vic's manager, accustomed to accommodating big men. We were joined by Ushiomaru, a young trainee from Akebono's stable invited along, said the yokozuna, as a reward for good performance in training. Ushiomaru, who looked a bit bruised I thought, just about managed to fit into a chair.

Akebono ordered for them both: alcohol-free pina coladas – no drink during training. They arrived embellished with cherries, slices of fruit, and straws, such thoughtful additions for men with chests so huge that lifting a glass to the mouth can be awkward.

Was he really gentle or fierce?

'I'd say that I'm a gentle person,' he said.

'You don't look so gentle in the ring . . .' I replied naively.

'I try to break my character apart, to be fighter in the ring and a regular person outside,' he explained. The fighter part, while separate from the gentle man, is nevertheless sincere, like two sides of a coin, he added. Sometimes, he said, he really does feel that he wants to kill his opponent. It comes over naturally. 'It's like being in a different zone. If you are on top of the game, you just go into it,' he said.

Then followed a silence while Akebono studied the menu with satisfaction. 'Spare ribs before you get started?' suggested the manager. The yokozuna declined and settled on bongo bongo soup – oysters, cream and garlic – followed by Hawaiian chicken salad. 'I'm on a diet,' he said, laughing at my look of slight disappointment. I ordered the same.

Conversation proved less halting than I had feared. Sumo wrestlers are supposed to be reticent, part of the personal dignity, or *hinkaku*, required to rise to the top. But *hinkaku*, it turns out, does not oblige you to keep your mouth shut.Was he really on a diet? Perhaps he had eaten before he came. Akebono laughed again. 'Just joking . . . when you've reached your top fighting weight, you need to stabilize. When you start as a wrestler you need to eat and sleep a lot to build up your body. We are not all the same.' He gestured at the youngster. When Akebono, now 27, arrived in Japan in 1988 he was a mere 300lb, a fair weight for the basketball player he then was.

Now, he reckons, he does not want to put on much more weight for fear of repeating the knee and shoulder injuries he has suffered recently. So instead of sleeping after a heavy lunch, like younger wrestlers do, he likes to work out in the gym and then curl up with a book, preferably pulp fiction. His current reading, *Waiting to Exhale*, is a tale of the turbulent love lives of four professional black US women.

The bongo bongo soup arrived, in clam shells. A few loud slurps later it was gone. Likewise, the salad. A main course? I tentatively suggested. The waiter, no doubt expecting this, appeared without being called.

The yokozuna thought for a moment. He asked for two plates of lemon butter veal with yakisoba (fried noodles), with rice on the side, plus two more pina coladas for himself and the silent Ushiomaru. At this, the youngster perked up a bit. Sensing a challenge, I asked for the same.

As we waited for the veal, I asked Akebono what had been the hardest part of his lightning elevation to yokozuna. Only eight years ago he was Chad Rowan, with not much to show for himself beyond ball skills, a high school diploma and plans to go into hotel management. His main reason for accepting the invitation to train as a wrestler, from a family friend in the sumo business, was to learn Japanese, indispensable to anyone who wants a future in the Hawaiian hotel trade.

I had expected him to cite language as the highest hurdle. Surprisingly, Akebono replied that learning Japanese, while frustrating, was not the toughest bit. Like all unmarried wrestlers, he lives, sleeps and mostly eats in a stable with Japanese teammates. So there was no choice but to speak Japanese from day one. Now, he even talks Japanese in his sleep, according to dormitory stablemates.

The hardest thing, he said, was learning patience. 'I used to get very frustrated. There is this seniority system. I was 18 when I came to Japan and I had these 15-year-old kids telling me to scrub the toilet and take out the rubbish, just because they had joined the stable before me. I used to get frustrated, because in practice, when they wrestled, they were weak. I had to learn to respect them. It wasn't like that in Hawaii, where the strong one is the top right from the start. I used to be very quick to react to people and things. I had to learn to stop and think, not to react on the spur of the moment . . .'

The only thing that really annoys him these days, he said, is young wrestlers who fail to show respect for elders. Ushiomaru looked impassive.

What, apart from fame and wealth, were the rewards? The nice thing about sumo is that 'you get out of the game what you put into it'. What did you get out of it? I asked. Simply, Akebono said he had grown up. Not all foreign would-be wrestlers understand this, he added, with a touch of sadness.

'Foreigners think we [Japanese-trained wrestlers] are just big bullies. In the stable, you are broken down physically and mentally. But they only do this to new wrestlers because they see a future in you. Then they start again from the beginning to build you back up. Most of us who come here from America think they can change the sport. But it's not like that. You have to change yourself into the sport.'

Their plates were empty again, but not mine. The veal was delicious, but I couldn't even begin the rice. Akebono accepted my bowl, with a nod of his sumo topknot, and passed it to his junior, who dispatched it quickly.

Having assimilated so well, did Akebono consider himself Japanese? In some ways, yes, he said. He became a Japanese citizen six months ago, hopes to marry a Japanese soon and wants to retire in Japan and run a stable in six years. By then he will have been a yokozuna for a decade, a rare accomplishment.

But there are parts of him that will never leave Hawaii. First, his mum. He returns home once a year to keep an eye on his mother and her sumo gift shop – 'golf balls with little sumo faces on top, T-shirts, knick-knacks' – which Akebono set up to keep her occupied after his father died four years ago. She makes a wonderful macadamia nut and toffee pie, he added. By great good fortune, it happened to be the dessert of the day at Trader Vic's. Two helpings each for the wrestlers; just the one for me.

Another part of Akebono that remains distinctively non-Japanese is his fighting style. While most Japanese wrestlers tend to grapple or lift their opponent out of the ring, Akebono charges like a bull to make best use of his superior size and speed.

'Yeah. Push! Push! Push!' he exclaimed, pushing his forearms into the air. The glasses rattled. The trouble is, he added, that his best opponents have got wise to this and just step out of the way when they see the charge coming. 'In that case, I just step back and when they step in again, I hit them. Think basketball . . .'

As the yokozuna stood for the photographer, I paid the bill and watched Akebono trying to quell his natural inclination to laugh and respond to the photographers' request to look fierce. This was going to be difficult. He could only put on his 'ring face' in the ring, he said. So we stopped talking to let Akebono concentrate. The smile gave way to calmness, and then that murderous look, eyes glistening.

I nervously shook hands, wondering whether he would note the sweatiness of my palms. 'You might have made a good wrestler,' he said, as we headed towards the lift. I doubted I could manage the *hinkaku*, at which the yokozuna smiled again. Demonstrating *hinkaku*, he stopped at the pay-desk and offered to pay the bill. When I said I would not dream of it, he bowed and said in Japanese, 'That was a feast.'

On the ground-floor lobby, Akebono headed straight for Louis Vuitton's New Otani branch to pick up a green leather folder, a present to himself, he said. I watched him being driven away, in a Chevrolet Suburban, an electric blue pick-up truck with smoked-glass windows. The muffled boom of rock music could be heard from the Suburban, and the last I saw of the yokozuna were his meaty fingers, tapping out the beat on the bodywork. Think basketball . . .

Imran Khan

'Cricket seems so small and far away'

The US war on terrorism has put a strain on the natural confidence of the Pakistani cricketer-turned-politician

By Edward Luce

I t is not often one gets to meet a childhood hero. But Imran Khan, Pakistan's finest-ever cricketer, and still the heart-throb of a million adolescent girls, is not in the mood for nostalgia. There is a strong atmosphere of foreboding in Islamabad, Pakistan's gleaming modern capital, following the country's decision to back the US in its war on terrorism.

'For the first time in my life, I'm starting to feel rather old,' said Imran. 'I've always been a natural optimist. But the terrorist attacks and America's declaration of war on terrorism both trouble me deeply.'

Dressed elegantly in a white shalwar kameez, the UK-educated leader and founder of the small Justice Movement party looks much younger than his 49 years. But there was also an air of wistfulness about the former Pakistan captain. And it took some effort to coax him off the subject of the US and what everyone in Pakistan assumes to be the impending war in Afghanistan.

We met, appropriately enough, at the Kabul Restaurant, a threadbare Afghan outlet in the centre of Islamabad. Imran's presence did not raise an eyebrow. 'I love Afghani food – the mutton you get here is the most tender in the world,' he said.

Imran ordered for us both: a simple meal of kebabs, stewed spinach, and unleavened Afghan bread. Although he was born in Punjab, Imran's family originally came from the Pathan tribal areas that border and spill over into neighbouring Afghanistan. The hardline Taliban regime of Afghanistan is dominated by Pathans.

Romanticized by Kipling and others as the least repressible people in the British Raj, the 'martial' Pathans of the north-west frontier province have also supplied many of the fast bowlers that have brought Pakistan such success on the cricket field. Imran, of course, is the most celebrated of them all.

Our conversation inevitably turns to General Pervez Musharraf's recent decision to back possible US-led action against Afghanistan. 'Afghanis are our cousins, we share the same blood,' said Imran. 'Any attack that results in the death of innocent Afghani civilians will provoke an enormous backlash in Pakistan. It would be deeply immoral.'

As a graduate of Politics, Philosophy and Economics from Keble College, Oxford, Imran is well placed to observe the miscommunication that often curdles relations between Islamic countries and the west and expresses anxiety that the terrorist attacks on the US could provoke broader conflict between Islam and the west.

At the same time, he is dismissive of the religious hardliners in Pakistan who have come out on the streets to chant 'Death to America' and 'Long live Osama' – in support of Osama bin Laden, prime suspect for the outrages.

'These people are not representative of most Pakistanis,' said Imran. 'But the western media, especially the TV outlets, have been focusing almost exclusively on the Islamic hardliners.

'All it does is reinforce the stereotype of the Muslim as a mad fanatic.'

Although broadly secular in his philosophy, Imran says he has also been the target of western media stereotyping, especially when, in 1995, he announced his engagement to Jemima Goldsmith, daughter of James Goldsmith, the late Anglo-French industrialist and Eurosceptic.

Imran flinches at the memory. 'I could not believe the British press coverage of my engagement to Jemima. They said I was going to lock her up in a room somewhere in Pakistan and never let her out.'

Imran was also vilified by most of Pakistan's Urdu-language newspapers over his bride's Jewish background. 'The coverage over here was equally upsetting. I was accused of being a Zionist and working for the Israelis. The whole episode was very disillusioning.'

Imran eats deftly with his fingers, an elegant contrast to my clumsy efforts with the knife and fork. He sips from a bottle of cola. I ask whether his experiences with the media have made him pessimistic about the possibility of Islam and the west ever peaceably co-existing.

Imran seems troubled. 'What the terrorists did in New York and Washington has nothing to do with Islam,' he said. 'The west doesn't blame Hinduism when the Tamil Tigers launch suicide bombers in Sri Lanka so why are they so quick to blame Islam when there are actions such as this?'

But Imran is also keen to emphasize that the west, especially the US, has done much to create the breeding grounds for people such as bin Laden. 'America's support of what Israel is doing in the occupied territories, and the sanctions on Iraq that are killing thousands of innocent children, give Muslims the impression that America has serious double standards.

'Of course it is vital that the guilty are punished for the terrorist attacks on America but it is also important that America removes some of the deep causes of resentment that many Muslims feel.'

So, tough on terrorism and tough on the causes of terrorism?

Imran agrees emphatically.

We polish off what remains of the mutton and he orders some green Afghan tea with sugar.

What, I asked, had persuaded him to turn to Pakistani politics? It seemed so far removed from the world of cricket and the glamorous life that Imran was reputed to have enjoyed whenever he was outside Pakistan.

Imran says he became interested in politics when the 'deep corruption' of Pakistan's 'ruling mafia families' began to dawn on him in the mid-1980s. At the same time, in 1985, his mother died of cancer. Her death – 'the most life-changing thing that has ever happened to me' – prompted him to re-evaluate his philosophy.

Imran spent much of the next decade raising money for the construction of a specialist cancer hospital in Lahore that is named after his mother. 'When you go out on the streets asking people for money it has a profound effect on your character. It brings you out of yourself,' he said.

'That experience also opened my eyes to the role money plays in Pakistan politics.'

With Imran having been falsely accused of siphoning off donations from the cancer hospital – in spite of the fact that he was the largest donor to the charity – his young party ran on an anti-corruption ticket in the 1997 election. A lack of money meant it failed to get anywhere, he says. Even today, it merits barely any press coverage in Pakistan. 'To get media coverage in Pakistan you need to have a lot of money.'

But Imran's natural optimism – some would say innocence – is irrepressible. Against all the evidence, Imran predicts his party will come to power at the next general election in Pakistan.

'Optimism works,' he said, smiling broadly. 'In my first Test match I thought I was going to get 100 runs and 10 wickets. If I thought I would get nowhere in politics I wouldn't bother.'

It was time for a parting of the ways. At just $5, the bill for lunch seemed unjustly small.

'Leave them a big tip,' Imran advised. As we were getting up, I asked him if he missed the world of cricket and international stardom.

He thought for a moment. 'The world of cricket seems so small and far away,' he said. 'What I am doing now with the cancer hospital and through politics gives me a much, much greater sense of fulfilment.'

David Millar

Back in the saddle

Doping brought the cycling champion to the brink of losing it all. Now he is a 'clean' crusader – but will two bottles of wine over lunch scupper his chances in the Tour de France?

By Tom Robbins

I t is 1.30pm and Scott's of Mayfair, a renowned fish restaurant on one of London's smartest streets, is buzzing. White-aproned French waiters dance between tables at which expensively dressed men and women are toasting their latest successes. At one end of the small room former snooker world champion Ronnie O'Sullivan is entertaining a group of friends; at the next table society designer Nicky Haslam makes a glamorous journalist laugh, and to my right some executives from Louis Vuitton are engaged in deep conversation with a prominent magazine editor. My table, however, is silent.

David Millar is late and, as I sit re-reading the menu and examining the cutlery, I start to worry whether he's coming at all. After all, professional cyclists are not known for their hearty appetites, especially in the run-up to the Tour de France, the biggest race of the year, which starts this weekend. Fans are familiar with whippet-thin figures hunched over their bikes and articles in cycling magazines describe obsessive regimes to reduce body fat, and thus avoid carrying unnecessary weight up the Tour's vicious mountain climbs. But Scott's menu features oysters with wild boar sausages, fresh Devon crabs and lobster thermidor: if Millar does turn up, will he insist on a protein shake and stick of celery?

My fears are unnecessary. When Millar rushes in, 30 minutes late, he

apologizes, blames the traffic, orders a beer and starts discussing the menu. 'I've been looking forward to this all day,' he says, eyes gleaming. 'I love restaurants like this, that classic French service, all so business-like.' I gingerly push the wine list across the table. We are meeting three weeks ahead of the Tour and I can't help feeling that I might be leading him astray. But Millar doesn't demur, and orders a bottle of Viognier Sainte-Fleur 2008.

In fact, being led astray is a large part of what people know about Millar. In 2004, he was reigning world time-trial champion, leader of French team Cofidis, with a string of race wins to his name, a million-euro annual contract and a playboy lifestyle. And then, on a summer's evening in one of Biarritz's best restaurants, a team of policemen burst in, grabbed Millar and bundled him into a police van. After two days in a cell, he confessed: he had repeatedly used performance-enhancing drugs. 'I knew I was going to lose everything – the house, the car, the lifestyle, the job, the respect . . .'

I suggest we leave the drugs until we have ordered – seared scallops with garlic butter for him, smoked salmon for me, followed by cod with Padrón peppers and chorizo for both of us – and ask him what it was that first attracted him to cycling. He says he took up mountain biking in his teens, having gone to live with his airline-pilot father in Hong Kong, but then, aged 15, road cycling began to fire his imagination.

'I started learning about the sport, reading about it, and I was just enchanted,' he says. 'It seemed romantic but also tragic – people would be winning but then lose it all, or crash but fight on, break bones but get back on their bikes and try to finish. Just getting to the end was seen as an achievement in itself. It's somehow old-fashioned, gladiatorial . . .'

Masochistic? 'Absolutely – it's all about suffering. Often the best guys are just those that can suffer longer, who don't give up. And it's so easy to give up, when you're on a mountain and it's really hurting. We go through a lot physically.'

And, so . . . the attraction? 'Well, they say it's like hitting yourself in the head with a hammer – when you stop it feels great.'

He describes a race in Switzerland in which 200 riders started but only 15 finished: 'The course went up a mountain, then down the other side to the finish, and it started raining, then snowing. On the descent it was so cold my fingers couldn't work the brakes and guys were

crashing off at all the corners. When I crossed the line, I was hypother-
mic and started having full body convulsions.' I nod sympathetically, my
mouth full of rich smoked salmon.

Millar, 34, is wearing a charcoal-grey Paul Smith jacket, funky thick-
rimmed glasses, slicked back hair and a deep tan. When he began to
become known in cycling, French newspapers nicknamed him 'le
Dandy' – 'I hated that!' he protests – but he still looks more like someone
who works in graphic design, fashion or film. The tan comes from living
and training in Girona, Spain, but he is in London for the launch of his
autobiography, *Racing Through the Dark*, the pages of which drip with
visceral descriptions of the agonies of cycling.

In it Millar describes how, having decided to give himself two years
to see if he could make it as cyclist, he moved to France – alone, aged
19 and unable to speak French – to join an amateur team. If unsuccess-
ful, he would return to the UK to go to art college, but it soon became
apparent that suffering was something for which Millar had a prodi-
gious talent. His amateur performances were so strong that five
professional teams tried to sign him, he went on to win a string of races,
then in 2000, on the first day of his first Tour de France, he won the
stage and ended up in the leader's yellow jersey. But behind the scenes,
the dream was turning nasty: on the eve of his first pro race, a rider he
was sharing a room with started discussing how the team was asking
him to dope for the race. Shocked, and with no one to turn to for advice,
Millar called his mum back in England.

'It was heartbreaking. This was what I'd always dreamed about and
suddenly my eyes were opened. I made the decision quickly that I
wouldn't dope, that I would stand by my own value system, but you're
in this weird situation because you can't really tell anyone. Who would
I tell – my team boss? They don't care; they know what's going on. The
sport's governing body? They know what's going on. I didn't have any
friends, so I called my mum.'

The fact that cyclists have taken drugs is hardly news – but Millar's
book reveals the jaw-dropping scale of the abuse. On his second race
he noticed that other riders had their own little medical bags with
ampoules and syringes and would keep disappearing off to the bath-
room. Deliveries of ice would turn up at odd hours to protect supplies
of erythropoietin, or EPO, which boosts red blood cells. One rider fell

from his bike, fracturing his wrists, but was using so many drugs that he was able to carry on for another 200km, and finish in the top 10. So was anyone not on drugs? 'There were clean riders but the real question is, "How many clean guys were winning?" And the answer to that is very, very few.'

Amazingly, Millar did manage to win some races and was promoted to team leader, but more often he was congratulated at the finish line for being 'the first clean one back'. 'At first I'd be pleased, take it as a compliment, but then it kept happening. It chips away at you, there's this gradual degradation of your ethical standards. I felt like it was me against everyone else, and eventually I started to question why I was fighting so hard. I thought, "All I am is a professional cyclist – why am I being so stubborn when nobody cares?"'

His fall from grace came, he says, during the 2001 Tour. Injured and exhausted, he had abandoned the race on the mountainous stage to Alpe d'Huez, wracked with guilt about letting down his team. That night an older rider and a manager came to his room and suggested that he might like to 'prepare' properly for the next big event, the codeword for doping. Had they been waiting for his weakest hour?

'Well, I think they had been waiting for the right time but here's the thing: I think they thought they were helping me. In some weird way I think they thought, "Let's start making David's life easier, let's stop him traumatizing himself all the time by trying so hard." I think they wanted to put me out of my misery.'

Our cod arrives – plus Millar's side order of chips and a second bottle of wine – as he tells me about the effects of EPO, taken for a few weeks before competitions, far enough in advance that it isn't detectable during races. In short, the drugs do work – they can 'turn a donkey into a racehorse', as one of his teammates put it – but they also killed any sense of satisfaction. 'My epiphany came in that police cell: I realized I was about to lose everything and it didn't bother me, not in the slightest. I'd come to hate cycling because I blamed it for the lie I was living.'

Banned from professional cycling for two years (criminal charges were eventually dropped) Millar severed ties with the European racing scene, and moved back to England, to a cottage in Derbyshire. On long solo rides through the Peak District, he started to enjoy riding again and, within a year, was plotting his comeback.

Aware that he would always be associated with drug-taking, he realized that he would have to become an anti-doping crusader as well as a rider, proving with his results that it was possible to win clean. Some critics found this conversion rather too convenient, his new-found zeal hypocritical and his excuses self-pitying. After all, he hadn't voluntarily owned up to his misdemeanours but been caught.

To the casual observer, fighting drug abuse in cycling might seem a lost cause. This year's Tour starts amid yet more scandals. Lance Armstrong, a seven-time Tour winner and still the world's most famous cyclist, is facing a doping investigation by the US Food and Drug Administration, and has been denounced by several former teammates. Meanwhile Alberto Contador, winner of last year's Tour and favourite for this year's, is the subject of a legal battle over a positive drug test.

Perhaps it's inevitable in a sport that demands such super-human efforts that there will always be temptation. Speaking of which, would he like a pudding? Some dessert wine? Yes and yes – gooseberry crème brûlée and a glass of Sauternes for him, Eton Mess and Muscat for me. The car arrives to pick him up – it is 3.30pm – but he shoos it away, saying we need more time.

So is there any hope? What Millar says next is perhaps the most shocking thing about the entire story: 'Today ours is the cleanest of all the endurance sports.' I almost choke on my meringue. Really? 'You can go into the sport now as a young rider and never encounter doping, never see a syringe . . . Of course we still have the anomalous cheaters you get in any walk of life but they are a minority – for a long time they were the majority.'

How has this come about? Is it the result of technological advances in testing or various campaigns by the World Anti-Doping Agency, on whose committee Millar sits? 'To be brutally honest, it's simple economics. If they want to come into cycling, sponsors need to know the team they are funding is clean, otherwise the risk is just too great.' For years, sponsors would come in for a few years, get burnt by a scandal and pull out. Today, at least three teams – Garmin-Slipstream (which Millar played a key role in setting up), Sky and HTC-Highroad – make being clean a key part of their image. They ensure their riders deliver on that promise by constant blood-profiling and by providing support for young riders.

And so to the big question: is it now possible to win the Tour de

France clean? 'Yes, I think it is, but that's a very recent development.' How recent exactly? Even after a two-hour, two-bottle lunch, Millar spots the bear-trap. 'Well, I wouldn't like to put an exact year on it . . .' he says, smiling.

Scott's
20 Mount Street,
Mayfair, London W1

....

2 x sparkling water	£9
Pilsner beer	£4.75
2 x bottle of Viognier Sainte-Fleur 2008	£98
seared scallops	£16.50
smoked salmon	£14.25
2 x fillet of cod	£43.50
chips	£4
green beans with shallots	£4.75
raspberry Eton Mess	£8.50
gooseberry crème brûlée	£7.50
Beaumes de Venise 2007	£9.25
Château Partarrieu 2007	£12
2 x espresso	£6
2 x covers	£4

....

Total (incl. service)	£272.25

::

Does he regret, I wonder, not being born a few years later, into a clean sport and now that, instead of having to move to France and fend for themselves, young British riders have perhaps the world's best national development programme? 'In some ways I would love nothing more than to be 18 now, going straight into the British Olympic programme, winning medals on the track, then moving on to the road. But [then] I'd have been just another pro-athlete – well-off, successful, fêted and egotistical . . . Having lost it all, I understand how fortunate I am.'

In the five years since his comeback Millar has won stages of the Vuelta and the Giro (Spain and Italy's equivalent of the Tour), and become the only Briton to wear the leader's jersey in all three. But perhaps a greater achievement is that rather than being shunned for breaking the previous generation's *omertà* on drug use, he has emerged as an unofficial spokesman for the professional *peloton*, the eloquent voice of experience. When Belgian rider Wouter Weylandt died in a high-speed fall in this year's Giro, it was to Millar that the *peloton* turned, and he later met race organizers to discuss safety. 'Obviously, the circumstances were horrible, but it was one of the proudest moments of my career.'

The car is back, and this time Millar has to go. We say our goodbyes and, as I sit in the now empty restaurant, I think how differently it could have turned out. Floyd Landis, stripped of his 2006 Tour win after testing positive, protested his innocence for four years and has ended up discredited. Star cyclists Marco Pantani and Frank Vandenbroucke moved on from performance-enhancing drugs to recreational ones and both were dead before the age of 35.

It could have gone that way for Millar too but instead he will be starting the Tour as a pivotal figure in the sport, and even stands a chance of taking the yellow jersey after the time trial on day two. Then the rather long bill arrives. I just hope our lunch hasn't scuppered his chances.

Thinkers

Jacques Attali

Attali and the global labyrinth

Over oysters and sea bass, the *FT* learns about one of Europe's most controversial public figures, the former president of the European Bank for Reconstruction and Development

By Lucy Kellaway

> Dear Mr Attali, I would quite understand if you had no wish to have lunch with the *Financial Times*. However, I should assure you that readers of the *FT Weekend* are intelligent people who are interested in articles about intellectuals . . .

I t was a nice try, but I was barely expecting a response let alone an acceptance from Jacques Attali. After all, it was this paper's unflattering coverage of his private jets and the quantity of Venetian marble in the headquarters of the European Bank for Reconstruction and Development that cost him his job as president of that bank three years ago.

Yet barely had I sent the letter than I received a fax saying that Attali would be willing to have lunch, so long as I came to Paris. London, he explained, was not his favourite place.

It was a beautiful autumn day as I strolled along the Champs-Elysées on my way to Chez Edgar. Inside, the restaurant was dark red; traditional. In halting French I told the fat madame at the door that a table was booked for two in the name of Attali. 'Jacques Attali?' she said, her face expressing admiration, awe.

A little late, Attali hurried in, hair swept back, looking pleasantly scruffy, a sprinkling of dandruff on the shoulder. 'Champagne?' he asked. That would be lovely, I replied.

Attali surveyed the busy surroundings and greeted a couple of friends. 'Actually I am, in a certain sense, the origin of the success of this place,' he said, his accent heavy and his diction idiosyncratic.

'I'm sure you remember the *Rainbow Warrior* saga,' he continued. 'The minister of defence was a very close friend of mine – he had to quit. I was not happy about it. I wanted to say we are still very good friends.' So Attali, who was then adviser to President Mitterrand, phoned Chez Edgar, a well-known haunt of journalists. He told the patron that the two of them wished to be seen eating lunch there that day. Thus, a tradition was born.

'This is not the best cooking in Paris, but it is not very expensive. If I had invited you I would have taken you somewhere else, but this time you are inviting me.' He picked up the menu and turned past the *prix fixe* to the à la carte, and chose oysters and sea bass. Our orders were taken by *le patron* himself, who greeted Attali like a long-lost friend, and shook my hand with considerable enthusiasm. 'You like fish?' he asked and suggested that I too had the sea bass. Noticing that it was FFr190 (£25), and being a cheapskate, I said I'd have the tuna, which was only FFr115.

'What is your competence, if I might say so?' asked Attali once the orders had been given. Somewhat at a loss, I described my job on the *FT*. In return, I asked him about his brand-new book, an abstract volume called *Chemins de Sagesse*, Paths of Wisdom.

'The book is about labyrinths globally,' he explained. 'In the 18th, 19th and 20th centuries ideologies ran along straight lines, but now we are back to a time where the labyrinth is the way of organizing nature, literature, management, decision making, organizations, biology.'

Are you saying that things are more complicated now? I asked, struggling to understand. He gave a Gallic shrug. 'You can say that. But labyrinth is much more than complexity. It is a metaphor of human creation. The qualities which are needed to go through the labyrinth are the qualities needed for the 21st century. These are: 1. When you are alone you are not lost. 2. A failure is not a failure but a success. 3. Memory. 4. Minutiae. 5. Intuition. 6. Dancing.'

Not knowing how to reply to this bizarre list, I asked whether he himself possessed these qualities. 'I didn't even think about it. It's not about self!' He seemed exasperated at the question.

How are sales going? I asked, in an attempt to shift the conversation to more solid ground. He said the book had sold 50,000 in the first 10 days, which is par for the course. Many of his 25 books, he informed me, have sold more than 100,000 copies.

People like Jacques Attali do not exist in England. The English do not believe it is possible for someone to be a world authority on any subject they turn their hand to, and distrust anyone who tries. But in France they also seem to have doubts: Attali has become almost as famous for allegations of plagiarism as for the books themselves. I watched him suck an oyster off its shell, and ask if he had developed a thick skin.

'One of my weaknesses is that when I read something I think, "How can they say that?" And then afterwards I say, "Maybe they are right."'

Unable to resist, I asked if he now thinks they were right about the EBRD marble.

'Of course not!' he replied.

Would the same thing have happened in France?

'Certainly not!'

He has rationalized that unhappy chapter in his life by putting it down to macroeconomics. 'I can explain it to you. The reason is the elite is supposed to change when there is not full employment. The judges in the media play the same role as the guillotine played in the French revolution. But the guillotine was irreversible.' He gave a broad smile, pleased with his joke.

So is it a huge relief to be a writer, and no longer a manager?

'Writing books is a very small part of my activities,' he corrected me. 'I do not know how many other things I do. I cannot count them all. What I like is to create things, I create books. I launch projects. When I was with Mitterrand I launched lots of things. I launched Bangladesh. I launched La Grande Bibliothèque in Paris, which is my child.'

I had lost him.

'I am not relieved to have left the European Bank,' he went on. 'I am happy to have created it. It is the difference between designing a plane and being a pilot on a commercial airline. I happened to be – unwillingly – a trial pilot. But if I was doing it again, I would do it exactly the same.'

Our main courses arrived. I had been given sea bass, whether I liked it or not. I did not dare complain: in any case the fish was delicious.

Writing may only be a small part of the whole, but no fewer than three projects are reaching completion. 'I have just finished a play. I'm very excited about it. My next book is a novel that is almost finished. I am working on a book about futurology – the world in 50 years. And – er – that's it. For the moment.' He paused and added, 'Plus, of course, some screenplays.'

A waitress asked if we would like pudding.

'I should not because I have to lose weight,' he said and went on to order a glace noisette, one of the most fattening dishes on the menu.

While I dithered, he leaned across the table.

'Sorry, you have something in your hair.' With charm he executed the potentially embarrassing task of removing a twig from my fringe.

'I am teaching futurology at the University of Paris,' he continued, 'and writing. I am involved in French politics, advising governments in East Europe, Latin America, Africa. I am also advising companies on international strategy, mergers and acquisitions . . .'

I protested that all that is too much for one man; he attributes such disbelief to envy: 'People are not happy to see someone who has two or three lives.' And has he become good at dealing with so much envy? 'Yes. Bof!' he pouted. 'Of course. When people realize next year that there is going to be a play . . .' he paused, anticipating the reaction.

'I will be thrilled when I see it. One of my best feelings as a creator was being backstage when a very famous French singer was singing a song I had written for her.'

Songs too! It turned out that Schumann had written the music, he only did the words.

Could he do the music too?

'Bof!' he said again. 'I haven't tried.'

He is able to do so much because he sleeps three hours a night. 'Yesterday I worked till 2am – I got up at six to write and had a meeting on genetics at nine.' He gave another broad grin, as if disarmed by his own energy.

During the lunch, he revealed little love of Britain or things British – they do not like ideas; they think 'dream' is a dirty word; our journalists lie – but would not be drawn into being openly disparaging.

'I like London. I like the music. I wouldn't say anything else, but music.' His social life apparently left something to be desired when he was there.

He then expounded a theory about London being uncivilized because it lies on only one bank of the river. I demurred, but he took no notice. 'It is a fact,' he said.

I collected the bill and we prepared to leave.

Outside, his chauffeur was waiting to drive us a few hundred yards back to Attali's office so that he could give me a sample of his recent books, including a promising-looking children's story. As we parted, a look of unease crossed his face. 'This is not another *FT* trick?' he asked. 'No,' I assured him. 'It is not.'

Václav Havel

The playwright who became president

Too well known in Prague to eat out, the Czech intellectual invites the *FT* to his office to discuss globalization, rampant consumerism and his almost constant craving for cigarettes

By Stefan Wagstyl

Always a shy man, Václav Havel shuffles into view as if, even in his own office, he feels uncertain of his surroundings. Years of fame as a dissident writer, anti-communist revolutionary and president of both Czechoslovakia and the Czech Republic do not seem to have robbed the 71-year-old philosopher-king of his natural diffidence.

His welcome is warm but a little hesitant. His handshake is restrained. His voice, gravelled by decades of smoking that ended in lung cancer, is so gentle that it is hard to imagine him delivering the hundreds of speeches that he has made.

And yet the moment the conversation begins he comes alive. It is as if the mind inside this frail body has energy far bigger than the frame in which it is confined. He listens intently, pauses before speaking and shapes his answers with deliberate care – plus occasional flashes of the wit that brought him early acclaim as a playwright.

We sit down at a stylish cherry-red table in a space carved out of a period building in Prague's historic centre. It is a self-consciously modern office with glass bookshelves and walls hung with contemporary art. Havel wears jeans and an open-necked blue shirt. Around him are scores of books in Czech, German and English.

Coffee is served – a mug for Havel and a delicate china cup for me – and a plate of chocolate biscuits that go untouched. I had asked to meet in a restaurant for lunch, but was told this would be difficult because Havel is so well known that we would be constantly interrupted.

I quiz Havel about his pictures. He says they are largely gifts he received as president and points to a colourful Buddhist tapestry. 'There are small things here. But what is important is this carpet. It is a gift from the Dalai Lama, and only seven people all around the world have this kind of carpet,' says Havel.

For many other public figures this would be a boast. But for Havel it is a statement of the obvious: his time as president transformed his life into what he calls 'a fairytale' in which extraordinary events such as meetings with the Dalai Lama, not to mention Pope John Paul II, the Clintons and Robert Redford, became ordinary.

This year Havel published an English edition of his recollections of his presidency, entitled *To the Castle and Back*. It is not so much a memoir as a series of commentaries, interspersed with contemporaneous office notes and entries from a diary he kept in 2005 while working on the book. President Havel worries about everything from the future of the planet to the half-cooked potatoes served to the visiting Emperor of Japan and the bat that has taken up residence in his summer house. 'In the closet where the vacuum cleaner is kept there also lives a bat. How to get rid of it? The light bulb has been unscrewed so as not to wake it up and upset it.'

As he leaves the castle for the last time, he wonders about what happens to an ex-president in a country with little experience of ex-presidents. He writes: 'I have to smile to myself when I realize that people don't know how to address me. Some say "Mr President", others say "Mr former President", some say "Mr Havel" and it's only a matter of time before someone addresses me as "Mr former Havel".'

He also worries about the failure of ex-communist states to complete the revolutions of 1989 by reforming what he calls post-communism – the domination of former communists in positions of economic power. I ask him how the reform of post-communism is progressing. He says the fight is still on, with victories in popular revolts in Ukraine and Georgia and more sedate gains in central Europe. 'As the young generation grows up, society needs to rid itself of the power of the people deformed by communism, people who had succeeded in quickly establishing themselves in the new regimes and in occupying various powerful positions.'

Havel is, however, disappointed that ex-communist societies have followed the west in embracing globalization and rampant consumerism. At our meeting he makes clear that there is little that can be done about this in free societies. 'But I feel there is no reason why we shouldn't reflect upon this trend. It is a two-faced trend: on the one hand it brings people thousands of advantages and joys and pleasures; on the other, it is endangering the human race.'

I wonder whether there isn't some intellectual snobbery hiding behind this anti-consumerism and put it to him that if people wished to use their freedom to go to McDonald's, why shouldn't they? He responds, 'I don't want to prevent anyone from being able to do that. What I want to say is something different . . . I get the sense that we are the first civilization in the history of mankind that is completely atheist. Human existence now isn't metaphysically anchored in any way in a code of moral conduct, from which we could then derive a legal code.

'That doesn't mean I don't enjoy the delicacies I can buy at the local supermarket . . . What I'm talking about is the underlying atheism and anti-spirituality of our civilization. We don't know where it's going to go from here and what it will bring for the human race.'

Pointing to a mobile phone, he says, 'Fifty years ago, I wouldn't have imagined this little device could be used to make calls all over the world, to make video recordings and to send images. If someone had told me about this then, I would have thought the future world would be a wonderful one when people would have these things and would be able to communicate better. But that didn't happen. The world today is worse, and it is full of more traps and contradictions than it was 50 years ago.'

I am shocked to hear him go this far. Surely, at least in ex-communist central Europe, the world is incomparably better than it was 50 years ago? Havel answers patiently: 'Yes, of course it is a good thing that the Iron Curtain fell and that communism ended, but that still doesn't mean that the world is a better place. The big differences between the developed world and the developing world are deeper than ever. The unifying forces of globalization incite various forms of chauvinism or nationalism. Terrorists almost have the capacity to fire nuclear missiles. The world is full of various dangers, including ecological ones in the form of climate change, and so on.'

He continues: 'I'd say that it is a good thing that the world is no longer divided in two, but new superpowers are emerging, and who knows what this will bring? China today is more powerful than Russia. Russia is witnessing the rise of a strange, special sort of dictatorship with strong imperialist demands, albeit dressed more elegantly than before.'

I ask Havel why, in his book, he is so rude about his fellow Czechs. He writes of the 'bitter provincialism' of the 'little Czechs'. Elsewhere he writes: 'What they [Czechs] consider ideal is the capacity to enjoy various blessings – as far as possible with no struggle, no work and no cost.'

Although Havel does not say so, a prime exponent of 'little Czech' politics is the Eurosceptic Václav Klaus, his rival and successor as Czech president. Havel describes in his book how the Thatcherite Klaus made an uneasy political companion for Havel and other mainstream liberals who led 1989's 'Velvet Revolution'. When Havel became president and Klaus prime minister, Klaus's well-known arrogance caused repeated conflicts even over the most trivial incidents, such as Havel's decision to express officially his regrets at the death of Frank Zappa. Havel writes that Klaus would have been 'happiest if I had submitted everything to him in advance for approval'.

Despite these barbs, many Czechs are disappointed the book does not say more about the Havel–Klaus relationship. Havel says, 'I am very much opposed to reducing the last 20 years of our history to personal tiffs between myself and Václav Klaus. And I don't like it when people get the impression that I did nothing but fight with him. I don't like that, and it doesn't reflect reality.'

Havel denies that *Leaving*, the first play he has written since the end of communism, has anything to do with Klaus, even though many Czechs think it has. The work concerns a leader who has lost power but is reluctant to admit it and refuses to surrender his official residence to a successor named Vlastik Klein. Havel insists he conceived the idea in 1988, before the Velvet Revolution.

I ask Havel about his controversial second wife, the actress Dagmar Veškrnová. Many Czechs were upset when Havel married Ms Veškrnová, his long-standing girlfriend, in 1997 in what they saw as indecent haste within months of the death of his first wife, the widely admired Olga

Havlová. I suggest that having become a moral authority far beyond his country's borders, he might have behaved with greater care. He shoots back, 'Yes, but even a moral authority has the right to marry a second wife when his first wife dies, no? It was about something else . . . These campaigns [against Dagmar] had a strange element of jealousy, as though the public felt abandoned or betrayed when I remarried, as if society were an abandoned lover. It's an interesting phenomenon.'

We turn to Europe. Havel, a passionate pro-European, is keen that the European Union's constitutional treaty should be kept alive despite its rejection in the recent Irish referendum. He is convinced the EU will muddle through, and, ignoring President Klaus's misgivings, says the Czech Republic should press on with ratification. Only then, he believes, should the EU consider a simpler treaty: 'It would be best now to quietly select some three or four people who could create a beautiful, simple constitution that children could learn about at school.'

His book has more to say about the US than Europe, and I ask Havel about his admiration for America. He says, 'The US, and especially New York, is a sort of a bazaar of the entire world. Everything is there, mixed together. It's a view upon the entire world, isn't it? I find that atmosphere appealing. It's a truly free country.'

Václav Havel's office
Prague

....

2 x coffee
1 x water

I ask him whether his fascination with the US is compatible with his concerns about consumerism and globalization, in which American companies are prominent. He insists there is no contradiction: 'Global corporations are by definition global, so it is not just a US invention or a US job, even though obviously the US plays a bigger role in this than the Czech Republic, for instance,' he says. 'It is a phenomenon of our civilization. I don't think it's good to associate it solely with America or even with America as a country that invented this.'

A last question. Has he, I ask, since he is photographed on the cover of his book with a cigarette in hand, stuck to his promise to stop smoking? 'I haven't smoked in 12 years,' he says, 'but about 40 times a day I feel like having a cigarette.'

Paul Krugman

'We ought to apologize to the emperor'

The Nobel Prize-winning professor of economics and controversial newspaper columnist writes fast but eats slowly. Over salade niçoise he discusses what Japan got right, what the Federal Reserve got wrong and how the eurozone can be saved

By Martin Wolf

I enter the Landmarc restaurant, at the Time Warner Center on Columbus Circle, New York, where I have agreed to meet for lunch with Paul Krugman, the 2008 Nobel laureate in economics, Princeton professor of economics and international affairs, and liberal columnist of the *New York Times*. I know nothing about this bistro-style restaurant, which my guest has chosen for its convenience to a television interview he has just completed. The restaurant is impersonal and – it's a late lunch, at two o'clock – beginning to empty.

Krugman, 59, most hated and most admired columnist in the US, rumpled and professorial, is sitting at a small table in the middle of the restaurant, working on his laptop. It is Thursday and he is writing his column. What, I ask, is it on? 'It's going to be Europe,' he replies. 'Partly because it is coming to a head, partly because I am a little overstretched and that's what I'm ready for. So I'm going to do that one.' I understand the feeling of being overstretched: Krugman is writing two columns a week, posting regularly on his blog, writing popular books and teaching.

So, I ask, will the argument of the column be that 'it's all over' for the eurozone?

'No. I don't think they can save Greece but they can still save the rest if they're willing to offer open-ended financing and macroeconomic expansion.' But this would mean persuading the Germans to change their philosophy of economic life. 'Well, the prospect of hanging concentrates the mind; the prospect of a collapse of the euro might concentrate their minds.'

I change the subject to ask how he has coped with the shift from being predominantly an academic economist to being the leading spokesman for the liberal cause. How did this happen? 'Well, it was funny,' he responds. 'I was doing a column for *Slate* and then a bit for *Fortune*, towards the end, and then the [*New York*] *Times* came along with this offer. It was 1999. We thought I'd be writing about the follies of dotcoms and stuff like that and then it turns out that it's a much more awesome and ominous responsibility. It was nothing I ever planned.

'Really, the rough period was the first [George W.] Bush term when it seemed like the whole world was mad, save me, or vice versa, and it's gotten easier.

'I have to say, though, that the economic crisis has played into the things that I was worrying about 15 years ago. It's been almost alarmingly easy to figure out what to say. But it's a very strange thing: it's not at all what I was imagining I was going to be doing with my life.'

We have already gone straight into the issues. The conversation turns to the Japanese crisis of the 1990s. In retrospect, I suggest, the Japanese seem to have managed the aftermath of their crisis quite well.

He agrees. 'What we thought was that Japan was a cautionary tale. It has turned into Japan as almost a role model. They never had as big a slump as we have had. They managed to have growing per capita income through most of what we call their "lost decade". My running joke is that the group of us who were worried about Japan a dozen years ago ought to go to Tokyo and apologize to the emperor. We've done worse than they ever did. When people ask, "Might we become Japan?" I say, "I wish we could become Japan."'

At this point we order: salade niçoise for Krugman; foie gras terrine for me; and a bottle of sparkling water. This is definitely not going to be up to the gourmet standards of some lunches with the *FT*.

I return to our discussion. I ask whether he is not being unfair to Ben Bernanke, chairman of the Federal Reserve and a former colleague at Princeton. After all, Bernanke has avoided deflation in the US. Krugman responds swiftly: 'We don't care about deflation because having a small minus, instead of a small plus, makes a huge difference to the world. We worry about deflation because we think it is a reason why one has a persistently depressed economy. While we may not have deflation, we have a persistently depressed economy. So what difference does it make?'

But surely, I argue, the Fed did deliver negative real interest rates by cutting rates quickly and avoiding deflation. This prods Krugman into rare praise: 'I have actually very few complaints about monetary policy here through some point in 2009. I thought that Ben [Bernanke] responded aggressively and forcefully, which was the right thing to do. He stepped in with the original QE [quantitative easing] and stabilized the economy.

'The question is, what did he do as we started to look more and more like Japan? At that point the logic says you have to find a way to get some traction. Fiscal policy might be great. But if you're not getting it you should be doing something on the Fed side and I think that logic becomes stronger and stronger as the years go by. And it's sad to see that the Fed has largely washed its hands of responsibility for getting us out of the slump.

'I hope that some day Ben Bernanke and Janet Yellen [vice-chair of the Fed] will think that I've done them a favour. There's all this sniping from the hard money guys and somebody needs to say, "Actually, no, if we actually think about this realistically, you're doing too little and not too much."'

So what, I wonder, would he do if he were put in charge? He says he would add maybe another $2tn to the Fed's balance sheet, by purchasing a wider range of assets, including more private sector liabilities. 'But mostly,' he continues, 'you work on the expectations side. I think mostly what you really need to do is to signal that you're going to keep your foot on the gas pedal.'

It does not even matter, he believes, if people are not sure the Fed will carry through. They just have to believe it might happen. 'So if Ben Bernanke made a statement, or the board made a statement, saying that we are reconsidering our views about the inflation target, even if we don't have a credible commitment that they're going to deliver 3.7 per cent annual inflation over five years, that's still a help.'

In his new book, *End This Depression Now!*, Krugman dismisses contemporary macroeconomic theory. He is also critical of the idea that policy credibility matters. On this he says, 'Credibility sounds great, but the evidence that anti-inflationary credibility is actually an important thing in the real world is basically nil.'

We return, inevitably, to the topic of the day. Would he conclude that the European currency union was a mistake? 'Yes, I think we've been asking, whose fault is this crisis? And I think it was basically fated, from the day the Maastricht Treaty was signed. Now, I think it might be rescuable with a higher inflation target, which is a poor second best to having a fiscal union. But no, the setup is fundamentally not workable.

'What's interesting is that the euro itself created the asymmetric shocks that are now destroying it [via the capital flows it engendered]. Not only have they created something incapable of dealing with shocks but the creation engendered the shocks that are destroying it.'

By this stage, I have long since finished my terrine. I always eat quickly. But Krugman is eating his salad very slowly, as he talks. He has to wave away waiters several times. The restaurant is now quite empty. When the meal is finally cleared, I order a double espresso, while he orders a regular filter coffee.

We discuss briefly the future of macroeconomics: his hopes rest on younger economists doing empirical work. 'There are young people doing some really excellent research. Most of it, there are a few exceptions, but what's really driving the cutting edge is empirical work.' Krugman points out that the prestigious Bates Clark medal, awarded to economists under 40 (he won it in 1991), 'has been going overwhelmingly to people doing very empirical stuff. And I think that's the salvation of economics in the long run, if there is a long run, because things are going so badly.'

We turn to his view of US politics. How does he explain what is going on?

He responds that 'a couple of things do seem to operate here. One is money. There are think-tanks which don't actually do a whole lot of thinking but which are lavishly financed . . . You can have a lot of fun if you go back and look at what they were saying, and it's hilarious, about Iceland as a role model, or the wonders of the Irish system.

'And then there is something about the appeal of this hard-money, gold-standard thing and it's always had an appeal, but it seems even stronger now. I would have thought that the fact that people like me have been so much closer to [being] right on inflation and interest rates would move a substantial number of people into thinking that maybe their preconceptions were not right.' But no.

I ask whether he is disheartened by the failure of people on his side of the political argument to stand up for what they believe in. After all, I note, you must be disappointed by the willingness to accept the need to slash entitlement spending – rather than to raise taxes – when the federal tax ratio is exceptionally low and there have been extraordinary shifts in the distribution of income. Does Krugman think that's all about money?

'These things are always complicated but some of it is about money. Look, with even a few mild words of reproof, Obama has lost a huge funding source from Wall Street. And you have got to give the right credit: they play a long game. They've spent 40 and more years working on "government is bad" or "taxes are bad".'

But, he continues, 'there is an organized progressive infrastructure now in the way that there was not. It's tiny and ill-funded, compared with the other side, but it's actually also smarter than the other side. I certainly feel personally that, although I'm not getting the policies I wanted, I am getting listened to in a way that was not true even two years ago.'

So how does Krugman cope with the hatred he attracts? '2002 to 2004 were by far the worst, and that was mostly not about economics, that was about the fact that I was pretty much alone in saying we'd been lied into [going to] war. But you do need to develop a thick skin. I've partly developed the attitude that if I don't get a whole lot of hysterical pushback then I probably have wasted the space in the column.

'I've been in this a long time and it was really shocking in the beginning. But eventually you get acclimated. I think it scares a lot of people off. I think a lot of journalists, the first time they publish something even mildly critical of right-wing orthodoxy, they hit this firestorm and they never come back. They run scared ever after. But I'm long past that point.'

I ask him about his punchy and provocative style. How conscious is it? 'I had already done some of it in *Slate* so I had learnt some of it, but this [writing for the *NYT*] is even tighter. There is a craftsmanship of making it work so that somebody, whose ordinary instinct is to think, "Oh, economics, boring," will actually read through your piece.'

What fascinates me, I say, is how he manages the output, particularly the quantity of blogging he is doing. Obviously Krugman is quicker than most people but how does he get time for anything else?

'I am still teaching. I probably work 70 hours a week but not 100 hours a week. But I am damned fast. I write faster than just about anybody in journalism, it turns out, which is interesting.'

Krugman is famous for resisting structural explanations for the high levels of unemployment. But what does he think of the view that our economies are dangerously addicted to financial and asset price 'bubbles'? He replies by asking whether I have ever seen the satirical publication *The Onion*. 'Quite early on they had the perfect headline, which was, "Recession Ravaged Nation Demands New Bubble to Invest In".'

So how's his new book doing? 'It's good. It's funny. We're on the bestseller list in the US. But it's selling like hotcakes in Europe. We're in fourth printing in Spain and they're about to put ads on the sides of Madrid buses, apparently.'

This brings us back to the eurozone crisis. I remark that the Germans are now in a position of having to choose between permanently bailing out those they regard as deadbeats or breaking it up, causing an immense economic and political mess. I feel quite sorry for them.

Landmarc	
Time Warner Center, 10 Columbus Circle, New York 10019	
salade niçoise	$22
foie gras terrine	$17
sparkling water	$7
double espresso	$5
coffee	$4
Total (incl. tax and service)	$71.88

He responds, 'I remember there was a humorous column in the *Independent* which would have been in about 1992 or thereabouts, about the decision to give the Booker Prize to the Maastricht Treaty – a postmodern novel in strict treaty form. And throughout the novel one senses, in the background, powerful forces with unknown motives. Who are these forces, what do they want? We never learn.

'It was a wonderful satire.'

Coffees are finished. We walk out from an empty restaurant, Krugman to return to Princeton and his column, I to return to the New York offices of the *Financial Times*. The crises go on. He is the pundit conservatives detest and liberals cheer. In the US anybody can become anything. A Nobel Prize-winning economic theorist can even become the country's most controversial columnist.

Nouriel Roubini

'You must come to Cannes too!'

When the economist foretold the credit crunch, nobody believed him. Since then, 'Dr Doom' has been hailed as a prophet and become an intellectual pin-up with roles in two Hollywood films

By Gillian Tett

I t is not yet eight o'clock in the morning but already the ultra-trendy Soho Grand Hotel in Tribeca, New York, feels like a film set. The cavernous hall is dominated by concrete pillars, metal sculptures and vast leather sofas, on which a collection of unfeasibly beautiful, elegant people are draped.

It seems an odd place to meet an academic economist for breakfast. But then Nouriel Roubini is not your average egghead. Granted, until the financial crisis started three years ago, he had spent most of his career analysing economics and writing books with titles such as *Political Cycles and the Macroeconomy* (1997) or *New International Financial Architecture* (co-editor, 2005). He was also responsible for delivering a series of speeches on the fragility of the banking world so dour that they earned him the monicker 'Dr Doom'.

But in 2007, all this changed unexpectedly. The financial crisis exploded and, almost overnight it seemed, the world realized that Roubini was one of the few economists who had actually predicted the looming banking collapse. Today policy-makers around the world hang on his words, journalists flock to his speeches to hear his latest

predictions and clients pay big money to receive analysis from his consultancy company, Roubini Global Economics.

His influence has stretched beyond the business world and even into Hollywood: he appears briefly, as himself, in *Wall Street: Money Never Sleeps*, Oliver Stone's forthcoming sequel to his 1980s parable of markets gone mad, as well as *Inside Job*, a forthcoming documentary narrated by Matt Damon. He is even something of an intellectual pin-up: his Facebook page is adorned with numerous photos of Roubini attending star-studded parties, usually with a bevy of beautiful women. ('They love my beautiful mind . . . I am ugly but they are attracted to the brains,' he told a gossip columnist last year.)

A few minutes before eight, the 51-year-old nerd-turned-heart-throb materializes in the lobby, wearing black jeans and an open-necked pale yellow shirt. It blends in perfectly with the hotel decor. The only discordant note is struck by his brown leather shoes, which are shockingly, defiantly battered. Is he too cerebral to worry about trifles like shoe polish? Or simply too self-confident to care? Either way, it gives this famous economist an oddly arty air.

He drapes himself gawkily over a vast leather sofa, and explains that the trendy location could be his local. 'I only live five minutes away,' he shrugs, looking at me warily with spaniel-like, dark-brown eyes. A breakfast menu appears, offering minimalist, fashionable dishes. I select egg-white frittata, espresso and a protein power shake; Roubini orders granola, juice, yoghurt and a latte, though he seems totally uninterested in the food.

'So what is it like being a celebrity?' I ask, wondering if he feels smug. He pulls a face. 'Celebrity is just noise,' he mutters. 'People are talking as if I have come from nowhere, as if I was in a little office somewhere, by myself all those years, totally obscure but then suddenly became famous. But that is not true at all – I have been an economist for 20 years!'

Indignantly, he runs through the details of his career. It is unusual. Born in Istanbul in 1959 to Iranian Jewish parents, he spent his early years in Iran, before moving to Italy, where he attended school and university. He subsequently moved to the US and Harvard, where he did a PhD in economics, then taught at Yale and in New York. Roubini, who speaks Italian, Hebrew and Farsi, says he finally felt he had arrived in the US 'about 15 years ago, when I started dreaming in English'. During this period he also did stints at the International Monetary Fund, Federal Reserve, World Bank, the US White House Council of Economic Advisers and the Treasury department, before setting up his own consultancy firm.

Hardly the CV of a nobody, it's true. But Roubini was still far from being a household name when, in the autumn of 2006, with the world economy and credit markets booming, he gave a big speech to the IMF warning that the 'United States was likely to face a once-in-a-lifetime housing bust, an oil shock, sharply declining consumer confidence and ultimately a deep recession', along with 'homeowners defaulting on mortgages, trillions of dollars of mortgage-backed securities unravelling worldwide and the global financial system shuddering to a halt'. It was a bold call; so much so that many policy-makers and economists thought Roubini was slightly mad.

Indeed, when Roubini attended the World Economic Forum meeting in Davos in January 2007 to make similar prophecies, his warnings were widely dismissed. It was at this rarefied Swiss mountain resort that I first encountered him and I remember it very well. In the preceding months I had also started to write about the dangers of complex finance (albeit far less eloquently and dramatically than Roubini) and those pieces sparked criticism from some of the luminaries assembled at Davos, who accused me of being 'alarmist'. Though we had never met before – and have barely talked since – at one sun-dappled lunch in a stuffy Swiss hotel Roubini forcefully defended my articles. I tell him I was grateful; vocal Cassandras were very thin on the ground back then.

'I remember that,' Roubini laughs. He then recalls, with irritation, a column written by Michael Lewis, author of the acclaimed Wall Street study *Liar's Poker* (1989) as well as the recently published study *The Big Short* (2009), during that Davos meeting, which labelled Cassandras such as Roubini as 'wimps' and 'ninnies'. 'It is amazing how some people have changed their views,' he says, adding acerbically that 'there is a lot of Monday morning quarterbacking' now.

Why did the banking world spin out of control in 2007? Roubini has co-authored with Stephen Mihm, a professor of economic history, a book about the banking collapse, *Crisis Economics*, which seeks to answer this question and suggest what can be done to put it right. At first glance it covers similar ground to all the other 'crunch lit' books now being churned out by economists. What sets this one apart, however, is that unlike almost every other economist – exceptions include William White and Claudio Borio of the Bank for International Settlements – Roubini can claim to have got things right *before* disaster struck. So what made him so sure he was right? I ask, as our understated breakfast arrives on the low table next to the leather sofa. The only splash of colour is a vast strawberry adorning my power shake.

'Having spent 10 years studying emerging markets, I know that you have patterns repeated over and over again,' he explains. 'A bubble is like a fire which needs oxygen to continue . . . when you see there is no oxygen, things change.' More specifically, by the summer of 2006 Roubini could see that the housing market had peaked. That left him convinced that the system was about to unravel, because there was so much mortgage debt.

He has continued to issue warnings since the crash. In early 2009, he argued that the banking crisis might not be finished. He also suggested that there was a 20 per cent chance of a double-dip recession, because American growth would be so weak. In fact, the US economy has rebounded faster than he expected and bank share prices have risen too. All of which leaves some rivals gloating that Roubini was simply lucky with his 2006 call. He retorts, though, that it is still too early to conclude that the global economy is really on a recovery track. And at least one recent call has been correct: for the past year he has repeatedly warned about dangers stalking sovereign debt. In particular, he thinks that the dramas in Greece reflect a bigger problem facing the western world, since governments appear to lack the stomach to tackle spiralling government debt.

'What really worries me about the US right now is that there is this [political] gridlock,' he says, arguing that this prevents the government from taking the necessary tough decisions. 'The UK has the same problem. There is no real willingness to have spending cuts or tax increases.' As a result, 'there will be temptation to keep monetizing the fiscal deficit', which will ultimately produce inflation.

To combat those risks, Roubini wants policy-makers to co-operate across party lines and to break out of their old ideological boxes of 'left' and 'right'. 'I grew up in Italy in the 1960s and 1970s and it was a period of a lot of social turmoil, when even young teenagers were engaged in politics. I was slightly more left of centre then,' he says, stirring sugar into his latte, making elegant swirls of brown and white. These days he is 'centrist' on economic issues, since he believes that governments need to spend money in a crisis to support the system, in line with Keynesian economic ideals – but he believes that when a crisis is over, they should revert to free-market approaches, reflecting the so-called 'Austrian school' of economics. 'There is this big debate between the Keynesian school and the Austrian school. But I am pragmatic and eclectic. It is all about timing.'

So where would he suggest people put their money now? What does he do? He looks coy. 'I have never in my life bought an individual stock, bond or currency. I have my own 401k [pension and savings pot] in a passive fund – 100 per cent equity investment, half US, half non-US. All the extra income I have received in the past few years has gone into cash. At some point I will move that into riskier assets, but not now.' This caution seems typical of Dr Doom, I suggest. He disagrees. 'Dr Doom as a nickname was cute and I did like it for a while but what I keep saying now is that I am Dr Realist.'

In other words, Roubini now wants to be known as a sage who can proffer constructive advice, instead of predicting disaster. Indeed, on the day we meet he has written a column for the *FT* urging Europe to let Greece restructure its debt. And he has just returned from Washington, where he met a group of senior western finance ministers and central bankers. 'What is important to me is that when I write something, people listen to me. I provide my wisdom to people, whether they agree or not.'

As he dollops yoghurt on to his granola, I cut to the chase. How does such lofty economic 'wisdom' co-exist with his new-found celebrity, gossip-column status? 'Celebrity has become a burden,' he sighs, 'there are more demands on your time. People think it is glamorous to fly places. But it is not – even if you travel business class and stay in wonderful hotels, you end 10,000 miles away from home.' He reckons that he spends two-thirds of each year on the road; unsurprisingly, the new book was mostly written on planes.

I suggest that some of his rivals would struggle to feel much sympathy with the 'dilemma' of having to stay in luxurious hotels. In fact, many might feel a twinge of jealousy, when they look at the money, fame and parties (he recently posted some pictures of a party that he attended in the Caribbean, thrown by Roman Abramovich). And what about all those glamorous women constantly surrounding the permanent bachelor Roubini?

'I am just a normal human being – I am alive! Why is anyone surprised that I am human?' retorts Roubini. 'Like many New Yorkers, I have a multifaceted life. I collect art – I love modern art, film . . . in fact, soon I am going to Cannes because I am appearing in two films!'

I express surprise; the film stars who live in this part of New York might consider this entirely 'normal'. Most egghead academics do not. However, Roubini explains that both films – Stone's *Wall Street* drama and the documentary *Inside Job* – are essentially highlighting the role he played in predicting the credit disaster.

I suddenly recall that I also gave an interview for the latter, talking about complex credit instruments, and am apparently appearing in it too. Our conversation and the location begin to take on a surreal quality; suddenly the starry grandeur of the Soho Grand does not seem such a strange place to be chatting about mortgage-backed securities after all. Three years ago, it was hard to imagine that such complex financial tools would ever attract the interest of Hollywood. Or that a man such as Roubini would be hailed as a prophet, or go partying in Cannes. Yet now that this bizarre plot twist has occurred, he is clearly determined to enjoy it – whatever fellow academics think.

I ask for the bill. Roubini has been so busy talking that he has barely eaten. He gathers himself up, and we stroll through the lobby,

Grand Lounge
Soho Grand Hotel,
New York

1 x double espresso	$8
1 x granola	$9
1 x plain yoghurt	$2
1 x frittata	$16
1 x power soy drink	$9
1 x latte	$6
1 x large Saratoga juice	$8

Total (incl. service)	$58

surrounded by concrete, bottleglass and steel. 'You must come to Cannes too! We can be a wonk and wonkette together!' he says, laughing at such an odd thought. I laugh off his infectious enthusiasm. Then, as he leaves, find myself checking my diary; could I fit in a trip to the film premiere in Cannes? Should I? Sovereign debt crises and collateralized debt obligations never used to be this much fun.

Yuko Tojo

Let sleeping gods lie

Certain Japanese politicians want to disenshrine the executed wartime prime minister Hideki Tojo. But his granddaughter insists that he deserves his divine status

By David Pilling

The first inkling Yuko Tojo had of what really happened to her grandfather was when she was in fifth grade at school. Gripping her small white hands around her neck, the 65-year-old re-enacts the classroom scene of more than half a century ago when a boy stood on a chair before leaping to the ground with the cry: 'Tojo hanged.'

The young girl looked up the strange word, *kohshukei*, in the dictionary and found a description next to the picture of a hooded man with a rope around his neck. 'Then I knew the meaning,' she nods, releasing her grip to continue the dissection of her lamb fillet.

'Until then I had always believed he had died on the battleground,' she says, recalling her childhood fantasy about her grandfather, Japan's prime minister in the Second World War, who had in fact been executed for crimes against humanity. 'My mother had always told me he had fought vigorously for his country and died.'

Nearly 60 years after the armies Hideki Tojo marshalled perished on the battlefield or fled back to their devastated homeland, his ghost is still stalking Asia. He is the most famous of 14 Class A war criminals enshrined – along with another 2.5 million war dead – at the Yasukuni shrine, a quiet sanctuary in central Tokyo that has become a rallying point for the Japanese right.

Since Junichiro Koizumi became prime minister four years ago, he has made a point of visiting the shrine each year, provoking outrage in China, which likens the gesture to bowing at the tomb of Adolf Hitler.

Yasukuni has become a dangerous flashpoint in Japan–China relations, already poisoned by history and suffering anew as the two Asian giants jostle for influence. Some Japanese politicians, including former prime minister Yasuhiro Nakasone, want to defuse the situation. They have urged the families of Class A war criminals to disenshrine their relatives' souls from Yasukuni. (There are no bodies buried there.) In that way, the prime minister could honour Japan's fallen soldiers without appearing to condone those who sent them on their suicidal mission.

Yuko Tojo, stalwart defender of her grandfather's reputation, has chosen the Crown, a French restaurant overlooking the Imperial Palace, to discuss Tojo's legacy. A tiny, straight-backed figure, dressed in a green woollen suit with large, gold-trimmed buttons, she arrives with bullet-train punctuality clutching a miniature trunk in eggshell blue. Prim and with an old-world politeness, she reminds me of Miss Marple, Agatha Christie's straight-laced detective.

Almost as soon as she sits down, she starts disembowelling her little trunk, pulling out her grandfather's memorabilia, including 161 postcards that Tojo sent to her father, then a young boy, from Europe. Next comes a ream of grainy photographs and a battered notebook, in which Tojo kept a neatly handwritten diary of his parental experiences.

'There is one entry describing how my grandfather would hide behind a chest and tie a piece of string to a candy bar,' she says as I thumb through the yellowing pages. 'When the baby tried to grab it, he would pull it away.'

I decide to order while there is still room on the table. She leaves the choice to me, smiling benevolently as I scour the menu. 'Just something simple. Not so expensive. The view is nourishing enough,' she says, drinking in the imperial gardens, the verdant vacuum at the centre of Tokyo.

My eyes alight on Le Menu Affaire, a set lunch that requires only one decision. She opts for the wrapped fillet of lamb, I for the grilled sea bream. As the waiter brings our amuse bouche, a sliver of apple atop a quivering oyster, I ask if she can remember her grandfather. 'Just fragments,' she says, her eyes wrinkling kindly. 'I was six when the war ended.'

After Japan's surrender, Tojo was imprisoned, awaiting trial. 'I was a girl so I wasn't brought so often, but my brother, who is two years older, remembers sticking his hands through the bars and touching my grandfather's hand.'

Family anecdotes form the basis of her memoirs, later turned into a box-office hit called *Pride*, which portrayed Tojo as a patriot and the tribunal that executed him as a kangaroo court. A scene in the film shows prosecutors turning off the microphone as defence lawyers argue that the perpetrators of Hiroshima and Nagasaki should also be brought to justice. 'It wasn't a fair trial. It was the victors judging the defeated. To deem Hideki Tojo a villain would mean the war was bad and that all the soldiers who fought in the war were bad,' she says, sipping the fluffy haricot bean soup through pursed lips. 'I want to review the war and the actions of the soldiers so that their deaths are not meaningless.'

But isn't the point that their deaths were meaningless, I say. Tojo's campaign was barbaric and led to the near-annihilation of Japan. 'It's true that precious lives were lost and that Japan lost the war. But they fought desperately hard and stood proud,' she says, her smile fading slightly. 'As a result Japan is enjoying peace and an affluent life. I would be sorry to say they died in vain.'

We take to studying our main course intensely, before I venture to ask how exactly Japan's aggressive expansionism, admittedly learned at the knee of the Great European Powers, brought about peace. 'I think from the way you use the word "aggression", your stance is totally different from mine,' she says after a silence broken by the sound of her knife clinking against the plate. 'You are looking at this from the standpoint that Japan was an invader. I say it was a defensive war. Japan did not have resources.'

After a discussion of the Nanking massacre, accounts of which she rejects as Chinese fabrication, and my suggestion that being short of resources does not justify grabbing them, she says, 'I wish you had a deeper understanding of what happened. Please make it clear in your article that we have very different standpoints.'

I switch to what suddenly seems like the less controversial subject of

Yasukuni. 'China has no business in this internal affair,' she pronounces, revealing her dislike for that country with a sideswipe at its plumbing arrangements. 'The Americans and the British haven't complained. It is only China who is whipping the souls of the dead.'

Japanese politicians too should know better than to talk of moving the souls. 'Once a soul is enshrined, you can't tear them into bits and take them from the shrine,' she says. 'Once they are enshrined, whether they are generals or rank-and-file soldiers, they all become equal. They are all gods.'

As petits fours are brought to our table, she dips back into her trunk. Like a conjurer, she pulls out a succession of astonishing items: a little brown box that Tojo fashioned in prison while awaiting execution, pencil stubs he used to record his last thoughts, and even the ash from his final cigarette.

At one point she puts a little packet on the white tablecloth a few inches from a strawberry parfait I have been eyeing. She opens it to reveal a small clump of her grandfather's hair as well as his nail clippings – a parting gift he had prepared for his family before a bungled suicide attempt.

'He told his lawyer that he was living in shame because he failed to commit suicide,' she says. 'His whole purpose of continuing to live was to avoid the prosecution of the emperor,' she adds, referring to his testimony – disputed by many historians – that the emperor was largely ignorant of the details of Japan's disastrous war drive.

There's an argument, I say, with a nervous back-glance at the imperial palace, that it would have been better if the emperor had been prosecuted. That way Japan might have made a cleaner break with its past. It seems ironic that Tojo, by being enshrined at Yasukuni, became a Shinto god, while Emperor Hirohito,

Crown Restaurant
Palace Hotel, Tokyo

....

2 x sliced apple with oyster
2 x haricot bean soup
1 x wrapped fillet of lamb
1 x grilled sea bream
selection of petits fours
1 x coffee
1 x milk tea

....

Total   Y14,000

as the price of US exoneration, gave up his divine status to become a mortal monarch.

'The emperor had wished for peace and had wanted to avoid war,' she replies, echoing the testimony her grandfather took to the grave.

All of Tojo's relics are now safely back in their case. But, through her, his voice still ripples through the air.

James Watson

Animal instincts

Don't feel guilty about coveting your neighbour's wife, having plastic surgery or raising your IQ with gene therapy, says James Watson, the man who discovered DNA. After all, we are only human

By Christopher Swann

D on't feel guilty about coveting your neighbour's wife, having plastic surgery or raising your IQ with gene therapy, says James Watson, the man who discovered DNA. After all, we are only human. James Watson must rank as one of the world's least recognizable famous people. Fifty years ago, aged just 24, he guaranteed his immortality when he and fellow scientist Francis Crick discovered the structure of DNA. The eureka-moment came in 1953 when Watson cracked the code, changed our perception of life, and dealt a deathblow to the idea that living cells were animated by some mysterious force. Today it is hard to think of a field of human study that has not been either revolutionized or coloured by his revelation.

But if Watson's secretary had chosen to play a practical joke on me and send me to lunch with some other 75-year-old, I would have probably fallen for it. There is a striking disparity between the distinction of his achievement and the unfamiliarity of his face. Even his name is linked, Siamese twin-like, with Crick's, and loses its resonance in isolation.

As Watson drives me to lunch at the Inn on the Harbor in the heart of Great Gatsby country in Long Island, New York, I ask him whether this lack of public recognition ever bothered him. With a rueful smile he

reflects that discovering the structure of DNA did little to help him propagate his own genes. 'There were no groupies,' he says. 'Well, I suppose there were two but you wouldn't have wanted to get too close to either of them.'

Instead Watson's main reward was to see the discipline he co-founded start to mature. Munching on a breadstick, he muses on 50 years of genetics. It's not just about attaining abstract knowledge about life. The potential of genetics to enhance life is massive, he says.

'If God is not going to cure cancer then it's up to us to do it,' he says. If the Church really recognized miracles, he adds, it would have canonized Jonas Salk for his polio vaccine.

Outside religious circles, this is uncontroversial stuff. But Watson's vision for genetics extends well beyond curing disease and into the hinterlands of political correctness. If genetic engineering can make people better-looking or brighter then all the better. 'It is part of human nature for people to want to enhance themselves. When someone is good-looking or bright there is a tendency not to care about those who are not. Thirty years ago cosmetic surgery was almost amoral. Now hardly a politician can survive without it. To want your children to have a good throw of the genetic dice is extremely natural.'

From universal DNA fingerprinting to bizarre manipulations of animal DNA, Watson is prepared to endorse a range of uses for the technology that may make liberals blanch. 'If everyone's genetic fingerprint were taken,' he observes, 'it would take away our liberty to commit crime.'

More controversial still, Watson argues that if technology permits it, women should be able to abort homosexual foetuses. 'Most women want grandchildren and do not say with glee that their son is homosexual,' he says.

This kind of full frontal assault on political correctness has got Watson into hot water in the past. It is easy to see how his willingness to discuss the ethical vanishing point of genetics has sometimes obscured a genuinely humanitarian desire to limit human suffering.

As he ploughs through a veal escalope (I get the impression that this was a painful decision and that he had probably tried everything on the menu several times), Watson stresses that he wants genetics to be put in the hands of the user – more often than not, women.

'These kinds of issues should not be decided by a group of government-appointed wise men. We should leave it up to women and let them make their own choices.

'There is far too much regulation. If nobody is hurt, then what is going too far? The idea that there is some fundamental order arranged by God is the origin of the whole fuck-up.'

Watson also advocates an understanding of genetics as an antidote to some of the self-delusions to which humans are prone. The discovery of DNA was the final step in the Copernican revolution that displaced humanity from the centre of the universe. 'Human beings were even more mysterious before 1953 and psychoanalysis was taken seriously,' he says.

Watson seldom resists the temptation to spike his reflections with barbed jokes. The fact that we now understand that humans are animals, he says, should help us recover from some of the unnecessary guilt that accompanies many of our fundamental desires. 'You should not feel guilty about coveting your neighbour's wife if she is better-looking or more fun. You cannot really change what you like.'

There is a restless energy to Watson that helps explain why he refused to sit on his laurels after unearthing the Rosetta Stone of life at an age at which few scientists even have doctorates. (He winces at my suggestion that he is the Macaulay Culkin of biology, whose greatest glory also came at the start of his career.) 'This was not a time to rest,' he says. 'I still wanted to do something important.'

Watson wanted the grand slam. Having uncovered the structure of DNA he aimed to work out how genes provided the information to make proteins – the building blocks of living matter. He became convinced that DNA chains were copied on to strands of RNA, serving as templates to order the amino acids in proteins.

With barely a pause for breath, in 1953 Watson began his dual quest for RNA and a wife. (He later conceded that at the time he thought more about girls than genes.) As it happened, it wasn't until he was 39 that he married a dazzlingly pretty 19-year-old sophomore from Radcliffe College.

'I have always been in a hurry,' he says. 'The scientific community is not always in such a rush. If we are able to see the genetic basis of cancer or autism we will at least see the face of the enemy.'

Watson's impatience to make genetics practical was heightened by the illness of his son, Rufus, who suffers from a form of autism thought to be epilepsy of the thalamus. It was around the time of his son's diagnosis in 1986 that Watson was installed as the chief cartographer in charge of mapping the human genome. On the subject of his son, who is now in hospital, the ever-effusive scientist starts to clam up. 'I do not see the need for immortality. But I do have a sick son in hospital. If we knew enough science we could help him. Fame is irrelevant.'

For Watson, Rufus is a symbol of the genetic injustice that may be alleviated by the progress of recombinant DNA technology. 'So far,' he says, 'the biggest practical impact of genetics has been in paternity suits and forensics. But they have found two genes for autism . . . so one day autistic children may not be born.'

However laudable his motives, Watson's combination of impatience and almost total disregard for social pleasantries has ruffled more than a few feathers among fellow scientists. In his memoir of the period, Edward O. Wilson, the Harvard biologist with whom Watson clashed over university appointments, dubbed Watson 'the Caligula of biology'. 'Watson,' he said, 'radiated contempt in all directions,' and was the most unpleasant human being he had ever met.

Having grown quite fond of Watson's disarming honesty, I found this description hard to recognize. I ask Watson – who by now has finished his food altogether and is staring at my half-completed plate with an air of expectation – whether he has mellowed with age.

'People exaggerated my rudeness,' he says. 'I just wanted things to happen fast and I wanted Harvard to appoint the best people.' (Watson became a professor at Harvard at 28, not so much because of its biology department as because it was a 'girl-containing university' – in contrast with the 'girl-less Caltech'.) 'If you are appointed editor of a paper where the staff are lousy, do you just wait until they die off? Besides, academia is a bit like an officer training corps. You need to be robust.'

I get the impression that Watson would make a delightful friend but a truculent colleague. (It seems fitting that his favourite among a batch of films out over the end-of-year holiday period is *Bad Santa*, the story of a cantankerous and outspoken Father Christmas.)

At 75 Watson may be preparing for posterity, but there is no indication he wants to hog the credit or disparage the runners-up in the race for DNA. As the waiter removes the remains of my tuna steak,

I cautiously turn the conversation towards Rosalind Franklin, the brilliant crystallographer whose X-ray pictures of DNA helped Crick and Watson towards double-helix theory. Franklin died in 1958 from ovarian cancer four years before Watson, Crick and Maurice Wilkins were awarded the Nobel Prize. Watson's disparaging description of Franklin as the 'dark lady' of genetics helped ensure her status as a feminist icon, unjustly denied her share of the credit for a giant leap in science.

Although Watson was clearly not fond of Franklin – whom he describes as a massive snob – he makes no effort to conceal how close she came to taking the prize. 'Rosalind should have discovered the structure of DNA a year before we did,' he says. She just became interested in other things, he says. Relieved to get the question out of the way, I take a deep breath.

As the waiter arrives with the bill, Watson instructs me to leave a big tip. There are some social conventions that even Watson is happy to honour.

Inn on the Harbor

105 Harbor,
Cold Spring Harbor,
New York

....

1 x shrimp and lobster
1 x baked clams
1 x tuna
1 x escalopine
1 x glass of house white
1 x iced tea
1 x coffee

....

Total (incl. tip) $72.86

Acknowledgements

A number of colleagues helped to turn a good idea into a real book. I would like to thank Caroline Daniel, editor of the *FT Weekend, Life & Arts* editor Lucy Tuck and her deputy Neil O'Sullivan, not to mention all their predecessors who have commissioned and edited more than 800 lunches since the series was launched on 23 April 1994. Bhavna Patel and Peter Cheek, the *FT*'s ever patient librarians, helped to retrieve full versions of the older articles. Sally Gainsbury, Richard Pigden, Christina Brown and Hannah Bishop tracked down contributors who had long lost touch with the *FT*. Cristina Vere-Nicoll and Alexandra Boulton provided important background research, under the guidance of Leyla Boulton. Emma Gilpin-Jacobs and her communications team worked hard to make the book one of the highlights of the *Financial Times*'s 125th anniversary celebrations. I am grateful to all for their support on a project even more rewarding than a five-course lunch.

Lionel Barber

Contributors

JAMIL ANDERLINI

Jamil was appointed the *Financial Times*'s Beijing bureau chief in February 2011. In 2010 he was named Journalist of the Year by the Society of Publishers in Asia, and in 2008 he won a UK Foreign Press Association Award. Born in Kuwait, Jamil grew up in the Middle East and New Zealand. He speaks and reads Mandarin Chinese and has lived mostly in Shanghai and Beijing since 2000. He is the author of an *FT* ebook, *The Bo Xilai Scandal: Power, Death, and Politics in China.*
Bao Tong, p. 193

PETER ASPDEN

Peter is the *Financial Times*'s arts writer, having previously been its arts editor for five years. He joined the paper in 1994, as deputy books and arts editor and a general feature writer on what was then known as the *Weekend FT*. He has written on numerous subjects, including travel, religion, politics, history, most art forms and sport.
Michael Caine, p. 9

LIONEL BARBER

As editor of the *Financial Times*, Lionel has steered the *FT* to three Newspaper of the Year awards. He has co-written several books, has lectured widely and appears regularly on international TV and radio. In 2009 he was awarded the St George Society medal of honour. A long-time foreign correspondent in Washington, Brussels and New York, he is a member of the Board of Trustees at the Tate.
Martin Amis, p. 3; Stephen Green, p. 90

ROB BLACKHURST

Rob has written features and interviews for a variety of UK and American broadsheet newspapers and magazines. Since his first piece for the *FT* magazine in 2005, he has gone back to his old comprehensive to examine meritocracy, spent a week with Prince Andrew, met skateboarding friars, interviewed 9/11 families, and attended a camp for British creationists.
Ronnie Wood, p. 49

PILITA CLARK

Pilita is the environment correspondent at the *Financial Times*, with a focus on the impact of emerging environmental trends and policies on businesses and investors. Prior to this role, she was the aerospace correspondent from 2009 to 2011 and deputy news editor on the main news desk at the *FT*. Before that she was deputy editor of the *FT* magazine.
Michael O'Leary, p. 107

KIERAN COOKE

Kieran was a foreign correspondent for the *Financial Times* and BBC for many years. As *FT* correspondent in Ireland in the late 1980s and early 1990s, he was among those bombed and shot at by a Loyalist gunman in a Belfast cemetery. Although some were worried that his lunch with Martin McGuinness would give the Irish Republican Army (IRA) the oxygen of publicity, the group declared a ceasefire on the same day the piece was published. Kieran now teaches journalists in the developing world and specializes in environmental reporting.
Martin McGuinness, p. 175

ROBERT COTTRELL

Robert was a *Financial Times* correspondent in Hong Kong from 1982 to 1984, and in Moscow from 2000 to 2003. He was also a staff writer for the *Economist*. He left journalism to launch a website, The Browser, in 2008.
Anatoly Chubais, p. 73

ANDREW DAVIDSON

Andrew switched to writing the interview page of the *Sunday Times* business section in 2003 after writing a similar weekly interview for the

Financial Times. He has won awards for Business Writer of the Year and Magazine Writer of the Year. He has published three books, *Smart Luck*, *Bloodlines* and *Under the Hammer*.
Jeff Bezos, p. 69

WILLIAM DAWKINS

Will joined the *Financial Times* in 1981 and left in 2004 to become a head-hunter. His career at the *FT* included the roles of publishing editor and foreign editor, after postings to Brussels, then Paris, followed by four years as the Tokyo bureau chief from 1993 to 1997. In 2009 he moved from Odgers Berndtson to become head of the UK board practice at Spencer Stuart, another executive search firm.
Akebono Taro, p. 267

DANIEL DOMBEY

Daniel has been the *Financial Times*'s correspondent in Turkey since 2011. Before that, he was US diplomatic correspondent based in Washington DC. He previously covered diplomatic beats for the *FT* in both London and Brussels, as well as working as a financial markets reporter.
George Soros, p. 115

BEVERLEY DOOLE

After several years among the hard-working Antipodeans on the *Financial Times*'s news floor, Beverley was appointed chief sub-editor on the *FT* magazine and she jumped at the chance to interview her country's prime minister, Helen Clark, in 2006. Beverley is now a freelance writer specializing in environmental issues back in New Zealand.
Helen Clark, p. 213

JAMES FERGUSON

Born in Birmingham of Irish stock, James had a stint driving trucks because that's what Elvis did. But he always drew, eventually being drawn to the *Financial Times* in the late 1980s, remaining there as cartoonist for features and the *Weekend* section, with occasional forays into the pages of *Euromoney*, the *New Yorker* and the *Leicester Mercury*.

JONATHAN FORD

Jonathan is chief leader writer at the *Financial Times*, having previously written for the Lex column. Before that, he worked for eight years at the financial commentary service Breakingviews, of which he was a co-founder. Jonathan started his career in investment banking but moved into journalism as a financial reporter for the *Evening Standard*.
Eden Collinsworth, p. 137

VANESSA FRIEDMAN

Vanessa has been fashion editor of the *Financial Times* since 2003. She writes a weekly column on style and a daily blog, and is the editorial coordinator of the *FT*'s annual Business of Luxury conference. Before joining the *FT* she was the features director for the launch of UK *InStyle*. She is the author of *Emilio Pucci* and is on the advisory council of Princeton University's history department.
Domenico Dolce and Stefano Gabbana, p. 144; *Tamara Mellon, p. 151*

MATTHEW GARRAHAN

Matthew is the Los Angeles correspondent for the *Financial Times*. He has worked for the *FT* for nine years, previously covering the leisure industries beat and working as sports business correspondent. He was awarded the LA Press Club's Entertainment News Award in 2008 for his story on Hollywood and the credit crunch.
Angelina Jolie, p. 36

JAMES HARDING

James joined the *Financial Times* in 1994 as a graduate trainee. He worked in Westminster, opened the paper's bureau in Shanghai in 1996, returned to London as media editor, then went to Washington as bureau chief from 2002 to 2005. He joined *The Times* as business editor in 2006 and was appointed the paper's editor in 2007.
Sean 'P. Diddy' Combs, p. 16

ADAM JONES

Adam has been accountancy correspondent for the *Financial Times* since 2010. Previously he was the *FT*'s online business education editor and then senior companies reporter. He also worked as a correspondent in Paris and a consumer industries correspondent in London. He joined the *FT* in 2001 from *The Times*, where he had been US business correspondent, based in New York.

Henri de Castries, p. 77

LUCY KELLAWAY

Lucy is the *Financial Times*'s management columnist and agony aunt and an associate editor. In her more than 20 years at the *FT*, she has been energy correspondent, Brussels correspondent, a Lex writer, and an interviewer of business people and celebrities for the Lunch with the *FT* series. Lucy was also the creator of the infamous Martin Lukes.

Zaha Hadid, p. 25; *Twiggy, p. 158*; *Lord Lawson, p. 239*; *Jacques Attali, p. 287*

ROULA KHALAF

Roula is the *Financial Times*'s Middle East editor and an associate editor with additional responsibility for the *FT*'s Middle East edition. She joined the *FT* in 1995 as North Africa correspondent and was previously a staff writer for *Forbes* magazine in New York. Her specialist areas are Iraq, the Gulf, North Africa and the Palestinian-Israeli conflict.

Saif Gaddafi, p. 219; *Queen Rania, p. 248*

SIMON KUPER

Simon has been working for the *Financial Times* since 1994, and now writes a general column for the newspaper. He is British but lives with his wife and three children in Paris. He is the author of several books. including *Football against the Enemy* and *Ajax, the Dutch, the War: Football in Europe during the Second World War.* He was co-author with Stefan Szymanski of *Soccernomics.*

Prince Alwaleed, p. 63

EDWARD LUCE

Edward is the Washington columnist and commentator for the *Financial Times.* He writes a weekly column, *FT* editorials on American politics and the economy, and other articles. He has worked for the *FT* since 1995 as Philippines correspondent, capital markets editor, South Asia bureau chief in New Delhi and Washington bureau chief. He is the author of *In Spite of*

the Gods: The Strange Rise of Modern India and *Time to Start Thinking: America in the Age of Descent.*
Imran Khan, p. 272

CHRISTOPHER PARKES

Chris joined the *Financial Times* in April 1977 with a first job as deputy commodities editor. A long line of posts ranging from consumer industries editor to Germany correspondent ended with a decade as the Los Angeles correspondent. Since retiring in 2006, Chris has lived with his artist wife Marta in the Mojave Desert, California. He is now writing – and printing and binding – his memoirs, *Drinking Coors.*
David Hockney, p. 30

DAVID PILLING

David is the Asia editor of the *Financial Times*. He was previously Tokyo bureau chief from 2002 to 2008. He has also worked in London as an editor, in Chile and Argentina as a correspondent, and has covered the global pharmaceutical and biotechnology industry.
Shaw-Lan Wang, p. 122; *Yuko Tojo, p. 313*

GIDEON RACHMAN

Gideon was appointed chief foreign affairs columnist and an associate editor of the *Financial Times* in July 2006. He joined the *FT* after a 15-year career at the *Economist*, where he held several senior positions including deputy US editor, Asia editor, Britain editor and business editor.
Oleg Deripaska, p. 83; *Donald Rumsfeld, p. 252*

JOHN RIDDING

John has been chief executive of the *Financial Times* since June 2006, having been with the company for more than 20 years in both editorial and executive positions. Previously, John was the editor and publisher of the Asia edition of the *FT*, as well as chairman of Pearson in Asia. After launching the Asia edition in 2003, he led it to a series of commercial and editorial successes.
Yu Hua, p. 54

TOM ROBBINS

Tom began his career as an investigative reporter at the *Sunday Times*, specializing in crime, home affairs and consumer affairs (1998–2003). He went on to edit the paper's newly launched motoring section (2003–5), before moving to the *Observer*, where he was deputy travel editor, then travel editor. He was appointed *FT* travel editor in June 2010. He is a keen cyclist and skier and in 2008 published *White Weekends*, a book on winter sports.

David Millar, p. 276

ALEC RUSSELL

Alec is the *Financial Times*'s news editor, following his stints as comment and analysis editor, world news editor and Johannesburg bureau chief. Before joining the *FT*, Alec was the *Daily Telegraph*'s Washington bureau chief (2003–6). He was an assistant editor at the *Telegraph* and, as foreign editor, oversaw its coverage of the 9/11 attacks and the war in Iraq. *After Mandela: The Battle for the Soul of South Africa* is the latest of his three books.

F. W. de Klerk, p. 232; *Morgan Tsvangirai, p. 258*

AMITY SHLAES

Amity was a *Financial Times* columnist from 2000 to 2005. Nowadays, she directs the economic growth programme at the George W. Bush Presidential Center and is a syndicated columnist for Bloomberg. Her 2007 history of the Great Depression, *The Forgotten Man*, was a *New York Times* best-seller for 20 weeks and she is the author of *Coolidge*, a biography of Calvin Coolidge, the 30th US president.

Angela Merkel, p. 243

NIGEL SPIVEY

Nigel freelanced for the *Weekend FT* from 1988 to 2000, while a research fellow at Emmanuel College, Cambridge. He is the author of several books on Greek and Etruscan art, and lately *The Ancient Olympics*. In 2005 he presented the five-part BBC/PBS television series *How Art Made the World*. He is now senior lecturer in classical art and archaeology at the University of Cambridge.

Gavin Ewart, p. 22; *Lord Hanson, p. 97*; *Jennifer Paterson, p. 165*

CHRISTOPHER SWANN

Chris is a columnist for Reuters Breakingviews, based in New York, and previously worked for Bloomberg News. Before this, he was an economics correspondent for the *Financial Times* in London and then Washington DC. After joining the *FT* in 1998, Chris worked as a world stock-market reporter, foreign news editor and companies reporter.
James Watson, p. 319

GILLIAN TETT

An assistant editor and columnist at the *Financial Times*, Gillian served as the US managing editor until 2012. Before that, she was responsible for the *FT*'s markets coverage, and served as Tokyo bureau chief and deputy Lex editor. She was named Journalist of the Year (2009) and Business Journalist of the Year (2008) at the British Press Awards. Her book *Fool's Gold: How Unrestrained Greed Corrupted a Dream, Shattered Global Markets and Unleashed a Catastrophe* was a *New York Times* bestseller.
Nouriel Roubini, p. 305

MICHAEL THOMPSON-NOEL

Michael worked for the *Financial Times* from 1969 to 1999. He inaugurated Lunch with the *FT*, and his distinguished career at the newspaper included the roles of features editor, Sydney correspondent, travel editor and deputy editor of the *Weekend FT*. Since his retirement, he has tried creative writing (a novel and a screenplay), with no success.
Marco Pierre White, p. 169

ADAM THOMSON

Adam joined the *Financial Times* in 1997 as Bogotá correspondent, then worked as assistant features editor in London, Buenos Aires correspondent, and bureau chief in Mexico City. Before that, he taught English, played chess, worked as a part-time DJ and took photographs. He fell into print journalism by accident: he was asked to cover for a friend with the express promise that the publication in question would not need any copy. Two days after the friend's departure on holiday, the publication called, demanding copy.
General Rosso José Serrano, p. 179

JOHN THORNHILL

John is the deputy editor at the *Financial Times*. He was appointed the *FT* news editor in 2009. Prior to this he worked in Paris as the editor of the European edition, both in print and online. He joined in 1988 as a graduate trainee, and his roles have included Paris bureau chief, world news editor, Asia editor, Moscow bureau chief and Lex columnist.
Albert Uderzo, p. 43

STEFAN WAGSTYL

Stefan is the emerging markets editor at the *FT* and edits the beyondbrics blog on FT.com. Before that, he was East Europe editor. He joined the *FT* in 1983 and his other roles have included Tokyo bureau chief, New Delhi bureau chief and industrial editor.
Václav Havel, p. 292

WILLIAM WALLIS

William is the *FT*'s Africa editor and has travelled and worked in more than 35 countries in Africa and the Middle East. He joined the *Financial Times* in 1998 as West Africa correspondent based in Lagos, and went on to become the *FT*'s Central and East Africa correspondent in Nairobi, acting subsequently as the newspaper's Middle East correspondent in Cairo.
Mo Ibrahim, p. 102; *Paul Kagame, p. 225*

ANDREW WARD

Andrew has been UK news editor at the *Financial Times* since November 2011. Previously, he was the White House correspondent and subsequently the Nordic bureau chief. His US beat included the Bush administration and the 2008 presidential election campaign. Ward joined the *FT* in 1999 as a graduate trainee and was appointed media correspondent in 2000.
Jimmy Carter, p. 207

RICHARD WATERS

Richard is the West Coast managing editor for the *Financial Times*, and writes about telecommunications and technology. He was based in New York for nine years, where he was the Wall Street reporter and NY bureau chief. Richard previously worked in London, holding a number of posts

including international capital markets editor, securities industry correspondent, and accountancy and taxation correspondent.
Steve Wozniak, p. 129

COURTNEY WEAVER

Courtney has been a correspondent for the *Financial Times* in Moscow since 2011. She joined the *FT* as a graduate trainee in 2009 after studying Russian literature at Stanford University and covering the 2008–9 financial crisis in Russia for the *Moscow Times*. In London, she has worked on the *FT*'s companies and markets desks.
Ksenia Sobchak, p. 183

JONATHAN WHEATLEY

Jonathan is the *Financial Times*'s deputy emerging markets editor. He was Brazil correspondent from 2005 to 2011, when he moved to London. He lived in São Paulo from 1992, writing for the *FT*, *Business Week*, the Economist Intelligence Unit and many others. He previously worked in television news, current affairs and documentaries in London.
Fernando Henrique Cardoso, p. 200

MARTIN WOLF, CBE

Martin is the *Financial Times*'s chief economics commentator and an associate editor. He was awarded the CBE in 2000 'for services to financial journalism'. He was a member of the UK government's Independent Commission on Banking in 2010–11. Martin's most recent publications are *Why Globalization Works* and *Fixing Global Finance*.
Paul Krugman, p. 297